ORGANIZING FOR SOCIAL CHANGE

ORGANIZING FOR SOCIAL CHANGE
A Dialectic Journey of Theory and Praxis

Michael J. Papa
Arvind Singhal
Wendy H. Papa

Los Angeles | London | New Delhi
Singapore | Washington DC | Melbourne

First published in 2006 by

 SAGE Publications India Pvt Ltd
B1/I-1 Mohan Cooperative Industrial Area
Mathura Road, New Delhi 110 044, India
www.sagepub.in

SAGE Publications Inc
2455 Teller Road
Thousand Oaks, California 91320, USA

SAGE Publications Ltd
1 Oliver's Yard, 55 City Road
London EC1Y 1SP, United Kingdom

SAGE Publications Asia-Pacific Pte Ltd
3 Church Street
#10-04 Samsung Hub
Singapore 049483

Published by Vivek Mehra for SAGE Publications India Pvt Ltd, typeset in 10/12 pt. Baskerville BE by Star Compugraphics, Delhi.

Library of Congress Cataloging-in-Publication Data

Papa, Michael J.
   Organizing for social change: a dialectic journey of theory and praxis/Michael J. Papa, Arvind Singhal, Wendy H. Papa.
      p. cm.
   Includes bibliographical references and index.
   1. Community organization. 2. Community organization—Case studies. 3. Social action—Case studies. 4. Social change. 5. Dialectic. I. Singhal, Arvind, 1962– II. Papa, Wendy H., 19   58– III. Title.

HM766.P37   307.1'4–dc22   2006   2005025813

ISBN: 10: 0-7619-3434-0 (HB)   10: 81-7829-581-4 (India-HB)
      13: 978-0-7619-3434-9 (HB)   13: 978-81-7829-581-7 (India-HB)
      10: 0-7619-3435-9 (PB)   10: 81-7829-582-2 (India-PB)
      13: 978-0-7619-3435-6 (PB)   13: 978-81-7829-582-4 (India-PB)

The SAGE Team: Deepa Dharmadhikari, Ashok R. Chandran, Rajib Chatterjee, and Santosh Rawat

This book is dedicated to
Everett M. Rogers (1931–2004)
—mentor, colleague, and friend—
who originally (in 1997) suggested that we write this book,
and almost saw it to completion.

Contents

List of Tables

List of Figures

List of Plates

Preface

Our collaborative research on organizing for social change got underway in Fall 1990, when Arvind Singhal joined the faculty of Ohio University's School of Communication Studies (COMS).[1] Michael and Wendy Papa had joined COMS a year earlier. Being in relatively early stages of our academic careers, we were "dreaming" new research projects. On a beautiful October evening—while the autumn foliage radiated red, orange, and yellow hues—the Papas hosted the Singhals for dinner. Stirring a pot of ratatouille in the family kitchen, Michael overheard Arvind telling Wendy the story of the Grameen[2] Bank, a grassroots organization that empowered tens of thousands of poor women in Bangladesh through microcredit. Arvind, in turn, learned about the Grameen Bank from Mohammed A. Auwal, a Bangladeshi graduate student enrolled in Arvind's *Communication and Information Diffusion* class. Michael found the Grameen story so compelling that he left the simmering pot on the stove, turned down the gas burner, and joined the conversation. Those were the beginnings, some 15 years ago, of our research journey. Then one thing led to another.

Later that fall (1990), Mohammed Auwal wrote a term paper on the Grameen Bank in Arvind's class (Auwal & Singhal, 1992), and in the summer of 1991, Auwal and Arvind traveled to Bangladesh to learn more about the Grameen Bank's organizing activities for the poorest-of-the-poor, meeting for the first time Professor Mohammed Yunus, its charismatic founder. In subsequent years, Michael and Auwal traveled to Bangladesh for fieldwork, Auwal wrote his dissertation on the Grameen Bank (Auwal, 1994a), and we published our findings on the control and emancipatory organizing processes of the Grameen Bank (Papa, Auwal, & Singhal, 1995, 1997). In mid-2001, Arvind returned to Bangladesh to study the village mobile telephony project of the Grameen Bank in collaboration with Peer J. Svenkerud[3] and Einar Flydal of Telenor AS (Norway) (Singhal, Svenkerud, & Flydal, 2002). Telenor, a Norwegian telecommunication company, joined hands in 1996 with the Grameen Bank to launch GrameenPhone, a highly profitable company that provides millions of Bangladesh's urban and rural inhabitants with mobile telephony services. Through Grameen Bank's 99,987 village telephone ladies who operate in 51,000 of Bangladesh's 68,000 villages, some 80 percent of Bangladeshi people—who previously had never made a telephone call, now use a mobile telephone to find out the market price of agricultural produce, to schedule a transportation pick-up, or to request an ambulance (Malaviya, Singhal, Svenkerud, & Srivastava, 2004a, 2004b, 2004c).

While our research on the Grameen Bank was well underway, Arvind and Professor Everett M. Rogers became United Nations' FAO[4] advisors (from 1991 to 1996) to the National Dairy Development Board (NDDB) in India, an umbrella organization of 112,590 village-level dairy cooperatives with over 12.1 million farmer members. Each year, for the next five years, Arvind and Ev Rogers spent about eight weeks with the NDDB in India to speed up the diffusion of NDDB's Cooperative Development (CD) initiative in India (which included a strong component on empowering women dairy farmers). One concrete outcome of our five-year consultation with NDDB was the initiation of a Ford Foundation-funded research project on the empowerment of women dairy farmers.

Why the focus on women dairy farmers? In India, women dairy farmers carried out most of the day-to-day dairying tasks—such as feeding, cleaning, and caring for the animals. However, they had little involvement in managing the affairs of the dairy cooperative society. Milk cooperatives in India were mostly run by men, a situation that the NDDB was trying to change to honor the Rochdale principles of cooperation, which mandated that the primary producer (the woman, in this case) be the primary manager of the dairy enterprise.[5] As part of the research grant, two mid-level NDDB managers—Dattatray Ghanekar and Arun Wayangankar—came to Ohio University (where all three of the present authors were based) and the University of New Mexico (where Professor Rogers was based), respectively, to earn their MA degrees in communication. In August, 1997, Arvind, Michael, and Ev Rogers spent two weeks in India, visiting dairy cooperative societies in Rajasthan, Gujarat, and Maharashtra. Our field visits and data-collection activities in India, spearheaded by Ghanekar and Wayangankar (and their NDDB colleagues), yielded several insights on the dialectic of empowerment and oppression among women dairy farmers (Papa & Singhal, 1999;

Papa, Singhal, Ghanekar, & Papa, 2000; Singhal, Law, Kandath, & Ghanekar, 1999; Shefner-Rogers, Rao, Rogers, & Wayangankar, 1998).

Meanwhile (between 1996 and 1998), Arvind served as Principal Investigator (along with Professor Everett M. Rogers) on a project funded by the David and Lucile Packard Foundation to investigate the effects of a highly popular entertainment-education radio soap opera in India called *Tinka Tinka Sukh* [Happiness Lies in Small Things]. Through an entertaining storyline, *Tinka Tinka Sukh* (broadcast for one year during 1996–1997) promoted gender equality, small family size, and communal harmony to audiences in north India. In early 1997, Mrs. Usha Bhasin, the All India Radio official in-charge of producing *Tinka Tinka Sukh*, visited Athens, Ohio, and handed Arvind a copy of an unusual poster letter, written by listeners of the radio serial. In this colorful 30 by 24 inch poster-letter, 184 residents of Lutsaan village in India's Uttar Pradesh State signed a pledge not to give, or accept, dowry (an illegal but widespread social practice in India). These villagers also pledged to not allow child marriages (also an illegal but common practice), and pledged to educate their daughters equally with their sons. During our August 1997 India visit, Arvind, Michael, and Ev Rogers (accompanied by Ev's wife, Corinne Shefner-Rogers, Mrs. Usha Bhasin, and other field researchers) spent three days in Lutsaan village trying to understand how *Tinka Tinka Sukh* sparked conversations and dialogue among listeners, goading them to make certain collective decisions, and undertake certain community-based actions (Singhal & Rogers, 1999; Law & Singhal, 1999).

The Lutsaan study strongly suggested that entertainment-education interventions had their strongest effects on audiences when messages stimulated reflection, dialogue, and debate about the educational topic among audience members, and when services could be delivered locally (Papa, Singhal, Law, Pant, Sood, Rogers, & Shefner-Rogers, 2000). Arvind and Michael applied these insights from Lutsaan in co-designing and implementing (with various collaborators —Population Communications International, All India Radio, and Janani and Brij Lok Madhuri—two India-based NGOs) a follow-up entertainment-education radio project in four Indian states—Bihar, Jharkhand, Madhya Pradesh, and Chhattisgarh. The year-long (2002–2003) broadcasts of the radio soap opera, *Taru* (named after the social worker protagonist who fights for gender and caste equality), were dove-tailed with a series of on-the-ground activities in 25,000 villages through a reproductive health service delivery organization, Janani, which works through the local village-based rural health practitioners (RHPs). Pre-program publicity for *Taru* was widely conducted through Janani's extensive RHP rural health network in 25,000 villages of India's Bihar State, folk performances were held to stimulate interest in group listening to *Taru,* and listeners' groups were established in several communities to encourage dialogue on social problems.

Population Communications International of New York funded a research grant to Ohio University with Arvind as Principal Investigator to assess the synergistic effects of *Taru*'s on-air broadcasts with the on-the-ground community orchestration, group listening, and Janani's service delivery. Between 2001 and 2004, Arvind and Michael, along with other colleagues and graduate students at Ohio University, Michigan State University, and Johns Hopkins University's Center for Communication Programs (notably Dr. Kim Witte) made several field visits to Bihar, India to carry out research on *Taru,* aided on the ground by field researchers of the Centre for Media Studies (CMS), New Delhi, our long-time research partner in India.[6] Our involvement with the *Tinka Tinka Sukh* and *Taru* projects yielded several publications, and sharpened our understanding of the dialectic of dissemination and dialogue in organizing for social change initiatives (Papa, Singhal, Law, Pant, Sood, Rogers, & Shefner-Rogers, 2000; Singhal, Sharma, Papa, & Witte, 2004; Harter, Sharma, Pant, Singhal, & Sharma, in press).

Starting in 1998 (and continuing to this day), Michael and Wendy worked on a research study to investigate different approaches to feeding the homeless in the Appalachian region of the United States. With friends, colleagues, and graduate students, Michael and Wendy participated in preparing and serving community suppers at Good Works, a not-for-profit Christian Ministry in Athens, Ohio. They also participated in other community suppers and in soup kitchens in various locations in Ohio, Michigan, Kentucky, and West Virginia. Extensive qualitative data, collected during these community suppers and soup kitchens with homeless people, helped sharpen our understanding of the dialectic tensions between unity and fragmentation in organizing for social change processes (Papa, Papa, Kandath, Worrell, & Muthuswamy, in press).

Our various collaborative research projects—on the Grameen Bank in Bangladesh; the empowerment of women dairy farmers in India; the on-air entertainment-education broadcasts and on-the-ground community organizing in India; and on community suppers in Appalachia—inform our collective understanding of the process of organizing for social change, including the dialectical tensions represented therein. Interestingly, our understanding of the various dialectics in the process of organizing for social change evolved over time. Our study of the Grameen Bank in Bangladesh drew our attention to the dialectic of emancipation and control, and raised implications for a future study on the communicative dimensions of empowerment. When we next conducted our study on the empowerment of women dairy farmers in India, the dialectic of empowerment and oppression emerged. The *Tinka Tinka Sukh* and *Taru* projects in India provided an opportunity to conduct in-depth case studies of media-sparked social changes in village-based communities. These in-depth community-based explorations pointed us to the dialectic of dissemination and dialogue. Finally, our investigation of community suppers in Appalachia provided an opportunity to blur the line between the researchers and participants. This investigation pointed us to the dialectic of unity and fragmentation. Collectively, these four projects are both separate and connected. They are separate as each represents an independent investigation of the social change process. They are connected because the insights gained in one project informed our subsequent projects. Collectively, these four projects pointed us to the multiple dialectic tensions that co-exist in organizing for social change phenomenon.

Involvement in these research projects greatly influenced our thinking and approach to research. All three of us were primarily trained in quantitative methods. However, what captivated us most were the rich, nuanced, and often contradictory narratives of our respondents. We all re-trained ourselves in qualitative methods to be able to research and write from this perspective. In fact, Michael became so interested in qualitative approaches that he took a position in the Department of Educational Studies at Ohio University to build a graduate curriculum in qualitative methods. We also recognized that the linear knowledge–attitude–practice (KAP) approaches to describe the process of individual behavioral change did not address the complexity of the social change phenomenon that we saw unfold on the ground. Social change in Bangladesh, India, and Appalachia seemed to be characterized by non-linear, circular processes—fraught with paradoxes, contradictions, and dialectic struggles. Our previous writings have drawn attention to this humbling realization.

Writing this book has been a humbling experience too. We originally titled the book *Organizing for Social Change: A Dialectic Journey from Theory to Praxis*. This original title which included "from" and "to" implied a linear progression, beginning with theory and ending with praxis. When our colleague, Dr. Lynn Harter gently pointed this out, we changed the subtitle to *A Dialectic Journey of Theory and Praxis*. Our revised title embodies a reflexive and synergistic relationship between theory and praxis, recognizing that while theoretical sensibilities guided our fieldwork, our field experiences allowed us to refine our theoretical beliefs and concepts. The new subtitle better captures the dialectical spirit of our work, explaining how theory informs praxis and how praxis informs theory. We argue that there is value in embracing theory–praxis as a disciplinary dialectic.

Each chapter in our book contains several boxed case illustrations, each describing a key personality or organization or an event that we hope provides useful insights to the reader. We purposely chose our case illustrations from various organizing contexts—social justice, academic, corporate, artistic, and others—to emphasize the useful role of dialectical thinking in all walks of life. Further, each chapter includes several photographs with the purpose of humanizing the people and processes that characterize organizing for social change processes.

While the world is characterized by multi-dimensional problems, scholars and practitioners are often organized around narrow disciplinary boundaries. We expect this book to create conversations within and across these disciplinary boundaries. Thus the audience for this book includes scholars and teachers of development organizing, organizational communication, communication and social change, community mobilization, social work, and public health; global, national, and local policy-makers; project officials and social change practitioners belonging to international development agencies, NGOs, and local governments; activists and socially-conscious entrepreneurs; and the general reader.

■ About the Authors

The co-authors of this book represent a combination of different nationalities, backgrounds, and experiences. While we each bring somewhat different perspectives to the present task, we collaborate to produce integrative products. To date, we have co-authored over a dozen articles on organizing for social change initiatives, which include six Top Paper awards by the International Communication Association (ICA) and National Communication Association (NCA).

Michael J. Papa, son of a New York City sanitation worker, grew up in a working class neighborhood in the Bronx, one of New York City's five boroughs. Some of the city's poorest neighborhoods were a stone's throw away from his home. Michael saw the face of poverty, malnourishment, and despair on a daily basis. The homeless and hungry, often with blank expressions, inhabited many of the Bronx's sidewalks and curbs, often leaning against telephone poles or huddling under doorways of dilapidated buildings. Michael earned a bachelors' degree in Speech Communication from St. John's University in New York City, an M.A. in Speech Communication and Dramatic Arts from Central Michigan University, and a Ph.D. in Rhetoric and Communication from Temple University in Philadelphia. Michael is presently Professor and Chair of the Department of Speech Communication and Dramatic Arts at Central Michigan University. He teaches and conducts research on organizing for social change projects in Bangladesh, India, and the United States. He presently serves as a consultant to the Conflict Resolution Program at The Carter Center (TCC) in Atlanta, Georgia, developing an evaluation plan to document the approaches of President Jimmy Carter in negotiating peace around the world.

Arvind Singhal, son of an Indian Railways engineer, spent his childhood in several Indian states (Orissa, West Bengal, Bihar, Jharkhand, and Uttar Pradesh), before his father settled down in the capital city of New Delhi. As a boarding school student in Mussoorie, and later at St. Xavier's High School, Delhi, Arvind engaged in social work in various neighboring rural communities, and volunteered at Mother Teresa's home for destitute children. He earned his bachelors' degree in engineering from the University of Delhi, an M.A. in broadcasting at Bowling Green State University, and his Ph.D. degree in communication theory and research from the Annenberg School for Communication, University of Southern California. Arvind is presently Professor and Presidential Research Scholar in the School of Communication Studies at Ohio University, where he teaches and from where he conducts research on organizing for social change projects in Bangladesh, India, Thailand, Vietnam, Peru, Kenya, and South Africa. He has lectured in over 40 countries, held visiting professor positions in Thailand and Malaysia, and has conducted workshops on the role of communication in social change organized by the World Bank, UNICEF, UNFPA, UNAIDS, the Food and Agriculture Organization (FAO) of the United Nations, the U.S. Agency for International Development, Family Health International (FHI), Program in Appropriate Technology in Health (PATH), the International Rice Research Institute (IRRI), and BBC World Service Trust.

Wendy H. Papa is the daughter of a Presbyterian Minister and a physical therapist, who were both veterans of World War II. Despite being raised by a professional mother (who worked as a physical therapist for over 40 years), she was exposed to the conservative patriarchal values dominant in central Indiana during the 1960s and 1970s. Wendy saw many intelligent and ambitious young women "choose" to support their husband's careers, rather than pursue their own aspirations. These experiences informed her interest in studying aspects of women's empowerment—both among homeless women in Appalachia (with Michael), and among Indian women dairy farmers (with Arvind, Michael, and others). Wendy received her bachelors' and masters' degrees from Central Michigan University with a concentration in interpersonal and public communication. Her Ph.D. degree is from Ohio University in applied behavioral sciences and educational leadership. Wendy is presently an Associate Professor in the Department of Speech Communication and Dramatic Arts at Central Michigan University, where she teaches classes in group and organizational communication and directs the basic communication course.

■ With Our Sincere Appreciation

We owe gratitude to many individuals and organizations who helped us conduct the research that informs the writing of the present book: Professor Muhammad Yunus, founder and Managing Director of the Grameen Bank; Mr. Khalid Shams, the number two at Grameen

Bank; and hundreds of Grameen Bank workers and members;
Dr. Verghese Kurien, Ms. Amrita Patel, Dr. S.N. Singh, Tom Carter,
Dr. N.V. Belavadi, Dr. Arun Wayangankar, and Dattatray V.
Ghanekar of the National Dairy Development Board (some of these
individuals have retired or moved to other institutions); Dr. N.
Bhaskara Rao, founder and Chairman of the Centre for Media Studies
(CMS), New Delhi, Ms. Vasanti Rao, Director of CMS, and CMS
field researchers Mumtaz Ahmed, Chetna Verma, and Alok
Shrivastav; Mrs. Usha Bhasin, Controller of Programmes at the Prasar
Bharati Corporation; David Andrews and Kate Randolph, both
formerly of Population Communications International (PCI), New
York; Gopi Gopalakrishnan, Arisingh Dutt, Shejo Bose, Neelam
Vachani, Sourov Chowdhury, Pankaj Kumar Singh, Gopa Chatterji,
Akhilesh Kumar Sharma, and Sushil Kumar of the reproductive
health NGO, Janani, in India (some of these individuals have moved
from Janani since our collaboration); Karuna Shrivastav, Dr. Alka
Kumar, and Kamal Dutt of All India Radio; Pandit Ram Dayal
Sharma of Brij Lok Madhuri; Keith Wasserman, founder and Manag-
ing Director of Good Works in Athens, Ohio; Jerry and Monique
Sternin, co-founders of the Positive Deviance Initiative at Tufts Uni-
versity; Curt Lindberg, Henri Lipmanowicz, and Prucia Buscell of
the Plexus Institute; Dr. Brenda Zimmerman of York University in
Canada; Pat Kruse of Behrhorst Partners for Development; Eliana
Elías and Luis Gonzalez of Minga Perú; Drs. Shereen Usdin and
Garth Japhet of Soul City Institute of Health and Development Com-
munication in South Africa; and Suzanne Hanney of StreetWise,
Chicago.

Several of our colleagues served as co-partners on our various
research projects in Bangladesh, India, and U.S.A.—Professor Everett
M. Rogers, Peter Vaughan, Kim Witte, William Rawlins, Lynn M.
Harter, Nagesh Rao, Corinne Shefner-Rogers, Mohammed A. Auwal,
Subrata Das, Saumya Pant, Suruchi Sood, Sweety Law, Krishna
Kandath, Devendra Sharma, Ketan Chitnis, Ami Sengupta, Elizabeth
Rattine-Flaherty, Tracy Worrell, Nithya Muthuswamy, and countless
others. Do Kyun Kim created the artwork and figures for the present
book, and George Gathigi and Indu Sharma scanned and cropped
the photographs in each of the chapters. George also prepared the
book's indexes. We owe you all a debt of gratitude.

We especially acknowledge Dr. Katherine Miller, Department of
Communication, Texas A&M University; Dr. Patrice M. Buzzanell,

Department of Communication, Purdue University; Dr. Lynn M. Harter, School of Communication Studies, Ohio University; an anonymous Sage reviewer; and Dr. Mary Jo Lodge, Theatre Program, Lafayette College, for reading a draft version of the present manuscript, and for suggesting ways to improve the book. Also, thanks to Mr. Tejeshwar Singh, Managing Director of Sage Publications (India) for his support of this volume.

We thank Dr. Sue Ann Martin, Dean of the College of Communication and Fine Arts at Central Michigan University (where Michael and Wendy are based), Ms. Sheila Roupe, Executive Secretary of the Department of Speech Communication and Dramatic Arts, and the following colleagues at Ohio University, who supported our research projects in multiple ways: Drs. Kathy Krendl, Provost; Greg Shepherd, Interim Dean of the College of Communication; Nagesh Rao, Interim Director, School of Communication Studies (COMS); and COMS wonderful staff members, Wanda Sheridan, Julie Venrick, and Brenda Nelson.

A very special acknowledgement goes to our children—Andrew and Samantha Papa and Aaryaman and Anshuman Singhal—who saw us collaboratively work on these projects from Day One; and to Arvind's wife, Anuja, who lovingly "made possible" these research and writing journeys.

Our objective here is not small. We seek to strengthen our understanding of dialectic tensions in designing, implementing, and studying effective organizing for social change initiatives with the aim of fostering freedom, equality, and social justice for the vulnerable, marginalized, and disempowered citizens of the world.

Michael J. Papa, *Mount Pleasant, Michigan, U.S.A*
Arvind Singhal, *Athens, Ohio, U.S.A*
Wendy H. Papa, *Mount Pleasant, Michigan, U.S.A*

Notes

1. In the 1990s, called the School of Interpersonal Communication or INCO.
2. Grameen means "rural" in the Bangla language.

3. Peer J. Svenkerud also earned his Ph.D. from Ohio University's School of Communication Studies.
4. Food and Agriculture Organization of the United Nations.
5. The pioneers of cooperation from whom these principles emerged were known as the Rochdale pioneers. The Rochdale principles have gone through several incarnations through the oversight of the International Cooperative Alliance.
6. CMS was also Ohio University's India-based research partner on the *Tinka Tinka Sukh* radio project.

1 A dialectic approach to organizing for social change

Great truths are those truths the opposite of which are equally true.
—Carl Deutch (quoted in Johnson, 1996, p. 249)

Consider the actions of commercial sex workers in Kolkata, India. Although these women experience disempowerment and oppression on a daily basis, through their organizing actions they have carved out spaces of control and found paths to empowerment.[1]

The capital of West Bengal is a city with a history of powerful labor unions and a leftist (Communist) government. Some 6,000 commercial sex workers (CSWs) in the Sonagachi red-light district in Kolkata (previously Calcutta) are organized in a strong labor union, the Durbar Mahila Samanwaya Committee (Women's Collaborative Committee), formed in 1995. This unique organization has 30,000 members who each pay dues of 50 cents per year. This labor union of CSWs in Kolkata fights against police harassment, provides schools for the children of commercial sex workers, and creates savings plans for its members (Plate 1.1). The labor union is enterprising; in 2001 it smuggled Raja family planning condoms from Bangladesh, a neighboring country, into Kolkata, so that CSWs would have adequate supplies for use with their customers. The typical CSW in Kolkata keeps a small stash of condoms under her pillow.

Initially guided by Dr. Smarajit Jana, the slight mustachioed epidemiologist in-charge of the Sonagachi project, the Women's Collaborative Committee has taken the lead in promoting condom use, which increased from 1 percent in 1992 to 82 percent in 2001 (Figure 1.1). As a result, prevalence of STDs (sexually transmitted diseases) in Sonagachi is relatively low. Some 11 percent of Kolkata's

Plate 1.1
Kolkata's commercial sex workers organize for social change
Commercial sex workers in Kolkata's Sonagachi red-light district collectively fight against harassment by police and the mafia, routinely rescue under-age trafficked girls, and crusade against HIV infection. Armed with banners, torches, and placards they collectively demand their rights as sex workers, including the right to be HIV-free.
Source: Durbar Mahila Samanwaya Committee.

CSWs are HIV-positive, while in Mumbai, India's big port city on the west coast, the comparable figure is 70 percent.

The HIV-prevention program in Kolkata employs 180 CSW opinion leaders and 100 other outreach workers, each paid about $1 a day, and operates 12 health clinics for CSWs, funded by the Indian ministry of health. Wearing green jackets over their saris, CSW opinion leaders tell brothel "madams": "If you are to enjoy the fruits of the tree, you must keep the tree healthy" (Dugger, 1999, p. A1). The total cost of the intervention program with CSWs is $210,000 per year. Through the Committee, CSWs in Kolkata have become leading crusaders against HIV infection (Singhal & Rogers, 2003). They were the first group in India to ask for legalization of commercial sex work and dignity for their profession.

It is instructive to contrast the empowered Kolkata CSWs with CSWs in Mumbai. In Kolkata, CSWs talk openly in front of their

Figure 1.1
Rising condom use and declining STD rates among Sonagachi commercial sex workers
As a result of empowered commercial sex workers who routinely use condoms, and the availability of locally-available STD treatment, Sonagachi has a relatively low prevalence of HIV and other STDs when compared to commercial sex districts in Mumbai and Delhi.

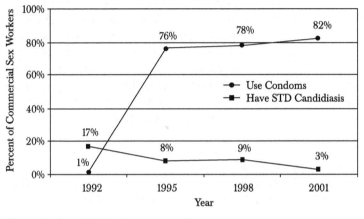

Source: Durbar Mahila Samanwaya Committee.

brothel madams; in Mumbai, CSWs listen attentively or speak quietly. In Kolkata, CSWs wear "decorous saris in muted colors and look like office workers waiting impassively at a bus stop." In Mumbai, by contrast, CSWs wear "shiny red lip gloss, midriff-bearing halters, skintight velvet pants, and gaudy saris. They pose aggressively with their faces set in a sulky come-on" (Dugger, 1999, p. A1).

The CSWs in Kolkata are *organizing for social change*, the process through which a group of individuals orchestrate their skills, resources, and human potential to gain control of their future. An individual sex worker in Kolkata has little power to change her life conditions; but organized collectively, the female CSWs accomplish a great deal. Hundreds of CSWs regularly *gherao* [encircle] the local police station, demanding action against pimps, hoodlums, and criminals who harass them.

When author Singhal visited Sonagachi in 2004 with officials of the West Bengal State AIDS Prevention and Control Society, the empowerment among Sonagachi CSWs was palpable. Minaal Kanti Dutta, the Project Director of the Sonagachi Project extended his hand in welcome and said: "I am Minaal K. Dutta, son of a commercial sex worker." Then he smiled and added: "And I am proud of it." Escorted by two outreach workers (both CSWs), author Singhal walked the narrow alleyways of Sonagachi, stopping to meet madams at Prem Kamal and Neel Kamal, two high class brothels, and then jostled across Inaam Box (I.B.) Lane. "This is the *mast* [sexy] lane," the outreach workers noted: "Here a prostitute charges about 50 rupees [one U.S. dollar] for a quickie." And, then instantly, they said: "Look, all the girls here are above 18 years of age." Sonagachi CSWs routinely intervene to rescue child prostitutes who are sold into the sex trade. In 1992, child prostitutes, under the age of 18 years constituted 25 percent of CSWs in Sonagachi. In 2001, with the organized interventions of CSWs, this number has dropped to 3 percent (Figure 1.2).

The present chapter frames our discussion of organizing for social change from a dialectical perspective. By taking such a perspective, we focus on the struggles and tensions that characterize individual and group efforts to betterment. We describe the main tenets of the

---

Figure 1.2
The decline of child prostitution in Sonagachi, Kolkata's commercial sex district
Sonagachi commercial sex workers regularly intervene in rescuing child prostitutes who are sold into the sex trade.

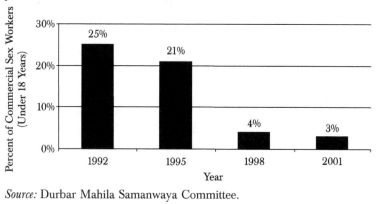

Source: Durbar Mahila Samanwaya Committee.

dialectical approach, provide an overview of the various contexts of organizing for social change explored in the present book, and introduce the dialectical tensions embedded in these social change efforts.

Organizing for Social Change

In aggregate terms, the world has progressed in alleviating poverty, promoting literacy, and improving health and sanitation. In the decade of the 1990s, the world's poor declined from 29 to 23 percent, primary school enrollments increased from 80 to 85 percent, 800 million people gained access to improved water supply, and 750 million to improved sanitation (UNDP, 2002). Further, in the past 25 years, 81 countries have taken significant steps to democratization; with 33 military regimes replaced by civilian ones.

However, the aforementions numbers mask stark inequalities. Of the 6.5 billion people living in 2005, 2.8 billion people live on less than $2 a day; and 1.2 billion survive on less than $1 a day. The richest 1 percent of the world's population earns the equivalent of the poorest 57 percent (UNDP, 2002). The richest 10 percent of Americans (28 million people) earn as much as 2 billion of the world's poorest (UNDP, 2002). Further, in 2005, over 73 countries still do not hold free and fair elections, and 106 governments still restrict civil liberties and political freedoms.

How can the poor, vulnerable, silenced, and marginalized people of the world gain in political, economic, and social power? How can they achieve freedom and equality through democracy and participatory governance? How can they express their views and participate in decisions that shape their lives? A poor farmer in Niger who cannot send his children to school, but has to send them to work in the fields, lacks agency, efficacy, and choice. So does a wealthy educated woman in Brunei, Oman, Saudi Arabia, and the United Arab Emirates, whose gender excludes her from casting a political vote (UNDP, 2002). Dignity comes from exercising some form of choice. For instance, in Porto Alegre, Brazil, poor citizens, since the early 1990s, have been participating in preparing local municipality budgets, and reallocating government spending to address *their* social problems. In the first seven years of this experiment in participatory democracy, households with access to piped water supply increased from 80 to 98 percent; and households with access to sanitation increased from 46 to 85 percent (UNDP, 2002). The tide can turn when the marginalized and the disfranchised collectively organize, thereby gaining in efficacy and agency.

■ What is Organizing?

A flock of geese, flying in a V-formation, provides important lessons in organizing (Plate 1.2). A goose flock can fly up to 1,000 miles without resting; whereas a single goose is exhausted after flying about 500 miles. The geese flying in the back utilize the air currents coming from the wings of the geese in front to lift themselves (Taylor, Taylor, & Taylor-Ide, 2002). The lead bird, which tires easily, routinely drops

Plate 1.2
A flock of geese flying in a V-formation provides important lessons for collective organizing
A flock of geese can fly up to 1,000 miles without resting whereas a single goose can fly only about 500 miles. The geese nurture, encourage, and support each other to reap collective gains.
Source: Personal Files of the Authors.

Box 1.1: Organizing a Holiday Feast

Humans are essentially organizing beings. Organizing is at the core what we do on a daily basis—whether in school, on the playground, in the workplace, or at home. Organizing is as much a part of routine events (e.g., preparing a family dinner) as it is of special events (e.g., preparing a holiday feast). Preparing a family dinner and/or a holiday feast involves a complicated set of organizational tasks: Processing inputs, making decisions, coordinating the efforts of diverse people, sequencing and timing activities, managing hierarchical relationships, addressing conflict, and generating synergistic outcomes.

Consider the holiday feast as an act of organizing based on author Wendy Papa's reminiscences while growing up in Indiana. Admittedly, the holiday feast described here is characteristic of middle-to-upper class U.S. households.

The process of organizing a holiday feast often starts with a family cook who takes a leadership role in planning and executing the dinner. Family members may be consulted about what they wish to eat. At the group level there may be negotiation as choices are considered, accepted, and rejected.

The next stage might represent a plan for purchasing and storing ingredients. A list might be drawn and decisions may be made regarding who will purchase what ingredient and when. Purchases may be spread over a few days. Fresh cream for strawberries, for instance, may be picked up only hours before the dinner. As ingredients come into the house, some go to the pantry, some to the refrigerator, and some to the kitchen counter.

The day before the feast, the cook may mentally rehearse a plan for cooking the dishes, including appetizers, soup, entrée, dessert, and wine. Recipes might be organized and placed in the kitchen for easy reference.

The day of the meal, the cook may assign roles to different family members. Some may chop vegetables; others may prepare a specialty dish. During this phase, the cook displays leadership, accomplishing tasks and coordinating the activities of others.

As time for the feast gets close, one or more family members will prepare the table, placing a tablecloth and distributing glassware, utensils, napkins, and serving dishes. Flowers or candles might be placed on the table, and a musical score may be selected for the evening. The cook may then direct family members in the final presentation of the various dishes, ensuring they are served in a way that is pleasing and appetizing to the eye—a parsley garnish on the pasta, a touch of cilantro on the sauce.

Box 1.1: Organizing a Holiday Feast
(continued)

In the flurry of activities in the last hour, unexpected difficulties may arise. Perhaps someone forgot to put dinner rolls in the oven; or the champagne was not chilled. Tensions may rise as the celebration nears. Under these circumstances, spontaneous solutions to problems are hatched, and meal preparations come to a close.

What do we learn about organizing from the process of organizing a holiday feast? Organizing involves planning, and it is helpful if someone with experience guides the process. This planning and directing may be done by a single leader, who coordinates the actions of others, or may be more diffused as decisions and actions are implemented collaboratively. Complex organizing requires coordination and management of resources—both material and human. The execution of a plan requires focusing on the task at hand to achieve outcomes in a timely manner. However, one should expect difficulties to arise and prepare to resolve problems judiciously. The solution may not be optimal, but perhaps works to satisfy most people. Further, effective organizing should result in people enjoying one another's company at the holiday feast, including the fruits of collective labor. That is, the whole should become more than the sum of its parts.

---

behind in the formation to ride the draft, and the geese at the back sequentially move forward. If a goose moves out of formation, the increased drag on its wings encourages it to fall back into position. Further, geese honk loudly while flying to encourage others and to identify their respective positions in the V-formation. A tired, wounded, or sick goose is never left alone. Two or three geese descend with it to the ground to protect, nurture, and nourish it back to health, before joining another passing flock.

A flock of geese in flight can illustrate the distinction between *organization* and *organizing*. An *organization* is composed of a group of individuals who engage in interdependent cooperative actions. Organizational members take inputs (materials, energy, and information) from the environment, process them, and return them to the environment as outputs (Farace, Monge, & Russell, 1977). So a flock of geese constitutes an organization (as does Harvard University, Dow Chemical, and the United Nations). However, the term organization is used in a static fixed sense without taking time into account.

Organizing, on the other hand, refers to the process-oriented, time-varying nature of the behaviors of members in an organization (Farace, Monge, & Russell, 1977). So a flock of geese flying in a V-formation and regularly rotating its leadership is engaged in organizing. In essence, an organization results from the results of organizing.

■ Organizing for What Purpose

Organizing can serve various purposes. Under Hitler, Germany was good at organizing. The Nazis murdered six million Jews in the highly organized death camps of Auschwitz-Birkenau, Treblinka, Dachau, Sobibor, Belzek, and Majdanek. Hitler's insidious Final Solution involved a highly rational, systematic, and organized process of identifying Jews in Europe, transporting them to concentration camps over an intricate network of railroad junctions, gassing them, and disposing their remains with cold efficiency (Aly, Heim, & Blunden, 2003).

The insidious slave trade, which transported 30 million slaves from Africa to the New World from 1450 to 1850, was also carried out by cold, rational, organizing efficiency (Rogers & Steinfatt, 1999). Africans made for "ideal" workers in colonial plantations: They were physically strong, experienced in farm work and raising cattle, used to hot, muggy climates, and resistant to tropical diseases (Thomas, 1999). They were transported like cattle—chained, packed, and stacked in tight straight lines to minimize wasted space in the ship's hull (Eisenberg & Goodall, 1997). The barest minimum food and water was provided in a regimented schedule on these long, hot, oppressively stifling journeys over the Atlantic. Sick or dying slaves were tossed overboard for a water burial.

In the present book, our interest lies not in such cold, rational, oppressive organizing processes. Our book is about *organizing for social change*, the process through which a group of individuals gains control of its future. We focus on organizing for social change processes that are pro-poor, pro-disempowered, pro-homeless, pro-hungry, pro-women, and pro-vulnerable. Organizing, in this sense, is empowering and transformative: It orchestrates people's talents, resources, and skills to enhance their collective power. We believe

Box 1.2: Stickball in the Bronx
Playing as Organizing

Today, in the United States, when a child wants to play soccer or baseball, they join an organized neighborhood league. These leagues enlist the help of adults (often parents) who serve as coaches and referees. Children wear uniforms, often sponsored by local merchants, and are driven by parents ("Soccer Moms" or "Soccer Dads") on pre-determined days and times to a designated location for practice or play. For instance, when author Singhal's son, Aaryaman, played soccer in the Athens Recreation League in Spring 2005, the family drove over to West State Side Park's Field Eight each Monday and Wednesday at 5:30 p.m. Parents took turns bringing drinks and snacks during the games, and sat on colorful lawn chairs (carried from home), cheering their respective wards. A referee's long whistle signified the completion of the game, making room for another set of teams to take the field.

Contrast the aforementioned experience of organized play with author Michael Papa's experiences in the Bronx. Papa played thousands of games of baseball while growing up in the Bronx during the 1960s and 1970s. Only a fraction of these involved organized competition. One popular game was "stickball," played with a rubber ball and a bat made out of a broom handle. The rules governing these games were negotiated impromptu. A sewer cap on a street corner served as home plate. The next sewer cap located 100 feet away was second base. The door handles of parked cars often served as first and third base. If one hit the ball the distance of roughly two sewer caps (200 feet), a home run was scored. These games were played daily on Bronx city streets where play would temporarily halt to allow a car to pass by. The players made the best of limited resources. The idea of wearing uniforms was alien.

A game would start spontaneously, not at a pre-determined hour, by choosing two teams from available players. Player positions would be determined based on how many players were available. There were no whistles; the umpiring of games was left up to the players. Disagreements about "strike outs" and "run outs" were quickly resolved—through altercation, negotiation, or accommodation. Rather than being told by adults in authority, the players co-negotiated rules. Most of the time was spent playing; often multiple games were played until the daylight turned to darkness.

Author Papa's stickball experiences in the Bronx embody a dialectic of *improvisation* and *institutionalization*. Improvisation occurred when roles were negotiated based on the number of available players, when play

---

Box 1.2: Stickball in the Bronx
(continued)

halted due to passing cars, when participants served as umpires, and when balls bounced off cars, cracked pavements, and apartment walls. This improvisation, however, occurred within the framework of institutionalization, as most of the basic rules governing baseball were followed. For example, establishing a lineup of hitters, the number of outs in an innings, and how outs were recorded were all based on rules established over 100 years ago. Despite the established rules, playing on busy city streets required both improvisation and spontaneity.

"Organized play" and "playing as organizing" represent two contrasting approaches to organizing. What different lessons do children learn from each of these approaches?

---

that both the means and ends, or the processes and outcomes, of organizing should be just and humane.

Organizing for social change involves more than just mobilization, service, or charity. Handouts and charity are anathema to people's dignity. The Government of Mexico once decided to pay tribute to Mexican mothers. A proclamation was issued that every mother whose sewing machine was being held by the Monte de Piedad (the national pawnshop of Mexico) would have her machine returned as a gift on Mother's day. There was tremendous jubilation after this announcement. However, within a few weeks, the same numbers of sewing machines were in the national pawn shop (Alinsky, 1971). Saul Alinsky, a noted community organizer from Chicago, coined the dignity-centered "iron rule" of community organizing: Never do anything for anyone that they can do for themselves.

Dialectical Tensions

When a group of disempowered people organize for social change, the complexity of the enterprise becomes apparent. Those in power sustain their privileges by reinforcing control or further denying rights to the poor. A bit of empowerment in one sphere may lead to oppression in another sphere. Dialectic struggles between competing opposites are fundamental in organizing for social change processes.

Rhythm and blues artist Smokey Robinson wrote one of his most popular songs in the early 1960s entitled, "You Really Got a Hold on Me." This hit song expressed the dialectic tensions that people often experience in romantic relationships (Table 1.1). Although each pair of statements in Robinson's song is contradictory, being in love unifies these opposites into a single experience that many experience and understand. The people we love may cause us pain. However, romantic relationships often flourish through the co-existence of these contradictory impulses, as the pain is often subsumed by the joy of staying connected.

Table 1.1
The dialectics of romance in Smokey Robinson's song

Negative Feelings	Positive Feelings
I don't like you	But I love you
You treat me badly	I love you madly
I don't want you	But I need you
You do me wrong now	My love is strong now
Don't want to stay here	Don't want to leave you

Dialectical tensions also characterized the work Arthur Miller (1916–2005), noted playwright and author of *The Death of a Salesman* and *The Crucible*—hailed by many as the great American Domestic Tragedy and the great American Political Tragedy, respectively (Mamet, 2005). Miller's plays are tragedies as the protagonists are powerless, allowing us to participate in dilemmas of the repressed. For instance, in *The Death of a Salesman,* the protagonist Willy Loman, an elderly salesman, cannot bring home enough money. After 34 years of employment, his company discards him. The drama ends without solutions, allowing the audience members to reconcile that the destiny of the human lot is to try and fail. In so doing, Miller nurtures contradictory impulses finding beauty in sadness, hope in loss, and dignity in failure (Mamet, 2005).

Sports fans of the Boston Red Sox baseball team provide us further insight into the tensions, pushes and pulls of dialectics. Despite a stream of strong players, the Red Sox did not win the World Series until 2004, their first win since 1918, an 86-year dry spell. Part of their misfortune was being in the same Division as the most successful professional sports team in U.S. history: The New York Yankees.

Box 1.3: Leonardo da Vinci
Embracing Dialectics

Why did Microsoft founder Bill Gates pay $31 million for 18 hand-scribbled sheets from Leonardo da Vinci's notebooks in 1994? For one, da Vinci was no ordinary person (Bramly, 1991). As art critic Bernard Berenson, aptly noted: "Everything da Vinci touched turned to eternal beauty" (cited in Gelb, 1998, pp. ix–x).

A contemporary of Machiavelli, Michelangelo, Magellan, and Christopher Columbus, da Vinci (1452–1519) is best known as the artist of two of the most famous paintings ever produced—the *Mona Lisa* and *The Last Supper*. However, painting was only a small part of da Vinci's repertoire (Gelb, 1998): As an inventor, da Vinci drew diagrams for a flying machine, a helicopter, a parachute, the extendable ladder (used today by all fire departments), the adjustable monkey wrench, a snorkel, folding furniture, and a water-powered alarm clock. As military engineer, da Vinci designed weapons that would be deployed 400 years later—the armored tank, the machine gun, precision guided missiles, and submarines. As scientist, da Vinci was the first to draw body parts in cross sections. He pioneered modern botanical science, noting that a tree's age can be measured by counting the number of rings in its cross section. He was the first to document the phenomenon of soil erosion, noting: "Water gnaws at mountains and fills valleys" (Gelb, 1998, p. 44).

What made Leonardo tick? Gelb (1998) attributes da Vinci's genius to various attributes, especially *curiosità*, an unrelenting quest for continuous learning, and *dimostrazione*, the testing of knowledge through experience and experiment. However, Gelb argues that da Vinci's true genius lay in his engagement with *sfumato* (literally "going up in smoke"), a willingness to embrace ambiguity, paradox, and contradictory dialectic impulses. His search for beauty, for instance, led him to explore ugliness. He carefully observed "ugly" people, mapping their facial expressions, gait, and bodily contortions. Further, while painting, he would routinely use a flat mirror to look at unfinished images in reverse. The ongoing, iterative back-and-forth between the real and the mirror image, helped move his pictures along.

Da Vinci believed in exploring topics, beliefs, or objects from opposing points of view: To understand joy, one must know sorrow; and to understand change, one must know constancy (Gelb, 1998). That is why da Vinci dissected each body part from at least three different angles. He drew flowers, birds in motion, and the locks of his subject's hair, from several different angles.

Box 1.3: Leonardo da Vinci
(continued)

Da Vinci privileged dialectical thinking. To him, multiple and opposing perspectives yielded deeper understandings of any phenomenon. Further, da Vinci's work embodied dialectical thinking. Freud (1961), for instance, noted that *Mona Lisa's* smile "lies on the cusp of good and evil, compassion and cruelty, seduction and innocence, the fleeting and the eternal" (Gelb, 1998, pp. 146–147).

Some attribute the Red Sox's decades of failure to "The Curse of the Bambino"—referring to the questionable sale by the Red Sox of one of the greatest baseball players of all-time, Babe Ruth, to their arch rivals, the Yankees.

A championship drought lasting over eight decades involves countless factors including quality of team management, player abilities, good luck, or misfortune. However, what explains the deep allegiance that Red Sox fans continue to hold for their team despite 86 years of failure?

The answer lies in dialectics. Red Sox fans love their team dearly while they simultaneously experience heartbreaks as the team allowed a championship to slip through their fingers. The Red Sox were in the World Series Championship in 1946, 1967, 1975, and 1986 and each time they lost in the final seventh game. Further, they recorded many second place finishes to the New York Yankees in the American League Championship whose winner competes in the World Series. Nonetheless, Red Sox fans returned by the millions every year. Even in years when the Red Sox team was mediocre, the faithful would turn out for games cheering their players. For these fans, love and disillusionment, joy and anguish, pride and embarrassment were not separate emotions. These dialectical tensions co-existed, simmered, and reinforced themselves over time. What happened to these tensions when the Red Sox finally won the World Series in 2004? Were they resolved?

The depth of the dialectic tension felt by Red Sox fans is exemplified in the reaction of one fan soon after the victory. He recounted to us: "I felt numb. I didn't know what to feel. I never thought this would happen in my lifetime. I'm happy but I'm also confused. What am I supposed to feel next year?"[2]

■ Dualisms versus Dialectics

Dialectics are not dualisms. Dualisms are characterized by mutually antagonistic realities which cannot co-exist together. So, hot and cold represents a dualism. Dualisms are binary opposites that are characterized by an either/or relationship (Miller, 2002). In describing dualisms no assumptions are made about the interdependence, simultaneity, or possible unification of opposing forces (Fairhurst, 2001). From a dualistic perspective we come to understand "what something is by focusing on what it is not" (Fairhurst, 2001, p. 380). In contrast, a dialectic perspective focuses on simultaneous existence of each force, and the tensions that exist between opposing forces. Simply stated, rather than reducing tensions to binary decisions (either/or), a dialectical perspective urges us to think in terms of "both/and."

The distinction between a dualism and dialectic can be understood with the analogy of the difference between catching a ball and juggling multiple balls. When a ball is thrown at a person, he/she either catches it or not. However, when juggling multiple balls, a person has to simultaneously manage the interdependent tension of opposite actions—throwing and catching with each hand. Throwing from the left hand to the right requires an opposite action of throwing from the right hand to the left (Johnson, 1996). In order for juggling to occur, each hand has to throw and receive balls at the same time and on an ongoing basis.

■ Elements of Dialectics

The concept of dialectics has been conceptualized in various ways. Central to most of these conceptualizations are the following *four* elements: (1) contradiction, (2) motion, (3) totality, and (4) praxis (Conville, 1998; Dindia, 1998; Rawlins, 1992, 1998; Van Leer, 1998). *Contradiction* refers to the co-existence of oppositional forces. For example, in human relationships the forces of independence and dependence co-exist. Although these forces are antagonistic, they characterize the interdependent relational dynamics between participants. *Motion* refers to activities, movement, or changes that occur as people shift between the competing poles of action. *Totality* refers to the "constant interconnection and reciprocal influence of multiple individual, interpersonal, and social factors" (Rawlins, 1992, p. 7).

Totality implies that multiple dialectics can operate at once, each shaping and being shaped by the other. Totality also draws attention to relational interdependence, implying that a person's actions in a social system impact others within that system. *Praxis* "describes the human communicator as an ongoing producer and product of his or her choices within an encompassing cultural matrix" (Rawlins, 1992, pp. 7–8). Put differently, human beings are simultaneously subjects and objects of their own actions. They influence their environment and, in turn, their environment influences them.

■ A Short History of the Dialectic Perspective

Dialectical perspectives were advanced by Chinese philosophers some 3,000 years ago. The ancient Chinese symbol of *Yin–Yang* embodies dialectical thinking (Baxter & Montgomery, 1996). The interlocking black and white shapes within the circle represent the interaction of two energies—*yin* (black) and *yang* (white).While *yin* signifies the dark, passive, downward, cold, contracting, and weak forces, *yang* signifies bright, active, upward, hot, expanding, and strong forces. These energies are in continual, simultaneous movement, shaping outcomes and being shaped by them.

Some 3,000 years ago, Lao-Tzu (1988), a contemporary of Confucius in China, in his classic treatise, the *Tao te Ching* [Book of the Way], further emphasized the importance of contradiction-riddled dialectical tensions in our daily lives: "When people see some things as beautiful, other things become ugly" (p. 2); or "Because she has let go of herself, she is perfectly fulfilled" (p. 11).

In Western contexts, the concept of dialectics can be traced back to Plato and Socrates. However, it was Hegel in the late 18th century who significantly advanced the dialectic perspective in philosophy. Hegel, a professor at the University of Heidelberg, placed everything—logical, natural, human, and divine—in a dialectical scheme that repeatedly swung from thesis to antithesis and back again to a higher and richer synthesis (Rossi, 1989). He strongly opposed the view that human beings and nature are unidimensional, unconnected, and static phenomenon. To Hegel, the dialectic represents a unifying metaphysical process that underlies the apparent diversity of the world.

In abstraction, Hegelian dialectics can be understood by examining the dialectic of "being" and "nothingness." "Being" (thesis) can be contrasted to its opposite "nothingness" (antithesis). However, just to do so oversimplifies the relationship between the oppositional tensions. The more accurate observation according to Hegel is that there is an interaction or movement between being and nothingness which is "becoming" (synthesis). As Hegel (1969, p. 176) explained: "Becoming is the unseparatedness of being and nothing, not the unity which abstracts from being and nothing; but as the unity of being and nothing it is this determinate unity in which there is both being and nothing" (Hegel, 1969, p. 176).

Hegel's dialectics influenced German intellectual life in general, and in particular he impacted the thinking of his student Karl Marx. Drawing upon Hegel's work, Marx developed his treatise on material dialectics, a philosophical approach to emancipation of the oppressed by overturning the structures of oppression. In Marxist terms, the current structure (thesis) is overthrown (anti-thesis), leading to a resolution of structural inequities (synthesis).

Marx's views on dialectical materialism were developed fully in *A Contribution to the Critique of Political Economy*. Marx (1977, p. 78) argued:

> At times, people complain in frustration that they lack the *means* to achieve their *ends*, or alternatively, that they can justify their corrupt methods of work by the lofty aims they pursue. For dialectics, *means* and *ends* are a unity of opposites and in the final analysis, there can be no contradiction between means and ends—when the objective is rightly understood, the material conditions [means] for its solution are already present.

According to Marx, thoughts were not passive and independent reflections of the material world. Rather, thoughts were the products of human labor. Furthermore, he believed that the contradictory nature of our thoughts had their origin in the contradictions within human society. From Marx's perspective, dialectics were not something imposed on the world from outside. Nor could dialectics be discovered by the activity of pure reason. Instead, dialectics were a product of human labor trying to change the world. Substantive changes occurred through the practical struggle to overcome the contradictions between means and ends. Thus, by overturning the structures of oppression, structural inequities could be overcome.

Russian philologist and social theorist Mikhail Bakhtin extended and reshaped Marx's conception of dialectics. According to Bakhtin (1981, 1984), dialectic tensions are inevitable and present in all personal relationships. Further, Bakhtin believed that communication prompted by dialectic tensions allows partners to grow individually and together. Consequently, each relational impulse needs a contradictory one. By focusing on the idea of process in dialectics, Bakhtin (1981) argued that change is the only paradoxical constant in human relationships.

Bakhtin (1981) noted that everday human action occurred at the confluence of a "contradiction-ridden, tension-filled unity of two embattled tendencies" (p. 272). These are forces of unity (the centripetal tendency) and forces of difference (the centrifugal tendency). Bakhtin (1981) explained: "Every utterance participates in the 'unitary language' (in its centripetal forces and tendencies) and at the same time partakes of social and historical heteroglossia (the centrifugal, stratifying forces)" (p. 272).

Extending Bakhtin's centripetal/centrifugal thinking, Leslie Baxter (1988, 1990, 1992, 1993; Baxter & Montgomery, 1996; Montgomery & Baxter, 1998) developed and tested a dialectical theory of communication, explaining the inherent oppositional tensions in relationships. According to Baxter, *three* main dialectics exist in relationships. Each of these dialectics exists both between the individuals in the relationship (internal) and between the relationship itself and the larger context within which the relationship exists (external).

First, the dialectic of *integration* and *separation* focuses on the tension between wanting to be connected and separate in a relationship. The internal form of this dialectic is *connection* and *autonomy*. In a relationship this dialectic refers to the simultaneous desire to be close to another person while also wanting to retain a sense of autonomy. The external form of the integration/separation dialectic is *inclusion* and *seclusion*. This involves the tension between wanting to include others, such as friends, in the time spent together as a couple while also wanting to spend time secluded as a couple.

Second, the dialectic of *expression* and *privacy* involves the tension between wanting to be open and closed in a relationship. The internal form of this dialectic is *openness* and *closedness*. This dialectic refers to the tension of wanting to self-disclose to a relational partner while also wanting to remain private. The external form of this dialectic is *revelation* and *concealment.* This involves the tension to reveal the details of a relationship to others external to the relationship, while also wanting to conceal relational details from others.

Third, the dialectic of *stability* and *change* involves the tension between wanting both sameness and variety in our relationships. The internal form of this dialectic is *predictability* and *novelty.* This dialectic refers to the tension of wanting some degree of predictability so we know what to expect from our relational partner. However, too much predictability may become boring so we also want some novelty in our relationship. Too much predictability or too much novelty may both lead to relational dissolution. The external form of this dialectic is *conventionality* and *uniqueness.* This dialectic involves the tension between wanting a relationship to conform to social norms while also wanting a relationship to be unique.

One of the central tenets of Baxter's perspective on dialectics is praxis. According to this tenet, humans are simultaneously actors and objects of their own actions: "People function as proactive actors who make communicative choices in how to function in their social world. Simultaneously, however, they become reactive objects, because their actions become reified in a variety of normative and institutionalized practices that establish the boundaries of subsequent communicative moves" (Baxter & Montgomery, 1996, pp. 13–14). Thus, Baxter argues that everyday social realities are outcomes of concrete practices informed by our actions of the past. So the past informs the present and our present actions will inform our future actions. These linkages among actions occurring at different points in time make us both subjects and objects of our own actions.

Another prominent perspective on relational dialectics is advanced by William Rawlins, Stocker Professor of Communication Studies at Ohio University and a colleague of author Singhal. Focusing on interactional dialectics in friendships, Rawlins (1992) identified *four* primary tensions.

The first dialectic is between the *freedom to be independent* and the *freedom to be dependent.* The freedom to be independent refers to the pursuit of one's interests without help or interference from a friend. The freedom to be dependent is being able to rely on a friend in a time of need. This dialectic tension exists when one person needs to rely on another yet also wishes he/she could solve the problem independently.

The second dialectic involves the tension between *affection* and *instrumentality.* Affection occurs when caring for a friend is an end in itself. Instrumentality is present when caring for a friend is a means to an end. Dichotomizing these tensions is difficult because one may derive utilitarian rewards from a friendship regardless of the original purpose for engaging in that friendship.

The third dialectic focuses on *judgment* and *acceptance.* Judgment refers to evaluating another person's failings, weaknesses, or mistakes. Acceptance refers to liking someone who has strengths and weaknesses as well as charming and irritating qualities. These two forces exist in dynamic tension with one another because we often value acceptance from friends while also appreciating judgment from people who genuinely care about us.

The fourth dialectic is between *expressiveness* and *protectiveness.* When we are expressive in friendship we reveal personal thoughts and feel free to comment on the messages and actions of that friend. When we exhibit protectiveness we shy away from self-disclosures that may make us vulnerable. We also may choose to preserve a friend's confidence or exercise restraint in commenting on sensitive issues. The tension between these forces may arise in many situations. For example, if a friend engages in potentially harmful behavior, we may be expressive in describing the problem yet restrain ourselves from commenting upon the most sensitive aspects of that behavior.

In summary, the concept of dialectics has been explored by many scholars. In philosophy, Hegel advanced a perspective that placed everything in a dialectic scheme that swung repeatedly from thesis to antithesis and back again to a higher and richer synthesis. Marx took this perspective into the material world by advancing the argument that current political and economic structures (thesis) may be overthrown (antithesis), leading to a resolution of structural inequities (synthesis). Bakhtin extended and reshaped Marx's views by looking at how dialectic tensions are present in all personal relationships. Finally, Baxter and Montgomery and Rawlins developed specific perspectives on how personal relationships involve dialectic tensions between competing poles of communicative action.

In the next section, we outline why it is important to examine the process of organizing for social change from a dialectic perspective.

■ Dialectics and Social Change

To describe the process of organizing for social change requires consideration of the nuances, contradictions, and dialectics that emerge when people attempt to change their behavior at the individual or collective level. Social change is seldom a neat and tidy process that flows linearly or can be predicted. It rarely flows directly and immediately from participation in organizational activities that involve a specific group of people. Rather, social change emerges in a nonlinear, circuitous, and dialectic process of struggle between competing poles of communicative action. It is a rather complex process, if not downright messy.

While organizing for social change, people often create a social learning environment in which new behavioral options may be considered only to later discover that what seems possible in theory may not work so easily in real-life. Certain community members may develop a sense of collective efficacy in solving a social problem, but the solution they devise may not be effective. A person may say that they believe in performing a certain action, yet these beliefs may not be reflected in his or her actions.

Leading organizational and communication scholars share this viewpoint. Many scholars have drawn attention to the dilemmatic character of organizational life and how change processes of any sort must be understood from a perspective that recognizes contradictions, paradoxes, ironies, and dialectics (e.g., Ashcraft, 2000, 2001; Ashcraft & Trethewey, 2004; Handy, 1994; Harter, 2004; Harter & Krone, 2001; O'Connor, 1995; Poole & Van de Ven, 1989; Putnam, 1986; Stohl & Cheney, 2001; Tracy, 2004; Tretheway, 1999; Tretheway & Ashcraft, 2004; Wendt, 1998). Furthermore, struggles between competing poles of communicative action may be intensified with a social justice mission or with the turbulent and complex environments characteristic of post-modernity. Such a focus disrupts the myth of rationality that has traditionally supported much theorizing about how people work interdependently in organizations. Simply stated, any contemporary theory of organizing for social change must account for the struggles and tensions that surface as people act together to accomplish individual and collective goals.

Contexts of Organizing for Social Change

In the present book, in chapters 2 to 5, respectively, we focus on four different contexts of organizing for social change. These include: (1) Grameen Bank in Bangladesh, (2) dairy cooperatives of India's National Dairy Development Board, (3) entertainment-education and community organizing in Indian villages, and (4) community suppers in Appalachia, U.S.A. In each of these social change contexts, we identify a set of dialectical tensions (discussed later in this chapter).

■ Grameen Bank in Bangladesh

The Grameen [rural] Bank in Bangladesh is an international icon of grassroots organizing, which mobilized the poor, landless, and vulnerable rural populations to come together, generate incomes through self-employment, and improve their socioeconomic conditions (Auwal & Singhal, 1992; Fuglesang & Chandler, 1988; Yunus & Jolis, 1999). The Grameen Bank provides its poor clients with collateral-free loans, loan utilization training, and various other social services, maintaining a loan recovery rate of 99 percent. Currently, 4.2 million families (comprising an estimated 25 million individuals) directly benefit from Grameen Bank's operation in Bangladesh (Grameen Bank, 2005). The Grameen Bank believes that credit represents a fundamental human right, allowing the poor an opportunity to unlock their own potential. Over 500 Grameen Bank replication efforts are underway in dozens of countries, including about 150 micro-enterprise based initiatives in the United States.

The Grameen Bank was the brainchild of Muhammad Yunus, a professor of development economics at Chittagong University in Bangladesh. In doing research in Jobra village (in the vicinity of Chittagong University), Yunus realized how poor people worked as "bonded" laborers to local moneylenders, who charged exorbitant interest rates—as high as 10 percent a day. Poor women with marketable skills (such as weaving, handicrafts, or sewing) had little hope of breaking the shackles of poverty without access to credit at reasonable rates of interest. So, in 1976, Yunus launched the Grameen Bank action research project in Jobra village to (a) provide collateral-free micro-loans to the poorest-of-the-poor women, (*b*) eliminate the exploitation by moneylenders, (*c*) create self-employment opportunities for the poor, and (*d*) organize the poor into a framework for their empowerment (Papa, Auwal, & Singhal, 1995, 1997). Initially, Yunus borrowed money from a local bank to lend to the poor women, as the bank was reluctant to lend to them for lack of collateral. The first loan recipients received very small loans for self-employment and repaid the loans with conventional interest in weekly installments. Initial successes led to expansion of the project to different poverty-gripped districts in Bangladesh. Eventually, in 1983, seven years after the beginning of the action research project, the Grameen Bank became an autonomous organization authorized by the Bangladesh government.

The Grameen Bank has since grown in magnitude and importance, continuously experimenting with new ideas to solve social problems and devising and adapting its policies to meet local needs. In the late 1990s, for instance, the Grameen Bank launched the innovative village mobile telephony project with the idea of placing one mobile telephone in each of Bangladesh's 68,000 villages, providing telephone access in remote areas that were previously unserved or underserved. By 2005, over 51,000 villages, comprising some 100 million rural people, who had previously never used a telephone, had achieved access to telephony.

In chapter 2, we examine in-depth the dialectic tensions in the Grameen Bank's efforts at organizing for social change in Bangladesh.

■ Dairy Cooperatives of India's National Dairy Development Board

The National Dairy Development Board (NDDB), the umbrella organization for 112,590 village-level dairy milk cooperatives in India with a membership of 12.1 million farmer members, is perhaps one of the world's biggest programs in organizing for social change. Its charismatic founder, Dr. Verghese Kurien started as an employee of dairy farmers in Gujarat's Kaira District, and launched the NDDB in 1965, on the insistence of the then Prime Minister, Lal Bahadur Shastri, to replicate the famous Anand dairy milk cooperative in Kaira

District. Starting from a small cluster of dairy cooperatives in Kaira District, Kurien slowly expanded the network of dairy cooperatives to include 12.1 million dairy farmers in 2005, directly influencing the livelihoods of 70 million people.

The village-level dairy cooperatives are networked in mutually supportive networks with district level milk unions and state and national level dairy cooperative federations (Kurien, 1997a). Together, these unions market close to 15 million liters of milk everyday, delivering clean, hygienic milk and milk products to urban consumers, and providing steady incomes and support services to the rural poor. Nearly $1 billion is paid out annually to these milk producer families, many of whom represent poor, landless, and small and marginal farmers.

In 1988–89, NDDB launched the Cooperative Development (CD) program to create stronger and more viable dairy cooperatives that were responsive to the needs of its millions of farmer members. The CD program (and its many incarnations) have since endeavored to strengthen village-level dairy cooperative societies in India through member education and leadership training, especially concentrating its educational activities on women dairy farmers. The money that dairy farmers receive from milk sales is generally controlled by men, who are usually the official members of the village-level dairy cooperative society (DCS) and make up most of the elected officers at the village, district, state, and national levels. The patriarchal dominance of Indian dairy cooperatives results from the prevalence of traditional Indian rural values and cultural norms (Chen, Mitra, Athreya, Dholakia, Law, & Rao, 1986; Sen & Grown, 1987; Sharma, 1991; Papa, Singhal, Ghanekar, & Papa, 2000; Wayangankar, 1994). Although some 85 percent of the daily dairy tasks associated with dairying are carried out by women, they constituted about 10 percent of the total membership in India's dairy cooperatives in the late 1980s (Philip, 1994; Wayangankar, 1994). Thanks to the CD and other affiliated programs, these numbers have risen to about 25 percent in 2005. In fact, of the 112,590 village-level dairy cooperatives in 2005, 18,500 are all-women dairy cooperatives, where women are not just members but also its elected leaders.

In chapter 3, we examine in-depth the dialectic tensions in NDDB's social change efforts at empowering women dairy farmers in India.

■ Entertainment-Education and Community Organizing in India

Entertainment-education (E-E) media programs are designed purposefully to both entertain and educate audience members. The educational objectives involve increasing audience members' knowledge about an educational issue, creating favorable attitudes, shifting social norms, and changing overt behavior. All India Radio (AIR), the Indian national radio network, has been responsible for developing and airing a number of E-E soap operas—which are then disseminated to a mass audience. We were involved in studying the community mobilizing aspects of two of these E-E radio serials: *Tinka Tinka Sukh* [Happiness in Small Things] broadcast during 1996–97; and *Taru* (named after the female protagonist) broadcast during 2002–2003.

The starting point for social change linked to E-E programming occurs when audience members become interested in the storylines and characters of the media program. Many audience members may strongly identify with media role models and begin to emulate them. Many become so attached to certain characters that they develop relationships with them that simulate face-to-face interpersonal relationships. This phenomenon is called *parasocial interaction* (Singhal & Rogers, 1999).

Audience members' interest and involvement with an E-E storyline, including identification with certain characters, is not sufficient to prompt social change, however. E-E programs appear to have their strongest impact on audience members when the messages embedded in the programs spark conversations and debate about the topic among listeners. For instance, listeners to the *Tinka Tinka Sukh* radio soap opera in Lutsaan village of northern India said that they were "emotionally-stirred" by Poonam's character in the program. Poonam, a young bride, is beaten and verbally abused by her husband and in-laws for not providing an adequate dowry, the payment by a bride's parents to the groom's parents, in whose home she lives after marriage. In recent decades, dowry payments in India have become exorbitant, usually including cash or gold, a television set, or a refrigerator (Singhal & Rogers, 1999). If the dowry payments are inadequate, the bride may by mistreated by the husband's family. In extreme cases, the bride is burned to death in a kitchen "accident," called a "dowry death." In the radio soap opera, Poonam was humiliated and sent back to her parents after incorrectly being accused by her in-laws of infidelity to her husband. In desperation, she commits suicide. These episodes generated a lot of discussion and debate among the radio listeners of Lutsaan village, who then wrote a letter to AIR, outlining their discussions and actions: "It is a curse that for the sake of dowry, innocent women are compelled to commit suicide. Worse still…women are murdered for not bring-ing dowry. The education we got from '*Tinka Tinka Sukh*', particu-larly on dowry is significant…. People who think differently about dowry will be reformed; those who practice dowry will see the right way and why they must change" (Singhal & Rogers, 1999, p. 5).

Our examination of E-E sparked community organizing was centered in several rural communities of India, including Lutsaan village in Uttar Pradesh State (during 1997–98), as also Abirpur, Kamtaul, Madhapur, and Chandrahatti villages in the state of Bihar (during 2001–2004). The organizing appeared to be prompted by conversations among peers that stimulated social learning. People learned from one another possible options for changing their behavior and improving their communities. We also learned about collective actions taken by community members to address social ills (e.g., establishing schools for *dalit* or lower caste children). *Unlike other social change contexts discussed in the present book, these community-organizing activities were created solely through the initiatives of disempowered community members.*

In chapter 4, we examine the dialectic tensions in community organizing sparked by E-E media initiatives in India.

■ Community Suppers in Appalachia, U.S.A.

Community suppers are held each day in thousands of locations across the U.S.—in churches, neighborhood pantries, and community centers. Typically, volunteers prepare meals alongside the poor and the homeless, viewing community suppers as a community building process. Community suppers usually incorporate certain rituals that may help network and inspire the poor. Grace might be said col-lectively to thank God for the meal. The poor may participate in meal preparation, in laying the table, or serving food—giving them a sense of dignity and agency. Community building occurs as the poor and the homeless form relationships with others who are experiencing similar problems. Such connections may raise collective possibilities. For instance, two homeless people may be able to pool resources to afford an apartment jointly.

The poor and the homeless also forge new connections with other well-to-do community members, who serve as volunteers or participants in the community supper. When people from different socioeconomic classes connect, the poor person may potentially access ideas, resources, and possibilities for action that they may have never considered. Perhaps even more important for the rehabilitation of the disconnected is the realization that the poor and the well-to-do, at a certain level, are one community. Social change becomes possible only when the poor and oppressed recognize that they have a support network much broader and deeper than they thought was possible. When well-to-do community members show their willingness to work alongside their poorer neighbors, there is a restoration of hope among the poor. The poor people's fear of failing may be lessened if they are assured that there are others who support their cause.

Social change is also prompted by the specific nature of the support provided by organizers of the community suppers. Help may be given to the homeless in finding shelter. Guidance may be given concerning job training and employment opportunities. Available medical care services may be identified. Through such assistance, the homeless are able to concentrate less on day-to-day survival and more on planning for the future. Being able to plan for the future represents an important step toward self-sufficiency.

In chapter 5, we examine the dialectical tensions in organizing the poor and the homeless through community suppers in the Appalachian region of the United States.

Dialectics in Social Change Processes

Our investigations of the four organizing for social change contexts (described in the previous section) suggested that many dialectic tensions surface as a group of disempowered people attempt to change their thinking and behavior with or without the assistance of external agents. Based on our analysis, we argue that four dialectic tensions are central to the process of organizing for social change: (1) *control* and *emancipation*, (2) *oppression* and *empowerment*, (3) *dissemination* and *dialogue,* and (4) *fragmentation* and *unity.* The dynamics of these dialectic tensions are described next.

■ Dialectic of Control and Emancipation

Organizing for social change efforts embody a dialectic tension between *control* and *emancipation.* The process of organizing for social change requires the disempowered to embed their actions in some control system that guides them to move from dependence to self-sufficiency. Although the control system may vary, the poor must engage in coordinated activities that are embedded in some organizational structure. The activities the poor perform are guided by rules and expectations that are reinforced by organizational members and the organizational structure in place. Although rules and expectations limit freedom on the one hand, emancipation becomes possible as the poor act together to build capital (economic and social) and free themselves from oppressive relationships.

The relationship between control and emancipation is not a simple one, however. Control systems make emancipation possible, but can simultaneously be problematic. If membership within the organization brings with it rewards that outweigh the costs of internalizing the control systems, then continued membership is justified. Alternatively, even in emancipatory systems control may be exercised in ways that raise questions about fairness and human dignity. If emancipation carries with it the requirement that one work 14 hours a day, 7 days a week, is one really free?

To illustrate the dialectic of control and emancipation, consider the case of Tasmiah, a Grameen Bank member in Bangladesh who experienced difficulties in loan repayment. Shortly after receiving her first loan Tasmiah's husband took her loan money. When she told her story to a friend who was also a Grameen member, she received criticism rather than sympathy. Tasmiah's friend was concerned that her own loan request would be jeopardized if Tasmiah failed to repay her loan in a timely manner. Tasmiah felt so humiliated and accountable to her other group members that she went to a village moneylender for a loan. Although Tasmiah's emancipation is linked to her membership in the Grameen Bank, the Bank's control mechanisms—that are unsympathetic to loan defaults—inadvertently oppress her further.

■ Dialectic of Oppression and Empowerment

Organizing for social change efforts also embody the dialectic between *oppression* and *empowerment*. This dialectic tension emphasizes that the process of social change is seldom linear or unidirectional. A person may act in a way that is empowering in one context but simultaneously oppressing in another. Alternatively, a plan that seems to have the potential to empower actually backfires and a person becomes further oppressed. Further, external forces may deny access to power no matter how well a strategy for empowerment is devised. So, to understand social change requires us to look at the tensions that pull people back and forth between forces that both empower and oppress.

Importantly, the experience of being pulled between the competing poles of oppression and empowerment is not an isolated experience for the poor; rather it is a central part of how the social change process unfolds. For example, the practice of *purdah* [veiling] in some parts of India demonstrates how women struggle with enabling and constraining forces to empower themselves. While the system of *purdah* mainly reflects an oppressive patriarchal code that keeps women in the domestic domain, it also bestows respect and honor on women. Thus, *purdah* simultaneously empowers and oppresses. Young unmarried women in village India do not practice *purdah* in front of adults or other women (Plate 1.3), negotiating an empowered gendered space in the face of overwhelming gender inequality.

■ Dialectic of Dissemination and Dialogue

The dialectic between *dissemination* and *dialogue* is also present in communities struggling with social change. When a group of oppressed people rely on outside, expert-disseminated information to guide their empowerment, it often creates a dependency relationship that might actually limit or derail empowerment. Perhaps the outside source directs, cajoles, or manipulates the poor to behave in certain ways without completely understanding them.

Why shouldn't the poor rely on their own ingenuity to realize empowerment? In the context of organizing for social change, dialogue involves a sharing of information, ideas, stories, and experiences

Plate 1.3
The practice of *purdah* is empowering and oppressing for Rajasthani village women in India
Note how young unmarried women do not practice *purdah* [veil], carving out a unique empowered space in the midst of overwhelming gender inequality.
Source: Personal Files of the Authors.

among the poor. Dialogue validates the local knowledge and resources of oppressed groups by facilitating a social learning process that is reflective, critical, and transitive. By developing a consciousness of oppression through dialogue, the oppressed can develop the power to transform reality.

Our stance is that the relationship between dissemination and dialogue is more complicated. There may be instances when information dissemination manipulates the poor or limits their potential. However, what about instances where the poor take the seed of an external idea and then develop that idea into a unique strategy for social change based on internal dialogue and conversations. Further, even when the poor dialogue with one another, isn't there an element of dissemination present? Some members may know more about the topic, and may express it more persuasively. Is such internal dissemination manipulative? The answer is not simple. Sometimes manipulation may be present, other times it may not be present. The answer depends on whose vantage point is being considered and with what understandings of context.

We argue that both dissemination and dialogue exist simultaneously in a dialectic tension with one another. For example, in the Indian radio soap opera *Taru* (described in chapter 4), the character Neha starts a school for *dalit* (low caste) children. Motivated by this story, young men and women in Bihar's Abirpur village established a school for lower caste children, despite initial opposition from some community members. Over the course of multiple conversations, they were able to persuade community members, including their own parents, to change their views toward people of lower castes. Importantly, although this social change was sparked by institutionalized information dissemination in the form of a purposively designed radio soap opera, this change would not have occurred without dialogue between and among listeners of *Taru* and other community members. Clearly, a dialectical tension between information dissemination and dialogue is present in the process of social change.

■ Dialectic of Fragmentation and Unity

Finally, we examine the dialectical tension between *fragmentation* and *unity* in organizing for social change efforts. Poverty and homelessness often leads to the separation and isolation of the poor from one another, and from members of other socio-economic groups. As will become apparent through the multiple narratives in this book, one path to building community is to connect the isolated to other people. As connections multiply among the poor and the homeless, and between them and other groups, a diverse community is developed. To survive, this community must locate and secure ties that bind the collective together.

However, differences (in ideas, actions, and socioeconomic status) between people will always be present in any community. Fragmentation occurs when there are multiple voices and interpretations present in a community. Often this multi-vocality separates people from one another, rather than unifies them into a consensus. On one hand, such fragmentation may be necessary to preserve diversity. On the other hand, these differences may create tensions and separate people rather than unify them. Is it possible to sustain forces of fragmentation and unity in a way that preserves the connections between people? In some instances communities may remain intact despite

---

Box 1.4: An Adhesive that Does not Stick

Dialectical tensions can be viewed as frustrating or unproductive. Or they can be welcomed as opportunities. Identifying and managing dialectics is as important for social change organizations as it is for corporations. Innovative organizations encourage, nurture, and manage dialectical tensions with aplomb (Fletcher & Olwyler, 1997; Johnson, 1996). Consider the case of 3M (Minnesota Mining and Manufacturing Company), hailed as a champion of innovation and creativity (Peters & Waterman, 1988).

In 1968, Dr. Spencer Silver, a scientist at 3M Company was trying to make an adhesive with high stickiness, and ended up with an adhesive that did not stick well. Rather than shelve his project as a failure, he experimented with the properties of this adhesive. An adhesive that does not stick embodies a dialectical tension, a literal push and pull.

Six years later, in 1974, Silver's friend, Art Fry, also a 3M scientist, was looking for a sticky bookmark. While singing in the Church Choir for dif-ferent services, the bookmark in Fry's book of hymns kept falling off, leading to an embarrassing scramble during services. Knowing about Silver's "failed" adhesive, Fry made a bookmark that was sticky enough to not fall off from a page, but not tacky enough to rip paper apart. The sticky bookmark was both temporarily-permanent and permanently-temporary. It was unique in that is was a repositionable adhesive. Nobody before had thought that adhesives could be repeatedly repositioned. Spence Silver and Art Fry had invented the sticky yellow Post-It note.

In 2005, 3M markets over 600 Post-It products, including note pads, flip charts, and easel pads. Post-it notes are available in eight standard sizes, 25 shapes, and 62 colors; and sold in over 120 countries. They earn 3M annual revenues of over a billion dollars.

The Post-It note exemplifies that dialectical thinking can pay rich dividends for entrepreneurial corporations. Why not then for social entrepreneurs?

---

forces that fragment. In other cases the forces of fragmentation may overwhelm the ties that bind people together.

To demonstrate the tension between fragmentation and unity consider the story of Bill, a poor elderly man who frequently attends a community supper in a small college town in the Appalachian region of the U.S. Bill was clearly connected to many people around him at the community suppers. He engaged in animated discussions with

Figure 1.3
Organizing for social change processes embody multiple, co-existing dialectical tensions

The poor, the homeless, and the disempowered experience contradictory tensions that both support and negate attempts to bring change. Our research suggests that the following four dialectics characterize organizing for social change phenomenon: The dialectics of *control* and *emancipation, oppression* and *empowerment, dissemination* and *dialogue,* and *fragmentation* and *unity.* These dialectics interact and intersect within a meta-dialectic of stability and change.

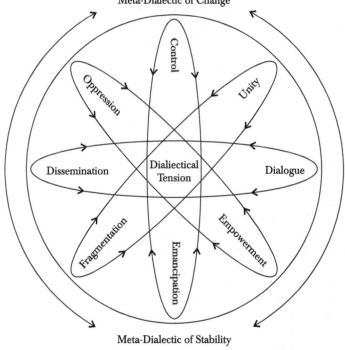

others, both fellow poor people, and the relatively well-to-do members of the community. However, when he referred to the college students who frequently prepared the community dinners, he demonstrated how he experienced fragmentation. Bill supported his parents financially from the age of nine when he first went to work in the mines of Kentucky. He supported them until they died about a decade ago. Bill argues that college students of today do not understand him when he talks about financially supporting one's parents. He believes these students are different from him; they take from their parents rather than giving to them. For Bill, the meaning of a harmonious family is everyone chipping in. As Bill engages with the various people who attend the community supper, he simultaneously experiences the forces of fragmentation and unity.

Although we will examine each of the four dialectics heretofore described as reflecting separate tensions, these dialectics may be unified by a meta-dialectic of stability and change (Baxter & Montgomery, 1996) or permanence and change (Burke, 1954/1984) (Figure 1.3). Specifically, control, oppression, dissemination, and fragmentation may represent the forces of stability or permanence that dominate the lives of the poor. Oppositional forces of change may then surface when the poor participate in social change programs and encounter the forces of emancipation, empowerment, dialogue, and unity. This meta-dialectic totality clarifies the interconnection and reciprocal influence of multiple and competing poles of communicative action.

Conclusions

Organizing for social change is a complex process that requires the coordinated and individual actions of many people—the poor and the privileged, outsiders and insiders, and expertise and local knowledge. The organized activities range from disbursement and utilization of micro-credit to empower the poor, to coordinating the actions of community members to prepare and share food with one another, to coordinating actions to establish a school for lower caste community members. Individual action is also an important part of fostering social change whether through a champion such as Muhammad Yunus of the Grameen Bank, or a local hero such as a poor woman who opposes the actions of an unscrupulous moneylender.

Dialectics are, as well, a central part of the experience of organizing for social change. The poor, the homeless, and the disempowered often experience contradictory tensions as they are pulled between competing poles of communicative action. This occurs because the process of organizing for social change seldom unfolds in a neat and tidy manner. Rather, people are pulled between forces that oppose one another in a dynamic tension. These forces both support and negate attempts to bring change to a community. The four dialectic tensions that we explore in this book are: *control* and *emancipation, oppression* and *empowerment, dissemination* and *dialogue,* and *fragmentation* and *unity.*

In the subsequent chapters, these four dialectics are examined in four different social contexts where the poor attempt to organize for change: The Grameen Bank of Bangladesh, the dairy cooperatives of India's NDDB, village-based communities that are exposed to entertainment education radio broadcasts in rural India, and community suppers in the Appalachian region of the United States.

In the concluding chapter, we embark on the journey of theory and praxis, reflecting on the lessons learned about organizing for social change from a dialectic perspective.

Notes

1. This description draws upon Singhal and Rogers (2003) and author Singhal's fieldnotes while visiting the Sonagachi Project in Kolkata in March, 2004.
2. Clearly, not all the fans of the Boston Red Sox share the same feelings of our respondent. However, our respondent reflects the feelings of many Red Sox fans whose affection for a team is based in part on that team's perennial quest to win yet always coming up short.

2 Dialectic of control and emancipation in Bangladesh's Grameen Bank[1]

We should not reconcile dichotomies, but rather recognize the complementarity of representation of events.
—Niels Bohr, Noble Prize-winning physicist and a self-avowed dialectical thinker (quoted in Holton, 1973, p. 118)

Several years ago we interviewed Tasmiah, a poor rural woman in Bangladesh. Her story provided us a deep understanding of the dialectic of control and emancipation when the poor attempt to lift themselves out of poverty. Tasmiah had three young children; her husband worked as a daily wage laborer on the farm of a wealthy landowner. After toiling in the sun for 10 hours each day, his compensation was a handful of rice. Tasmiah, her husband, and young children suffered hunger pains day and night. Malnutrition was setting in and Tasmiah worried how long her children would be able to survive such hunger and deprivation.

When Tasmiah approached her husband about the possibility of working outside the home to supplement the family income, he refused. His position was that his honor would be compromised and he would be subject to ridicule in the village for not being able to support his family. The practice of *purdah* [veiling] also restricted Tasmiah's mobility outside her home.

One day Tasmiah learned about the microlending programs of the Grameen Bank. If she could become a member, she would be given a loan to start a small business and the income could be used to support her family. However, when she asked for her husband's permission to enroll, he refused.

As her children's health deteriorated, Tasmiah, now desperate, mustered enough courage to attend a Grameen Bank meeting. She met many other women who were in a similar state. In a few weeks, she received her first loan of approximately $30 (U.S.). Her hands shook as she accepted the money from the bank worker. Her eyes were moist, overwhelmed by the emotion of being in a position to feed her children.

When Tasmiah was stirring the evening meal, her husband returned home from work. Not able to restrain her exuberance, and clutching the wad of *Taka* bills in her trembling hand, she told her husband about her membership in the Grameen Bank. The color of his face changed; he flew into a rage. Admonishing Tasmiah for disobeying him, he said: "I divorce you, divorce you, divorce you." Her marriage ended. He took her loan money, threw Tasmiah and the three children out of the house, and remarried within a few months.

In the course of a single day Tasmiah experienced a shift from exuberance to shock, to sorrow, to desperation. How could her husband be so heartless? How would she now feed and clothe her children? Where would she live? A sea of questions floated in Tasmiah's head. With her children by her side, Tasmiah went to the home of her closest friend, the woman who had introduced Tasmiah to the Grameen Bank. She was expecting sympathy and compassion. Instead, she received criticism. Her friend's main concern was that her own loan request would be jeopardized if Tasmiah failed to repay her loan.

Humiliated beyond words, and feeling responsible for her friend's welfare, Tasmiah went to the village moneylender for a loan. After assessing her precarious position, the moneylender refused her loan request. He was unsure that Tasmiah would ever be in a position to repay the loan. Then Tasmiah walked five kilometers to the Grameen Bank branch office to explain her situation. She remembers not being able to look directly at the bank worker; she was too embarrassed. Fortunately, the bank worker understood Tasmiah's distress. After consulting with the bank manager, Tasmiah was encouraged to apply for a second loan.

How did Tasmiah feel about her friend's criticism? Saddened and hurt initially, Tasmiah realized that her friend's response was understandable. They had joined the Grameen Bank together. Tasmiah's friend had also endured sleepless nights with hungry, crying children.

Tasmiah noted: "My misfortune is my responsibility. How can I ask someone else to suffer? We pressure one another to repay our loans, but what other choice is there? If one member does not repay a loan, other members suffer because their credit opportunities are limited. I do not want to hurt the lives of my fellow members." Tasmiah's statement demonstrates the strong sense of interpersonal identification that exists between and among Grameen's members. Grameen members push themselves and one another to work responsibly and be accountable. This interpersonal identification compels Grameen members to act in ways that insure continued credit opportunities for fellow group members.

Tasmiah's story gives us intimate insight into the dialectic of control and emancipation. To benefit from membership in the Grameen Bank, members must submit to the policies, procedures, and control systems of the organization. These control systems might restrict individual choices and freedom—illustrated by Tasmiah's turning to an unscrupulous moneylender to retain her membership in the Grameen Bank at any cost. However, it is only by submitting to the policies and control systems of the Grameen Bank that emancipation becomes possible.

Tasmiah's story illustrates that control and emancipation co-exist in a dialectic relationship (this dialectic is the main focus of the present chapter). However, readers may also note that Tasmiah is caught in a web of intersecting relational dialectics (Baxter & Montgomery, 1996; Rawlins, 1992). For instance, Tasmiah is torn between the need to share her dilemma with friends (*expressiveness*) and the need to keep her affairs private because of the shame she feels at being abandoned by her husband (*protectiveness*). Although expressiveness may be emancipatory, the control offered by protectiveness preserves dignity. The dialectic of *affection and instrumentality* also operates for Tasmiah and her fellow group members. They genuinely care for one another as friends (affection) and they need to continue their relationship to access continued loans from the Grameen Bank (instrumentality). Although affection may be emancipatory, instrumentality introduces elements of control. Further, the dialectic of *judgment* and *acceptance* also comes into play between Tasmiah and her friends. Tasmiah knows that her behavior of defaulting on the loan will always be subject to evaluative judgment, even as she is accepted back into her peer group. So while acceptance may be emancipatory, evaluation and judgment introduces control.

Box 2.1: Muhammad Yunus
The Poor Man's Banker

When Bangladesh became independent in 1971, Muhammad Yunus (Plate 2.1) resigned his university position in the U.S., and returned to Bangladesh. While teaching development economics at the University of

Plate 2.1
Muhammad Yunus, founder of the Grameen Bank, at a United Nations event in New York
Known as "Banker to the Poor," Yunus has led the global microcredit movement to free credit from the bondage of collateral. His dream is to end poverty and put it where it belongs—in museums. In this photo, Yunus is wearing a *Grameen Check* shirt, a brand of clothing marketed and distributed by the Grameen Bank social change conglomerate.
Source: United Nations.

Box 2.1:   Muhammad Yunus
(continued)

Chittagong, Yunus saw first-hand the debilitating effects of hunger, poverty, and famine. When author Singhal first met him in Dhaka in the summer of 1991, some 14 years ago, he recounted: "Here I was teaching the elegant theories of economics in the classroom.... I felt I knew everything…had all the solutions. But outside of the classroom people were dying of hunger and poverty" (personal conversation, July 2, 1991).

Questioning his economics training, Yunus more or less "abandoned" his academic life, and became interested in learning about poverty not from textbooks, but first hand from the lives of poor people. He relinquished his "birds-eye" view of poverty, embracing a ground-centered "worm's-eye" view (Yunus & Jolis, 1999).

In the mid-1970s, Yunus met a poor woman in Jobra village who made bamboo stools. However, after working for some 10 hours a day, the woman earned a profit of only two (U.S.) pennies daily. "How could anyone work so hard, make such beautiful bamboo stools, and earn so little," Yunus wondered (personal conversation, July 2, 1991). The woman explained to Yunus that she borrowed money from a local moneylender to purchase the bamboo, and was bonded to sell him the stools at a discounted price. Yunus figured that if he gave the woman 25 cents (U.S.), she would be free from the clutches of the moneylender. But were there other woman in Jobra village who were in a similar situation?

Yunus and one of his students went around Jobra village for the next several days and identified 42 such people. When Yunus calculated the total amount these 42 women needed to free themselves from bondage, he gasped: Only 27 dollars! He noted: "I was ashamed of being a member of a society that could not provide 27 (U.S.) dollars to 42 skilled, hard-working women" (personal conversation, July 2, 1991). To overcome his shame, Yunus pulled out $27 from his pocket and asked his student to give it to the 42 woman as a loan.

Next, Yunus went to meet the local bank manager (the bank was located on the Chittagong University campus), suggesting that he lend money to poor people. The manager thought Yunus was crazy. Nobody lends money to the poor for they are not credit-worthy. The bank's rules did not permit providing loans without collateral. And the poor had no collateral. Shocked by the apathy of bankers, and banking rules that were seemingly designed to keep poor people in poverty, Yunus offered to guarantee the loans of these poor people. Reluctantly, the bankers agreed,

---

Box 2.1: Muhammad Yunus
(continued)

---

telling Yunus he had made a bad investment. Such were the modest beginnings of the Grameen Bank action-based research project in 1976. Beginning with Jobra village, Yunus expanded microlending operations to 2 villages, then to 5, then to 10, then to 50, and then 100 villages. The results were astounding. The so-called "good-for-nothing," "credit-unworthy," poor people paid back every single penny. In October 1983, Yunus institutionalized his credit operations to become a formal for-profit Grameen Bank.

The Grameen Bank demonstrated that the poor could be organized through microcredit, launching a microcredit revolution around the world to address poverty. Some 500 replication projects of the Grameen Bank are underway in some 75 different countries.

In 1997, Yunus helped organize the global Microcredit Summit in Washington, D.C. Over 2,900 people, representing 1,500 organizations from 137 countries, attended the Summit. Its purpose: To mobilize resources to reach 100 million of the world's poorest families by 2005 through microcredit, and to take the necessary steps to send poverty to museums (where, Yunus believes, it belongs). In his opening speech, Yunus noted: "This summit is a grand celebration—we are celebrating the freeing of credit from the bondage of collateral. This summit is to pronounce goodbye to the era of financial apartheid" (Yunus quoted in http://www.grameen-info.org/mcredit/speech2.html).

What is the report card of the Microcredit Summit Campaign? By December 31, 2003, seven years after the campaign got underway, microcredit was disbursed to 81 million poor people, of which 55 million represent the poorest-of-the-poor. Of these poorest clients, 45 million are women. Assuming five persons per family, the 55 million poorest clients reached by the Microcredit Summit Campaign includes some 275 million family members (Daley-Harris, 2004).[2]

In the present chapter, we focus on investigating the dialectic of *control* and *emancipation* by focusing on the experiences of members (loan recipients) and workers of the Grameen Bank in Bangladesh. Understanding the dialectic requires that we examine these personal experiences from the theoretical perspective of concertive control. Before we begin our discussion on concertive control theory, let's learn more about the Grameen Bank in Bangladesh.

Plate 2.2
**Grameen Bank members chanting the Sixteen Decisions during their
weekly center meetings**
This collective ritual of chanting slogans, enacted week-after-week, builds
solidarity, cohesiveness, and trust among Grameen Bank members. These Sixteen
Decisions, including "We shall not live in dilapidated houses," "We shall grow
fruits and vegetables all year around," and "We shall send our children to school,"
represent the Social Welfare Constitution of the Grameen Bank.
Source: Personal Files of the Authors.

Grameen Bank: Organizing the Poor
for Social Change

The Grameen [rural] Bank in Bangladesh, founded in 1976 as an
action-based research project by Professor Muhammad Yunus, is a
system of lending small amounts of money to poor women so that
they can earn a living through self-employment. No collateral is
needed, as the poor do not have any. Instead, the women borrowers
are organized in a group of five friends. Several groups coalesce into
a Grameen Bank Center at the village-level. Each group member
must repay their loan on time, while ensuring that other group members do the same, or else their opportunity for a future loan may be
jeopardized. This delicate dynamic between "peer-pressure" and
"peer-support" among Grameen borrowers is at the heart of its
widespread success (Auwal & Singhal, 1992; Papa, Auwal, & Singhal,

1995, 1997; Yunus & Jolis, 1999). In short, interpersonal networks are effective collateral for poor women. The scope of Grameen Bank's operations go beyond microlending. It is a full-service social change organization. For instance, in every village-level center meeting Grameen Bank members renew their pledges to fight socio-economic, health, and nutritional problems by reciting various slogans (Plate 2.2), including the Sixteen Decisions (the Social Welfare Constitution of the Grameen Bank—see Table 2.1).

Table 2.1
The Sixteen Decisions representing the Social Welfare Constitution of the Grameen Bank

1. The four principles of Grameen Bank—discipline, unity, courage, and hard work—we shall follow and advance in all walks of our lives.
2. Prosperity we shall bring to our families.
3. We shall not live in dilapidated houses. We shall repair our houses and work towards constructing new houses at the earliest.
4. We shall grow vegetables all the year round. We shall eat plenty of it and sell the surplus.
5. During the plantation seasons, we shall plant as many seedlings as possible.
6. We shall plan to keep our families small. We shall minimize our expenditures. We shall look after our health.
7. We shall educate our children and ensure that they can earn to pay for their education.
8. We shall always keep our children and the environment clean.
9. We shall build and use pit-latrines.
10. We shall drink tubewell water. If it is not available, we shall boil water or use alum.
11. We shall not take any dowry in our sons' wedding, neither shall we give any dowry in our daughters' wedding. We shall keep the Center free from the curse of dowry. We shall not practice child marriage.
12. We shall not inflict any injustice on anyone; neither shall we allow anyone to do so.
13. For higher income we shall collectively undertake bigger investments.
14. We shall always be ready to help each other. If anyone is in difficulty, we shall all help him.
15. If we come to know of any breach of discipline in any Center, we shall all go there and help restore discipline.
16. We shall introduce physical exercise in all our Centers; we shall take part in all social activities collectively.

Source: Papa, Auwal, and Singhal (1997).

Box 2.2: Global Moneylenders

One reason why poor countries can't provide decent education and health care to their citizens is because they are "bonded" to global moneylenders like the International Monetary Fund (IMF), the World Bank, and other such institutions. Most countries have paid back in interest more than they originally borrowed, but the principal remains untouched, continuing the insidious debt cycle. In 2005, sub-Saharan Africa pays $1.30 in servicing debt for every dollar it got in aid, four times what it spends on health care for an average citizen (Watkins & Woods, 2004).

For the $5 billion that Nigeria had borrowed until 1986, it has already paid back $16 billion in debt servicing, and still owed $28 billion. President Obasanjo of Nigeria noted: "If you ask me what is the worst thing in the world, I will say it is compound interest" (*Herald Tribune*, 2004, October 2–3, p. 8).

Further, creditors like the IMF and the World Bank advocate democracy as a condition for extending loans, but one may argue that they do not practice it themselves. Many criticize these institutions as beings the government of the many, by the few. The 50 plus African countries account for a quarter of the membership of IMF and World Bank, but hold only 4 percent of its vote. The tiny European nation of Belgium, with a population of 10 million, has more voting power in these institutions than Nigeria, Ethiopia, Zambia, Tanzania, Mozambique, and South Africa combined (the total population of these six African countries is approximately 300 million) (Watkins & Woods, 2004).

By early 2005, the Grameen Bank had loaned the equivalent of $4.7 billion (U.S. dollars) to 4.2 million poor borrowers (of which 95 percent are women borrowers) in over 50,000 Bangladeshi villages, and had an enviable loan recovery rate of 99 percent (Figure 2.1). The Bank had 1,393 branch offices and employed 15,000 staff members (Table 2.2) (Grameen Bank, 2005). The idea of micro-lending, based on the Grameen Bank experience, has spread throughout the world, and has everywhere proven effective in gaining a high rate of loan repayment.

Figure 2.1
The growth in the number of Grameen Bank members
Grameen Bank started as an action-based research project in 1976 and was formally institutionalized in 1983. By mid-2005, it had enrolled 4.2 million members, of which 95 percent were women. Its loan recovery rate continues to be an astounding 99 percent, pointing to the creditworthiness of poor people.

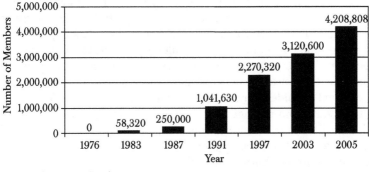

Source: Grameen Bank.

Table 2.2
Grameen Bank's reach and impact in Bangladesh

Cumulative Amount of Loans Disbursed since Inception	U.S. $4,692 Million
Rate of Loan Recovery	99%
Cumulative Number of Houses Built with Grameen Housing Loans	612,788
Number of Members	
Female	4,031,570
Male	177,238
Total	4,208,808
Number of Grameen Groups	705,277
Number of Grameen Centers	83,654
Number of Grameen Bank Villages	50,023
Number of Grameen Branches	1,393
Number of Branches with Computerized Accounting and MIS	1,242
Cumulative Number of Village Telephones	99,987

Source: Grameen Bank (2005).

Theory of Concertive Control

In contemporary organizations, decentralized, participative, and democratic systems of control are becoming more common, leading some observers to call the current era the "postbureaucratic" age (Ogilvy, 1990; Parker, 1992; Soeters, 1986). When control is embedded in the lateral, mission-centered, highly coordinated actions of a comparatively non-hierarchical organization, a system of "concertive control" exists (Tompkins & Cheney, 1985). In concertive control systems, control shifts significantly from management to workers who collaborate to create rules and norms that govern their behavior. This collaborative process can be stimulated by top management or by workers who produce a value-based corporate vision statement to guide their day-to-day actions (Barker, 1993). The irony of this shift from management-designed control systems to worker-designed systems is that workers may create forms of control that are more powerful, less apparent, and more difficult to resist than that of the former bureaucracy (Barker, 1993).

■ Empowerment in Organizations

Most descriptions of concertive control systems in organizations do not include a discussion of empowerment. We believe that empowerment is central to control systems. When members of an organization experience empowerment, their commitment to that organization becomes stronger and they are more likely to internalize its control mechanisms.

There are multiple ways to conceptualize empowerment. Empowerment is both a perception and a process. (e.g., Alvesson & Willmott, 1992; Blau & Alba, 1982; Conger, 1989; Conger & Kanugo, 1988; Pacanowsky, 1988; Vogt & Murrell, 1990). Albrecht (1988) observed that empowerment as a perception is a belief that one can influence people and events in an organization to achieve desired ends (see Greenberger & Strasser, 1986; Kanter, 1977). When individuals believe they can attain desired ends without interference from external forces (economic, political, or social), they identify ways they can act to secure those ends. In terms of process, the centrality of communication to empowerment is noted by Craig (1994) and

Deetz (1994a, 1994b), who claim that specific dimensions of empowerment are revealed when human decisions or actions are negotiated, coordinated, and codetermined. For example, a group of workers who have been sexually harassed by their immediate supervisor could meet to discuss whether or not to confront the harasser, present a formal complaint to upper management, and/or retain legal counsel.

The mere act of participating in workplace decisions, however, does not provide sufficient proof that workers are empowered (Cheney, 1995; Stohl, 1995). For authentic democracy and meaningful worker empowerment, employee decisions should cover a wide range of issues, and employees should be able to identify specific instances of producing and implementing decisions that they find meaningful (Ashcraft, 2000, 2001; Bernstein, 1976; Cheney, 1995, 2000, 2001; Deetz, 1992; Harter, 2004; Harter & Krone, 2001; Monge & Miller, 1988; Stohl & Cheney, 2001; Strauss, 1982). Also, participative decision-making should move from the lowest levels of the hierarchy through upper-management levels and should empower lower-level employees to deal with higher-level issues (Cheney, 1995).

In the Grameen Bank, the process of empowerment evolves as workers and members collaborate with one another to uplift the poor. Both Grameen workers and members participate in training programs to develop their knowledge, skills, and confidence to perform their specific organizational roles. These programs address the perceptual dimension of empowerment by building confidence among workers and members so that they can achieve desired goals. Empowerment is also displayed as an interactional process in the activities of workers and members. For example, Grameen workers participate in discussions in which they design social and economic programs for the poor. The workers are empowered to design these programs because top management believes that the best ideas emanate from field level employees. In addition, members (loan recipients) are required to devise their own small business ideas. Proposals for these businesses are generated in meetings among members. Member discussions focus on identifying potential business ventures, negotiating individual responsibilities, and determining the amount of capital needed to initiate business. Thus, the Grameen Bank offers clear opportunities for workers and members to empower themselves through making their own decisions and determining their own courses of action to reach individual and collective goals. Although concertive control systems can empower workers in ways that elude them in traditional bureaucracies, these systems can also limit behavioral options open to employees.

■ Identification in Organizations

For concertive control systems to be effective in regulating worker behavior, the workers must *identify* with a set of organizational values and factual premises that guide their decision making and work activities (Barker & Tompkins, 1994). These decision premises are accepted in exchange for incentives offered by the organization such as wages, salary, recognition, and praise. Concertive control systems emerge when visionary leaders produce a value-based organizational mission that is intended to serve as a guide for member behavior and decision-making. Workers exhibit *identification* with this vision when their decisions are aligned with the organization's values (Tompkins & Cheney, 1983). When considering decision options, a member is limited to alternatives linked to his or her identifications; "other options will simply not come into view, and therefore will not be considered" (Tompkins & Cheney, 1985, p. 194). Through identification, the decision makers' range of "vision" is narrowed and alternatives for action are limited to meeting the organization's values.

In addition to worker identification with an organizational mission, another form of identification surfaces in interpersonal relationships within organizations (Tompkins & Cheney, 1983). To accomplish tasks and reach goals, organizational members must act together. In acting together, although a feeling of camaraderie may develop among system members, the interests of each party may not be mutually served (Barnard, 1938). When two people collaborate in an endeavor, "who is to say, once and for all, just where 'cooperation' ends and one partner's 'exploitation' of the other begins?" (Burke, 1950, p. 25).[3] Organizational theorists must scrutinize those forms of identification that obscure the worker's vision and thereby prevent him or her from seeing the exploitation and oppression of the system in which he or she is embedded.

■ Disciplinary Techniques in Organizations

Organizations cannot operate without some form of discipline. As Barnard (1938) argued over a half-century ago, the master paradox of organizational life is that "to accomplish our individual goals, we must frequently relinquish some autonomy to the organizational system" (p. 17). However, discipline is also simultaneously constraining because it guides employee behavior in directions that are ultimately functional for the organization (Barker & Cheney, 1994). Concertive control systems are often characterized by micro-techniques of discipline to regulate and normalize individual and collective action in organizations. When members internalize these disciplinary techniques (because of their identification with the organizational value system), they become part of "standard operating procedure."

Foucault's (1972, 1976) views on power and the micro-techniques of discipline are central to concertive control systems. Born in France in 1926, Foucault was deeply involved in the radical movement characterizing French universities in the mid-twentieth century and founded an organization to get the voices of French prisoners heard by French society. A professor at the College de France and at the University of Berkeley, Foucault died of AIDS in 1984 (Kaufman, 2003). Foucault argued that discipline functioned as a social force in the organization sorting good behavior from bad, providing a context for organizational interaction, and shaping day-to-day organizational activity (Foucault, 1976; Barker & Cheney, 1994). Foucault contended that disciplinary discourses serve to control, govern, and "normalize" individual and collective behavior, leading organizational actors to the conclusion, "That's the way we do things around here."

Foucault provides us with insight into micro-techniques of discipline. Discipline is a social force that operates differentially and precisely on bodies. In fact, "discipline 'makes' individuals; it is the specific technique of a power that regards individuals as objects and as instruments of its exercise" (Foucault, 1976, p. 180). What Foucault means here is that the modern "individual," who so cherishes freedom and choice, also comes to internalize a whole set of ideas and practices that govern and shape him or her. These micro-techniques of discipline do not always involve crushing people; rather, discipline usually stems from training the docile body (May, 1993, p. 43).

How does Foucault's description of discipline as a social force operate in an organizational context? Consider a manufacturing organization in which a new employee is trained to operate a specific piece of equipment throughout the workday. A shift supervisor observes the employee to ensure that the proper sequence of operational steps is followed and that the work is performed at an adequate speed. The repetitive nature of this task eventually results in what Foucault refers to as a docile body. In other words, the workers' physical actions become so routinized that they are repeated automatically without variation. Eventually, mental docility occurs as well as the worker can perform actions without thinking through each step. When the disciplines associated with task performance are internalized in a docile body and mind, the worker governs his or her behavior, even if the supervisor is not watching.

Foucault's (1980a) triad of formative discipline includes rules of right, knowledge, and power. Rules of right are captured aphoristically by the statement, "That's the way we do things around here" (see Barker & Cheney, 1994). In the exercise of power, certain "truths" emerge and become the taken-for-granted knowledge base within a social system. The effects of this knowledge base reinforce and reproduce discipline within the system.

Micro-techniques of discipline both punish and reward. Micro-penalties accrue when making the slightest departure from correct behavior subjects the violator to punishment. Within this disciplinary apparatus, "[E]verything might serve to punish the slightest thing; each subject finds himself [sic] caught in a punishable, punishing universality" (Foucault, 1976, p. 178). Micro-penalties can be associated with time (lateness, absences), activity (inattention, negligence), behavior (impoliteness, disobedience), talk (idle chatter), and the body (lack of cleanliness, disrespectful gestures) (Papa, Auwal, & Singhal, 1997). Conversely, disciplinary systems also reward by means of awards. People are judged against a norm in a way that continually creates ranks. Those judged to be significantly better than the norm are rewarded by the judgment itself.

Constant surveillance (in the form of a supervisor's "normalizing gaze") eventually induces self-control on the part of organizational members and results in what some have called an organizational personality or an organizational conscience (Merton, 1968; Presthus,

1962; Reissman, 1949; Ruitenbeek, 1963; Scott & Hart, 1979; Thompson, 1961; Whyte, 1956). "Power no longer needs to unleash its sanctions and instead its objects take it upon themselves to behave in the desired manner" (Garland, 1990, p. 146). As Foucault (1976) explains, the perfection of power should tend to render its actual exercise unnecessary, for the objects of power should be caught up in a disciplinary apparatus of which they themselves are the bearers.

A strong relationship exists between micro-techniques of discipline and employee identification. Galbraith (1967) argued that member identification with organizational goals and values can be a powerful motivating force, particularly in nonprofit enterprises. For example, Galbraith explained that scientists, engineers, and technicians associated with the Jet Propulsion Laboratory (operated on behalf of the National Air and Space Administration by the California Institute of Technology) identified strongly with the goals of the lab and were deeply proud of their contributions to the enterprise. In fact, member identification with the goals and values of this organization may have been more important than financial compensation. Knoke and Wood's (1981) examination of member commitment in 32 voluntary associations in Indiana also supports this perspective. Specifically, they found that offering widespread opportunities for decision-making and influence significantly raised member commitment levels. Importantly, in both the Jet Propulsion Laboratory in California and in the voluntary associations in Indiana working long hours in service to the mission of the organization was expected, and workers met these "expectations" because of their strong identification with organizational values.

When workers identify so strongly with organizational values, they may lose critical distance in evaluating the fairness of the micro-techniques of discipline they have collectively created, or in which they have heavily participated. Foucault (1980b) recognized this very issue when he observed that "power is only tolerable on the condition that it masks a substantial part of itself. Its success is proportional to its ability to hide its own mechanisms" (p. 86). Thus, it is important for us to focus on how member identification with an organization may obscure a member's ability to evaluate objectively the micro-techniques of discipline that are part of concertive control systems.

Box 2.3: Concertive Control in Academia

Among industrialized nations, the United States has one of the worst policies toward maternity leave. If you are a full-time employee, most organizations offer only six weeks paid maternity leave for the mother, and none for the father. By comparison, Canada, Sweden, and Denmark offer mothers up to one year of paid benefits; further, paternity leaves are also common. Despite the limited time offered for maternity leaves in the U.S., many women informally pressure one another in ways that further restrict the time mothers spend with a newborn child. Consider the experiences of Elizabeth, a close friend of author Wendy Papa.

Elizabeth was working as a full time instructor at a reputable university on the east coast of the U.S. when she became pregnant with her second child. At that time she was teaching four classes per semester. With class preparation, teaching, grading, office hours, other service responsibilities, and taking classes toward her doctorate Elizabeth often worked 60 hours per week. When she approached her supervisor about maternity leave, she was exposed to the first of many conversations that showed how women control one another's choices.

Elizabeth's supervisor was a woman who told the story of her last maternity leave which she restricted to only three weeks so she would not miss teaching her classes and meeting other professional responsibilities. When Elizabeth indicated that she would like to avail the full six weeks (that her faculty contract allowed), the supervisor suggested that Elizabeth rearrange her teaching schedule and double the time she taught each week for the four weeks prior to the birth of her child. Given a present teaching load of 16 hours per week, this solution proved impractical in terms of time, room availability, and student schedules. The supervisor then reluctantly agreed to find other instructors to cover her classes for the remaining weeks.

Over the course of the next several weeks, several other women (university professors) in the department talked to Elizabeth about what they did during their maternity leaves. One colleague emphasized that two weeks of maternity leave was reasonable as it does not disrupt classes. Another colleague talked about taking only three weeks of maternity leave as she felt pressured from the faculty to continue to "pull her weight" in terms of teaching, service, and research. One of Elizabeth's closest friends in the department talked about limiting her leave to four weeks and bringing in a breast pump, so she could carry home breastmilk for her child. Elizabeth felt that the underlying message in all of these

---

Box 2.3: Concertive Control in Academia
(continued)

conversations was that a women's professionalism would be compromised, and her job evaluations may suffer, if she took a full six weeks of maternity leave.

Elizabeth carefully considered her options. Her annual contract was coming up for renewal. She was worried about the tone of the stories shared by her fellow women colleagues in the department, including her supervisor. Elizabeth felt that the standards set by these women restricted her choices in this situation. If she violated the standards, she might suffer professional consequences.[4]

So, a very effective system of concertive control was established in Elizabeth's academic department. At what cost?

■ Rationale for Studying Concertive Control in the Grameen Bank

Our rationale for selecting the theory of concertive control to analyze the dialectic of control and emancipation in the Grameen Bank is four-fold. First, the Grameen Bank has empowered its members and workers to participate in the creation of their own norms and rules for the execution of economic and social development programs. Also, Grameen members themselves meet to develop small business ideas and to decide how to handle such problems as loan defaults. The discussion fora in which these rules and norms emerge increase levels of identification within member and worker groups as well as provide clear examples of empowerment.

Second, the bank's loan programs establish a system in which members and workers monitor and control each other's behavior. For example, members pressure one another to repay loans since one member's failure to repay can jeopardize others' credit opportunities. Bank workers also have created a concertive control system by pressuring one another to work long hours and forego vacations to maintain the Grameen's successes in improving the lives of the poor. Top management does not *require* 12-hour workdays, or 7-day workweeks; rather, bank workers have created these norms.

Third, the theory of concertive control provided us with a framework for understanding how member identification with value-based appeals masks the mechanisms of discipline. Thus, by focusing on members and bank workers' stories, accounts, and metaphors, we searched for themes and examples that reveal the ways these two groups socially construct rule systems that govern their behavior.

Finally, the theory of concertive control illuminates the dialectic of emancipation and control in organizing for social change. Specifically, members are both emancipated from the oppression of poverty at the same time that they are embedded in control systems that not only limit their options but raise questions about fairness and human dignity.

Methods of Data-Collection

Using the conceptual scheme of concertive control, we interpreted and critiqued the Grameen Bank's approach to organizing for social change. In order to do this we integrate (*a*) our study of information materials and scholarly literature on the Grameen Bank; (*b*) our field study (observation and interviews) of the Grameen Bank completed by research team members over six visits, and involving a total time period of 20 weeks; (*c*) our communication with top-level Grameen Bank officials since 1990, including four personal interviews with Professor Muhammad Yunus, the founder and managing director of the Grameen Bank; and (*d*) several documentary films and reports about the Grameen Bank (e.g., Balkin 1989; Bornstein, 1996; Fuglesang & Chandler, 1988; Ghai, 1984; Hossain, 1988; Hulme, 1990; Rahman, 1988, 1989a, 1989b; Rogers & Singhal, 2003; Siddiqui, 1984; Yunus, 1984, 1997; Yunus & Jolis, 1999).

Our interviews consisted of open-ended questions that focused on the social and economic changes experienced by Grameen Bank members since their affiliation with the bank. Probing follow-up questions were asked when appropriate to gain a deeper understanding of member experiences. Some 350 Grameen Bank members in 12 village centers in five different regions of rural Bangladesh were interviewed in this manner. The interviews with bank members were conducted in their neighborhoods, workplaces, and homes. We photographed important events and gatherings, took notes on all significant conversations, and tape-recorded the in-depth personal interviews. At the end of each day, we discussed our informal conversations with the Grameen Bank members and recorded their impressions. We also conducted loosely structured focus group discussions with 20 Grameen Bank workers to gain different insights into the bank's operations. So, ultimately our analysis draws on the photographs, notes, and transcriptions of our in-depth and focus group interviews.

In addition to the personal interviews previously described, some 75 Grameen Bank members and an estimated 35 bank workers were interviewed informally in our various field visits. Thus, our analysis draws interview data from approximately 425 Grameen Bank members and 55 fieldworkers.

■ Analyzing Data

Readers may note that in each of the four contexts of organizing for social change that are explored in the present book (in chapters 2,3,4, and 5), we used the same approach to analyzing data. For the sake of efficiency this data analysis process will be described only in this chapter/context.

The data collected through participant observation, interviews, and informal conversations was analyzed in a continuous, cyclic process using Morse's (1994) four-stage conceptualization of data analysis: comprehending, synthesizing, theorizing, and recontextualization. The comprehending stage involved selecting the most appropriate methodological approaches, entering the field, gaining rapport with participants, and identifying when we had enough data to offer a "descriptive slice" of the project. After preliminary readings of the field notes, and interview transcripts, we conducted separate coding sessions with all available materials for the purpose of searching for dominant themes. Then we began an intensive reading of the preliminary codings together, clumping and re-coding until a tree of large order and small order themes emerged from the data (Lindlof, 1995). This allowed us to move to the latter stages of data analysis, which focuses on theorizing and recontextualization. Theorizing refers to the "constant development and manipulation of malleable theoretical schemes until the 'best' theoretical scheme is developed" (Morse, 1994, p. 32). In this way a grounded theory approach to understanding the data emerged, and then we moved to recontextualization, that is, finding ways in which theoretical explanations could be applied to other organizing for social change settings.

Dialectic of Control and Emancipation in the Grameen Bank

The dialectic of control and emancipation is clearly present in development organizations like the Grameen Bank. Both workers and members in development organizations must surrender some individual freedom in order to gain access to the resources of the collective. In this section, we turn to concertive control to explicate the dialectical tension between control and emancipation present in the Grameen Bank's activities. The theory of concertive control gives us insight into the Grameen Bank's program of participatory management for workers and mutual accountability for loan recipients. These programs sustain the dialectic by offering Grameen Bank workers and members economic and social rewards that can only be received if one abides by the rules and norms sustained by the organization. The theory of concertive control also helps us to understand member and worker identification with the Grameen Bank, aspects of empowerment, and the micro-techniques of discipline that regulate member and worker behavior. Finally, concertive control systems within the bank draw our attention to the paradoxes members and workers encounter in maintaining a democratic organization.

■ Concertive Control among Grameen Bank Workers

The Grameen Bank requires all fieldworkers and lower-level managers to attend motivational programs that describe the humanitarian mission of the organization. These programs present inspirational talks that illustrate employee contributions to alleviating human suffering and uplifting the poorest of the poor in Bangladesh. The motivational programs also highlight the recognition the Grameen Bank has received from international agencies, scholars, and entrepreneurs.[5]

The Team Metaphor and Identification   A "team" metaphor emerges that is central to both worker identification with the Grameen and the concertive control system that governs worker behavior. Indeed, our interviews with bank workers included frequent references to the ways in which the Grameen is similar to a team. For example, Muhammad Sobhan, a Grameen fieldworker from Chittagong, remarked: "We work in the field as a team to support and help one another to administer loan programs and deliver social services. We always know we can count on one another for help when a problem emerges" (personal interview, March 21, 1994). When the Grameen Bank receives an international award, each team member shares the glory, again strengthening worker identification with the organization. In fact, in one of our field visits, we observed that a *New York Times* article was posted on the bulletin boards of several branch and zonal offices. The title of this article was "Yunus Recommended for Nobel Prize by President Clinton." When one fieldworker was asked why this article was posted on the bulletin board, he responded: "It makes us so happy to be part of the Grameen Bank and to work with Professor Yunus. He deserves a Nobel Prize, and he is gracious in saying how all of us workers are part of what makes the Grameen Bank work" (personal interview, March 19, 1994).

The forms of worker identification revealed in our field interviews can be compared to Etzioni's (1961) description of moral involvement in organizations. Etzioni notes two types of moral involvement: pure and social. Pure moral involvement occurs when a worker internalizes work norms and identifies with authority. Such moral involvement is reflected in the workers' commitment to goals established by Grameen's founder Muhammad Yunus and in their strong work ethic. Social moral involvement refers to worker sensitivity to pressures from primary group members. Consistent reference to the team metaphor and the fact that workers push one another to succeed provides evidence of this form of involvement. Both pure and social moral involvement "designate a positive orientation of high intensity" (Etzioni, 1961, p. 10) and are most likely found in value-based and non-profit organizations such as churches, political parties, and social movements.

Box 2.4: Atiquar Rahman
Unquestioned Dedication

When bank workers use the team metaphor, they primarily frame their membership in positive terms and focus on how managers and field-workers labor together in pursuit of common goals.

Meet Atiquar Rahman, a Grameen Bank fieldworker who works on the outskirts of Dhaka. He regularly works 12-hour days, and he often works for months at a time without a single day off. When asked why he works so diligently, he stated: "How can I let down the other field-workers and the poor people we serve? We work together with management as a team, and in working together we help the poor to improve their lives" (personal interview, March 21, 1994). This dedication to working together permeates the entire organization and shows how strongly workers identify with one another and the goals of the Grameen. Atiquar could not imagine questioning his commitment to the Grameen Bank, realizing that he is a part of an incredible humanitarian effort. No other organization in Bangladesh offers the poor so much hope. No sacrifice is too great for him to endure to continue the success of the organization.

Worker Empowerment   Our examination of worker stories, such as the one shared by Atiquar Rahman, also provided us with clear evidence of empowerment. Grameen workers enjoy decision-making autonomy in branch and area offices where substantive planning takes place. Essentially, fieldworkers are the planners of Grameen's localized programs. Nine persons working in a branch create an annual plan and pass it on to their supervisory area office. The head office integrates the plans received from the grassroots level to facilitate overall organizational planning and to set realistic goals to be achieved within specific periods of time. The head office rarely interferes with the planning, aside from offering broad guidelines or linking local plans to the corporate vision of uplifting the poorest of the poor. By giving employees the responsibility for creating social and economic programs for the poor, the Grameen sustains a culture of empowerment. First, because the head office trusts and respects the judgments of Grameen's fieldworkers, the workers develop a sense of pride in their role in alleviating rural poverty. This is consistent with Albrecht's (1988) view that empowerment can be experienced as a perception since Grameen's workers have internalized

---

Box 2.5: Muhammad Sarkar
Self-Imposed Pressure

Although Grameen workers shared many stories with us that indicated how they were empowered to help the poor, other stories suggested that team membership has its costs.

Muhammad Sarkar is a Grameen Bank fieldworker who works on the outskirts of Dhaka. He told us about the pressure he feels from fellow fieldworkers to retain a high loan recovery rate. When he experienced problems with loan recovery in a particular center (two members had ceased loan repayment), he felt personally responsible for solving the problem. The two members had taken out a loan to manufacture and sell bamboo products (baskets and trays) and cane mats. However, due to the theft of their raw materials and the illness of one member, they were forced to close their small shop. Sarkar met with the non-paying members and attempted to persuade them to resume loan repayment. When that did not work, he offered to help them manufacture products for sale until they could find another worker. Sarkar eventually wound up working an extra two hours a day (added to his normal 12-hour day) so that the loan recipients could keep their business functioning (personal interview, March 23, 1994).

Perhaps the most revealing aspect of Sarkar's story is the guilt he felt whenever he walked into the local branch office. The loan repayment records of his centers were posted on a wall behind his desk for all the other fieldworkers to see. Sarkar felt that he was failing as a fieldworker; his disgrace was greatest when he compared his loan recovery record to the posted records of his co-workers. Although he had experienced immense *personal* satisfaction in working with Grameen, he, in fact, considered quitting his job because he felt incapable of sustaining the high standards his coworkers had established. When the members operating the small business finally resumed loan repayment, Sarkar decided to stay with the Grameen. He was both relieved and thrilled when the delinquent members returned to the center. As he stated, "I feel like I am again contributing to the success of the Grameen and that I am not a burden to my coworkers" (personal interview, March 23, 1994).

The preceding story shows how Grameen fieldworkers create an environment of concertive control. Upper management does not pressure the workers to sustain a 99 percent loan-recovery rate; however, the workers place incredible pressure on one another. Fieldworkers so strongly identify with the Grameen's continued success that they will

---

Box 2.5: Muhammad Sarkar
(continued)

---

work long hours, forego vacations, and do whatever is required to insure that members continue to repay their loans. Essentially, peer pressure is sustained through conversations in which workers exhibit their interpersonal identification with one another as team members, as well as their identification with the mission of the Grameen. Fazle Manik, a Grameen fieldworker from Comilla, offered us insight into these forms of identification: "We know our best efforts are needed for the social and economic programs to work, that is why we [workers] rely on each other so much. We know we can count on one another for help if we have a problem in a center. Our work with the Grameen is important because no other program in Bangladesh can help the poor as much as we do" (personal interview, March 22, 1994).

When a Grameen fieldworker experiences problems with loan recovery in a given center, the punishment is essentially communicative in form. Fieldworkers will criticize one another and make reference to the loan repayment records that are posted behind worker desks. The fieldworkers identify so strongly with the Grameen's goal of uplifting the poor that they socially construct standards for performance that place extraordinary pressure on everyone to succeed. For example, in many branch offices, Grameen workers have established a workload norm that consists of seven-day workweeks and 12-hour workdays. Muhammad Sobhan, a Grameen fieldworker from Chittagong, commented: "If we did not work as hard as we do, we would not be able to maintain a high loan recovery rate in our centers, and help loan recipients who are having problems with their businesses" (personal interview, March 21, 1994). As Barker (1993) explained, work norms can take on a heightened intensity in work teams. If workers violate one of these norms, "they must be willing to risk their human dignity, being made to feel unworthy as a teammate" (p. 436).

---

the belief that their personal actions influence the poor in a desirable way. Second, empowerment has an interactive dimension in the Grameen Bank, as workers collectively determine their own goals and the means of attaining them.

Muhammad Sobhan, a Grameen worker from Chittagong, gave us insight into the emergence of empowerment among fieldworkers. "I could never imagine working another job where I can have so much influence in helping others. Professor Yunus trusts us and respects our judgments. We decide together in the branch what needs to be done to help members, and we put the plan into action" (personal interview, March 21, 1994).

Paradox of Sociality and Control   Two types of paradoxes are linked to the control practices maintained by the workers. First, there is a "paradox of sociality" reflected in the intensity of worker commitment to the goals of the Grameen Bank (Stohl & Cheney, 2001). Grameen's fieldworkers feel a tremendous sense of pride in helping the poor improve their lives; however, to accomplish the goals of the bank the workers sacrifice almost every aspect of their personal lives, including other forms of participation in family and community. Workers are empowered to play an integral role in helping the poor to improve their lives; however, the level of work required to reach organizational goals borders on the inhumane.

Second, workers experience a "paradox of control" (Stohl & Cheney, 2001). This paradox surfaces when workers appreciate the perceived freedom that comes with creating their own control system, yet they actually experience less freedom within the work group because they must all keep an eye on one another to reach codetermined goals. In the Grameen Bank, the control paradox arises when fieldworkers collectively establish goals for their branches in terms of loan recovery. However, the workers experience less freedom in this system because of how carefully they monitor one another's performance. A worker who experiences a decline in loan recovery rates is criticized and made to feel unworthy as a fieldworker or teammate.

Worker Discipline   Despite the substantial pressure workers place on one another, they exhibit remarkable commitment to the Grameen Bank's goal of empowering the poor. Atiquar Rahman made this very point after sharing his story about some potential loan defaulters: "We do pressure one another to recover loans, but look at what we do. When we first enter a village we see such little hope and such suffering. We are part of a program that gives people hope and lifts them from suffering. We experience no greater happiness than seeing how Grameen membership helps the poor improve their lives" (personal interview, March 21, 1994). Another Grameen worker also linked aspects of the organization's disciplinary system to his success in helping the poor. Shamsul Hoque, a fieldworker in the Gazipur district, explained: "The Grameen is different from any other bank because of the discipline of its staff. I'm not allowed to accept even a glass of water at my client's doorstep, so that I'm not partial to them in the future. It is this discipline of the Grameen Bank which makes us tick" (personal interview, August 12, 1991).

Foucault's (1976) observations concerning the training of the body by subjecting it to disciplinary processes is relevant to how Grameen workers are trained, as well as to how they live in the field. In fact, one of the main purposes of Grameen's training programs for prospective fieldworkers is to eliminate by self-selection "those who do not have the stamina or inclination for the physically demanding nature of fieldwork" (Fuglesang & Chandler, 1993, p. 74). The problems and discomforts of living in rural Bangladesh (e.g., excessive heat and humidity, limited transportation and communications equipment, mosquito infestation, and pouring monsoon showers) are daunting even for the most dedicated person; hence, trainees are exposed to poor, rural living conditions early in their training experiences. Also, trainees and fieldworkers are encouraged not to use bicycles so they can better understand the hardship of the landless who are chronically without transport (Fuglesang & Chandler, 1993). However, even if bicycles were available, many workers could not use them because of poor road conditions. In fact, many workers walk barefoot for up to 10 miles a day because the mud on rural roads is so deep it would destroy their shoes (Counts, 1990). Thus, the daily life of a fieldworker is a physically strenuous and monotonous one that requires both a disciplined mind and body.

Another aspect of discipline that is central to the Grameen's operations is the strict system of monitoring worker performance. The performance of every bank worker is followed on a daily basis. If loan disbursement or repayment figures drop during a particular week, there is reason for concern and remedial action. This ongoing monitoring and evaluation of worker performance creates a situation of strong mutual accountability (Fuglesang & Chandler, 1993).

The monitoring and evaluation of worker performance became particularly clear to us in the branch offices when fieldworkers returned from their village centers. Although exhausted from a long day's work, bank workers would begin counting and recording the loan repayments as soon as they sat down at their desks. Each member counted the money in full view of the other branch members and the branch manager. The pace of the counting and recording operations is fast and clearly stressful. As we learned in talking with a number of fieldworkers, the stress they feel is linked to the immediacy of the evaluation they receive. "Lagging performance is quickly discovered and corrected, and good performance is quickly rewarded" (Fuglesang & Chandler, 1993).

The counting of loan repayments at the end of the day is reflective of Foucault's (1976) disciplinary apparatus. The public counting of loan repayments constitutes a daily *examination* for workers. *Hierarchical observation* occurs as the counting and recording of statistical information is performed in full view of the manager. The manager (and the other coworkers) then offers *normalizing judgments*—the feedback given to the worker about his or her performance.

Grameen workers willingly accept the various forms of discipline associated with their jobs because of their strong sense of identification with the bank. The interviews we conducted with fieldworkers provided evidence of two types of organizational identification. First, the workers identify strongly with the Grameen Bank's mission of uplifting the poor. As Shamsul Hoque, a Grameen Bank fieldworker from the Gazipur district, noted: "I feel like the engine of change. An engine that gets its fuel from the vision of Muhammad Yunus and water from the dreams of the poor and the landless" (personal interview, April 21, 1991). Motivation comes from the emotionally satisfying experience of helping others, by the sincere desire to right human wrongs.

The second form of organizational identification that was reflected in our interviews was how the workers strongly identified with their branch office co-workers or team members. They support one another, but they also criticize each other, particularly when loan recovery rates fall below the 99 percent repayment level. Mazibur Rahman, a Grameen worker from Madhabdi, addressed this issue: "We are always ready to help each other because fieldwork is so difficult. But we cannot forget what we are here to do. If some members default on loans, there will be less loans available for others. We keep track of each other's loan records and we pressure each other because the high recovery rate is what allows the Grameen to continue" (personal interview, March 22, 1994). This form of identification is more interpersonal in nature; however, as observed earlier, it raises the question of where cooperation among workers ends and exploitation begins.

How do these forms of worker identification influence their description and evaluation of the disciplinary techniques practiced within the organization? Our interviews with Bank workers indicate that they see only the positive aspects of discipline. Branch managers remind fieldworkers that if they break discipline, the Grameen Bank collapses (Fuglesang & Chandler, 1993). Atiquar Rahman, a fieldworker from the Dhaka area, expressed this very sentiment: "Discipline and self-control are demanded of us but it is the backbone of our success" (personal interview, March 21, 1994). Thus, bank workers do not criticize the disciplinary techniques that are part of the Grameen because they recognize that discipline is central to the success of the organization. Importantly, the absence of any critical comments concerning the disciplinary techniques used by Grameen workers may be reflective of a "paradox of consensus" (Stohl & Cheney, 2001), in that group cohesion is achieved at the expense of the vitality of oppositional or minority voices. Most of the fieldworkers we interviewed talked about the discipline that is maintained in the branches and described personal sacrifices that were required to meet loan recovery goals. Yet, no fieldworker criticized these practices and expectations. Seemingly, consensus has been reached among fieldworkers concerning the discipline necessary to reach organizational goals; however, how much are workers pressured to accept these demanding goals? Furthermore, if opposing views concerning discipline and goal attainment have been silenced, what prospects exist for sustaining workplace democracy within the Grameen Bank?

■ Concertive Control among Grameen Bank Members

Concertive control also works on the loan recipients. To obtain a loan, an applicant must form a homogeneous group with four other individuals of the same gender and of similar socioeconomic status (Yunus, 1983). As a five-member group, the new loan applicants regularly meet with the bank fieldworker to understand the philosophy and procedures of the Grameen Bank, to learn how to operate small businesses, to establish trust among themselves, and to learn how to sign their names. These meetings promote the perceptual component of empowerment, instilling confidence in new members and providing them with information on how they can establish and operate small businesses.

After approximately four weeks of training, the group, by consensus, selects two members from among themselves to receive an initial loan (the amount varies from 2,000 to 4,000 takas, the equivalent of $30–60). The group is empowered to make these nominations, but the corporate vision of the Grameen advises them to select the neediest members. This loan disbursement is subject to the bank worker's satisfaction with the group's ability to observe Grameen's discipline and refund the loan in time. After several weeks, when the first two borrowers have established their credibility by repaying their weekly loan installments, two other group members, who are also nominated by consensus, receive similar loans. The fifth person, usually the group chairperson, receives his/her loan when the second set of loanees has also established their repayment credibility.

Mutual Accountability, Identification, and Control   Because Grameen members share collective responsibility to repay loans, they sustain a system of peer support and peer pressure that replaces the need for material collateral in ensuring credit discipline. If one member defaults, the prospective loans of other members are in jeopardy. Usually, however, if one member defaults on repayment for a genuine reason, the other members collectively arrange to pay the installment, identifying strongly with Grameen's values (i.e., members must help one other to succeed). Grameen's system of collective responsibility for loan repayment creates a strong sense of material interdependence among group members.

For Grameen members, the group and the center provide fora for their individual and collective empowerment. The members share experiences about financial, health-related, educational, and other social activities directed by the bank. As members share their stories of success and renew their commitments to help one another, they realize that they have the power to make their lives better. Also, once members believe they can improve their lives through their own efforts, they can identify specific actions to bring about positive change. For example, women members in a town adjacent to Nageswari were concerned with the continuing practice of dowry in their community. They negotiated a solution among themselves by deciding not to give or take dowry in the marriage of their children. To avoid being victims of clandestine dowry practice, they arranged marriages between their sons and daughters. However, on one occasion, the Grameen members found out that a local bridegroom was demanding a bicycle and a radio as dowry. At the end of the wedding ceremony, the women of the center told the bridegroom that he could leave with either the bride or the dowry, but not both. To avoid social embarrassment, the bridegroom eventually left with the bride. This example underscores the social empowerment that emerges among Grameen members as they meet ritually in the centers to socialize, discuss ideas, and determine actions they can take in the face of demanding situations. In addition, this example shows how empowerment is an interactional process (Albrecht, 1988; Chiles & Zorn, 1995) in which members collectively identify specific courses of action to improve their lives socially and economically.

Although Grameen members empower themselves through collectively identifying and enacting solutions to solve personal and business problems, there are aspects of their participation in the bank that are not reflective of authentic democracy. For example, Stohl and Cheney (2001) describe a "paradox of formalization" that can occur in democratic organizations. A paradox of formalization occurs when certain aspects of democracy are institutionalized in a way that, in the long run, can actually inhibit the democratic process. Indeed, Cheney (1996) has found that the Mondragon cooperatives in the Basque Country of Spain are encountering some limitations to their own democratic practice now that some of their decision-making procedures are well established, legitimized, and even routinized. In this case, such a paradox is reflected in the regimented behavior that occurs in every center meeting when Grameen members recite the Sixteen Decisions and other slogans that are linked to socio-economic, health, and nutritional problems.

Grameen members have undoubtedly become empowered economically through their affiliation with the bank. The economic empowerment they have experienced is, in large part, related to a loan repayment system of mutual accountability. However, mutual accountability among center members has led to a powerful system of concertive control in which members themselves threaten delinquent borrowers with expulsion from the bank if they do not resume loan repayment.

Box 2.6: Shokhina and Rehana
Peer Pressure in Action

Consider the case of Shokhina, a mother of three children, who lives in Barmi-Sripur village. She took a personal loan of 5,000 takas ($75) and a house loan of 10,000 takas ($150) from the Grameen Bank. Shortly after receiving these loans her husband became seriously ill. His treatment bankrupted Shokhina and she could no longer afford her loan payments. Ashamed of her predicament, Shokhina stopped attending the center meetings. Instead of receiving support from her fellow center members, they began to chase and taunt her. The center chief eventually arranged for the branch manager to meet Shokhina. After listening to her problems, she was asked to surrender the house she had built with the housing loan; however, her personal loan was rescheduled and she was offered a small additional loan to continue her husband's medical treatment.

Despite the fact that Shokhina dealt with substantial personal hardships and eventually paid all of her debts, her group members wanted her expelled from the bank. They were worried that their future credit opportunities would be jeopardized by someone who was an unacceptable risk. Fortunately, the bank manager prevented this expulsion, and she received another housing loan (personal interview, August 9, 1991).

The level of peer pressure felt by members to repay their loans is also reflected in the story of Rehana, as told to us by her husband Azizar Rahman in the village of Chakjagatpur. Rehana had taken a loan from the Grameen Bank without her husband's knowledge. When she failed to repay the loan, she was insulted and threatened by fellow center members. Her feelings of humiliation and failure were so strong that she attempted suicide. Her husband prevented the suicide and later lamented: "When it is difficult to feed ourselves, how can we repay the installments?" (personal interview, August 11, 1991).

The stories of Shokhina and Rehana provide evidence of a control paradox that is linked to democratic processes within the Grameen Bank. Members have the authority to maintain credit discipline within the center, but to sustain discipline, they must closely monitor one another's behaviors and actions. The fact that Shokhina and Rehana were chased, insulted, and taunted by fellow members for not paying their loans reveals how control can get out of hand in a democratically-run organization. In addition, consider the fact that Shokhina's temporary cessation of loan repayment was linked to her husband's serious illness. Nonetheless, the members of her center wanted her expelled from the bank even after she repaid her loan. This is a clear instance of members' perceiving that control is more important than compassion, even when a person is genuinely in need of help.

Relief from Oppression Grameen members identify strongly with the organization. Before acquiring membership in the Grameen, they suffered from hunger, oppression, injustice, bondage, and servitude. After becoming involved in the Grameen's economic and social programs, they developed a sense of hope, gaining control of their lives. Rabeya, a woman whose husband is a Grameen member in the village of Barnal, provided us with an example of her family's life before and after affiliation with the bank:

> At the end of the day, what my husband brought from his wages did not make a full meal for us. We felt hungry all day. Those were really hard days. We had no peace at home. Nobody believed us. Nobody lent us anything, nor did the grocer allow us to buy anything on credit. Now we have peace at home. People believe us. We have a sense of community among the Grameen Bank members who consult with each other. Even though my husband is a member and I am not, we, the wives look after each other. This is a great sense of community that has happened due to the Grameen Bank. (personal interview, August 9, 1993)

Most Grameen Bank members share similar experiences. The Grameen Bank alleviates their wants and provides a smooth escape from poverty, vulnerability, and socioeconomic injustice. Given the incredible life transformation that occurs when members have access to capital, it is hardly surprising that they identify so strongly with the bank. Joygon Begum, a Grameen member from Nikrail village, provided the most succinct description of her identification with the bank when stating: "The Grameen Bank gave me life—so I will stay with it until the day I die" (Counts, 1990, p. 1).

Many of the stories we gathered described how Grameen's programs empowered and emancipated the members from oppression. The overriding theme was relief from poverty and hunger since they became members of the bank. Almost all the descriptions went somewhat like this:

> Previously, we suffered from hunger, now we do not; previously, my husband/wife used to work for others at nominal payment, now we are self-employed; previously, we could neither feed our children nor send them to school, now we do; previously, people did not believe us creditworthy, now they do; previously, we did not have a tubewell/pit latrine, now we do; previously we could not think of

living in a tin roof house, now we do; previously, we had only one piece of rag per person, now we can afford new clothes; previously, we had worries all the time, now we do not; previously, we did not have the courage to handle money, now we do; and so forth. (Auwal, 1994b, p. 164)

Paradoxes of Representation, Identification, and Control The level of identification displayed in member stories and accounts also provides us with evidence of a possible "paradox of representation" (Stohl & Cheney, 2001). Specifically, the active members appear to have become co-opted by the dominant interests that are behind Grameen's participative system of governance. They do not question worker directives or recommendations, and they express total commitment to Grameen's programs because the bank has played such a clear role in transforming their lives. When such strong levels of identification and commitment are present, how likely is it that members will identify options for their empowerment that are unique or in some ways disagree with the Grameen's particular approach to development organizing? Furthermore, if members never disagree with fieldworkers or bank officials, how democratic is the Grameen's approach to development organizing?

The strength of member identification with the bank shows clearly in their actions, especially in the discipline they exhibit in response to fieldworker directives. For example, when we met the Grameen Bank official in Barmi-Sripur village and told him about our interests in the organization, he sent word out for all branch members of the village to assemble at a designated place. Within 10–12 minutes, all the members had gathered. One of these members was Rokeya, who had not slept the previous night because of her sister's wedding. Despite her physical condition, Rokeya responded to the Grameen official's request, a reflection, according to the bank official, of her commitment to the bank. This event, however, could also be interpreted as a sign of rigorous and effective discipline fostered by the Grameen and reflect its control and command orientation. Members are conditioned to uphold the priorities of the bank over their personal lives. Such unquestioned commitment is reminiscent of Foucault's (1980a) observations concerning the taken-for-granted knowledge base in a social system. Discipline is so instilled in the bank members that they accept bank worker directives because these directives represent "rules of right," or, more simply, "the way we do things around here."

Member Discipline   A final aspect of member identification with the Grameen is reflected in the disciplined physical behavior of the members in the center meetings. Professor Yunus believes that the culture of poverty is represented in the physical stance and behavior of the landless. "It is expressed in the bent back, the fallen glance, and the low inaudible voice" (Fuglesang & Chandler, 1993, p. 86). Grameen workers train members to look at them directly when they talk, to stand straight, and to speak loudly and clearly. In addition, during the meetings, they shout slogans and carry out a program of physical exercises together. Taken collectively, these practiced behaviors are intended to create group solidarity and group success.

Given the strength of member identification with the Grameen, how do the members describe and evaluate the disciplinary techniques practiced within the organization? Our interviews with bank members indicate that they see only the positive aspects of discipline. When Tasmiah recounted her struggles with loan repayment, she noted that it was discipline that allowed her to succeed. "I may be exhausted at the end of a long day's work, but this discipline is necessary for us to provide for our families" (personal interview, March 22, 1994). Fazila Bewa, a loanee from Dhopajani village, advanced a similar perspective: "Indiscipline tends to lead to defaults in loan repayment" (Ray, 1987, p. 101). Discipline, on the other hand, allows members to stand together and move forward together (Fuglesang & Chandler, 1993).

The absence of criticism concerning the discipline that members must exhibit to maintain their membership in the bank is suggestive of a "consensus paradox." In our interviews, members talked repeatedly about the discipline that is needed to maintain their membership in the bank and to operate small businesses. Yet, no member offered criticisms of the disciplinary standards. It appears that consensus has been reached among center members concerning the discipline that is necessary to remain in good standing within the organization.

Grameen members' dedication to maintaining credit discipline is central to their financial success and to the continued operation of the bank. However, the members' complete commitment to these disciplinary standards may also provide evidence of how their

Box 2.7: The Grameen Social Change Conglomerate

The Grameen Bank piggybacks several synergistic social change initiatives on its microcredit operations. For instance, consider Grameen's information technology initiatives in remote, rural Bangladesh.

In 1997, the Grameen Bank established a non-profit organization called Grameen Telecom with the vision of placing at least one mobile phone in each of the 68,000 villages of Bangladesh. At that time, there was one telephone in Bangladesh for every 400 people, representing one of the lowest telephone densities in the world.[6] There was virtually no access to telephony services in rural areas. Professor Yunus realized that while it was not possible for each rural household to own a telephone, it would be possible through mobile telephone technology to provide access to each villager.

Thus the Grameen Telecom's Village Phone Project (VPP) was born. In 1997, Grameen Telecom formed a joint venture company called GrameenPhone Ltd (GP) in partnership with Telenor of Norway, Marubeni of Japan, and Gonofone Development Corporation of the U.S.[7] The Company, GP was awarded a license to operate a nation-wide GSM-900 cellular network on November 11, 1996. GP started its operation on March 26, 1997.

The business model of the VPP was deceptively simple and a potential win-win for everyone involved, including the service providers and the end users (Singhal, Svenkerud, & Flydal, 2002). Four business entities were involved in the VPP: GrameenPhone (the for-profit business), Grameen Telecom (the not-for-profit business), Grameen Bank (for-profit microcredit bank), and the mobile handset owner in the village (Plate 2.3), commonly referred to as the Village Phone Lady (who was a member of Grameen Bank) (Malaviya, Singhal, Svenkerud, & Srivastava, 2004a, 2004b, 2004c).

GrameenPhone sold bulk airtime to Grameen Telecom at half the regular rate that was levied in the urban areas. The handsets were made available to villagers through Grameen Bank loans. Grameen Telecom was responsible for the sales, marketing, servicing and administration of the village phones. This arrangement meant that GrameenPhone avoided the costs of billing and bill collection from the village phone users, and had a steady revenue stream from Grameen Telecom. Grameen Bank benefited by cross-selling to villagers (who were existing Grameen Bank borrowers) the opportunity to start an additional business of providing mobile phone services in their village. Because the initial loan for a mobile

Box 2.7: The Grameen Social Change Conglomerate *(continued)*

Plate 2.3
A Village Telephone Lady (right forefront) in Chaklagram village of Bangladesh with other village women, who now have access to telephony services locally
The mobile telephone confers status and prestige on the village telephone lady. In rural Bangladesh, technological gadgets (such as cameras or transistor radio sets) are usually appropriated by men. The Village Phone Project consciously places the mobile phone in the hands of a rural woman. So, now even a rich, male landlord has to come to her home to access the telephone service. *Phone Bari*, the home of the village phone lady, is now an important location on the village map.
Source: Personal Files of the Authors.

phone set was about $390, an amount few villagers could invest on their own, these Grameen Bank members took loans to lease or purchase the mobile telephone sets, thus, generating additional income for Grameen Bank (Malaviya, Singhal, Svenkerud, & Srivastava, 2004b). In addition, villagers settled their monthly telephone bills while repaying their loan amounts.

For Grameen Telecom, the VPP set-up meant that it could be optimistic about fulfilling its promise of providing mobile telephony in villages for the rural poor of Bangladesh. While most telephone companies targeted only the rich living in the cities, Grameen Telecom's VPP targeted the

	Box 2.7: The Grameen Social Change Conglomerate *(continued)*

rural poor, particularly women, because 95 percent of Grameen Bank borrowers are women. The Village Phone Ladies benefited because they now had an independent source of revenue. The villagers who used the mobile phones to make and receive calls benefited because they were now "connected" to the rest of the world, using one of the most modern cellular technologies of the world, while paying one of the cheapest cellular rates in the world. And from the perspective of the Government of Bangladesh, with the "mobile" presence of the village telephone lady, rural residents could receive and make telephone calls, obviating the need to install expensive large-scale telephone exchanges and digital switching systems.

Since its inception in 1997, GrameenPhone's subscription rate has doubled each year to reach over 2 million subscribers by December, 2004 (Malaviya, Singhal, Svenkerud, & Srivastava, 2004b), which represents the biggest subscriber base and coverage of any mobile telephony operator in Bangladesh, and in South Asia. The company turned a profit in 2000 of $14 million, which steeply climbed to over $110 million in 2002, and over $200 million in 2003 (Malaviya, Singhal, Svenkerud, & Srivastava, 2004b, 2004c). Many believe that even brighter business prospects lie ahead: Demand for mobile telephony services in Bangladesh is estimated at about 5–6 million subscribers (out of a population of 130 million people). GrameenPhone's growing mobile telephony network in the country and its financial viability also helps the Grameen Telecom's VPP to piggyback on it.

By early 2005, some 99,987 village phones were operating (about 5 percent of all GrameenPhone's subscribers) in about 51,000 Bangladeshi villages. These village phones were serving an estimated 100 million rural inhabitants, more than 80 percent of Bangladesh's rural population. The village phones, on average, generated 2–3 times more revenues for GrameenPhone than a personal use city subscription, although the total revenue from these village phones was a relatively small percent of total GrameenPhone revenues (6 percent) (http://www.telecommons.com/villagephone, 2000).

Although the village phones contributed a small percent toward GrameenPhone revenues, they yielded a very high social impact in terms of reaching 100 million rural Bangladeshis who previously did not have access to telephony services. Studies indicated that the VPP had a very positive economic impact in rural areas, creating a substantial consumer

Box 2.7: The Grameen Social Change
Conglomerate   *(continued)*

surplus, and immeasurable quality-of-life enhancements.[8] For instance, the village phone obviated the need for a rural farmer to make a trip to the city to find out the market price of produce. The village phone accomplished this task at about one-fourth the cost of taking the trip to the city and almost instantaneously (as compared to the hours of time it can take to make the trip to Dhaka). Further, the village phone helped families to keep in touch with relatives overseas, to know about remittances sent to them from migrant workers overseas, and to arrange appointments with doctors in the cities.

Rural women in Bangladesh also became increasingly empowered through the VPP. Usually, technological "toys" (such as cameras, radios, cassette players, and others) are appropriated by rural men. However, through the VPP the mobile phone was placed in the hands of rural women. Now even a rich landowner had to come to her home to access the telephone service. He had to wait in line for his turn, if another villager was using the phone at that time. The home of the Village Phone Lady became an important location on the village map, often being referred to as the *Phone Bari* (or "home of the phone"). The VPP thus conferred status and prestige on rural Bangladeshi women.

So what have been the overall effects of the VPP in rural Bangladesh? The VPP makes telephony services accessible and affordable to poor, rural Bangladeshis, spurs employment, increases the social status of the village telephone ladies, provides access to market information and to medical services, and represents a tool to communicate with family and friends within Bangladesh and outside (Bayes, Braun, and Akhter, 1999; Quadir, 2003; Richardson, Ramirez, and Haq, 2000). Thus by synergistically combining its microcredit operations with information technology initiatives, the Grameen Bank has empowered its poor client base.

Another information technology venture of the Grameen Bank is the Village Internet Program (VIP), a pilot project in which borrowers obtain loans to purchase and operate "cyber kiosks" for profit. The purpose behind the "cyber kiosks" is for Grameen borrowers to have increased access to agricultural and market information for business use, to provide distance and virtual education through remote classroom facilities, and to provide computer-based employment (such as data-entry, transcription services, etc.) in rural areas, as an alternative to massive migration to the cities (Yunus & Jolis, 1999).

**Box 2.7: The Grameen Social Change
Conglomerate** *(continued)*

The VIP is supported by established infrastructures and technologies within the Grameen family of companies (Table 2.3). For instance, Grameen Shakti [Energy] has developed photovoltaic solar systems to provide electricity to villages that lie beyond the national grid of central station electricity. The plan of VIP is to have cyber kiosks that run on solar power and connect to the Internet by mobile wireless, microwave, and laser connections. Each cyber kiosk is run as an independently-owned and operated franchise of Grameen Communications, in which the borrower will earn money by selling Internet, telephony, and other computer-related services (Yunus & Jolis, 1999).

The key lesson of the Grameen Bank approach to the use of mobile telephony and Internet services is that poor people should not just be the passive consumers of communication technology, but rather its owners. When poor people own communication technology in ways to provide increased access to information to the resource-poor and, in so doing, create a viable business proposition for themselves, they help bridge the digital and economic divide in society.

In conclusion, the Grameen information technology operations in Bangladesh, demonstrate how "penny" capitalism and organizing for social change processes can operate creatively to bridge the digital divide and serve the underdogs of society.

---

empowerment opportunities are limited. As noted earlier concerning the fieldworkers, there appear to be limits on the range of issues that can be addressed by loan recipients. Although Grameen's members are clearly empowered to design their own economic development activities, they are *not* empowered to negotiate different standards of credit discipline within their centers.

Our observations of women chanting the Sixteen Decisions of the Grameen Bank clarified for us the dialectical tension that exists between emancipation and control in development programs. Clearly Grameen's economic and social programs are emancipatory for its members. Through its loan activities and social programs the Grameen Bank transforms the lives of its members. However, in order to achieve economic self-sufficiency individual members may at times subordinate some of their personal desires (e.g., to design a personalized development plan) to the collective will of the organization. As Barker (1993) concluded, "for individuals to achieve larger goals they must actually surrender some autonomy in organizational participation" (p. 409).

Table 2.3
The Grameen social change conglomerate

Grameen Bank	A for-profit bank. Specializes in collateral-free credit and other financial services for the "poorest of the poor."
Grameen Krishi [Agriculture] Foundation	A for-profit company like the Grameen Bank. Unlike the Grameen Bank that deals only in cash, the Krishi Foundation lends and accepts repayments in cash as well as in agricultural input and produce.
Grameen Uddog [Industry]	A not-for-profit company. Works with tens of thousands of poor hand-loom weavers in Bangladesh. Organizes and networks these village-based weavers into a large business which exports more than one million yards of hand-loomed cotton "check" fabric a month.
Grameen Motsho [Fisheries] Foundation	A not-for-profit company. Operates hundreds of hectares of fish farms and shrimp farms as well as dozens of fish seed multiplication farms.
Grameen Fund	A not-for-profit company. Provides finance to ventures that are risky, technology-oriented, and deprived of credit from formal financial institutions because the poor entrepreneurs are deemed not credit-worthy.
Grameen Kalyan [Rural Welfare]	A not-for-profit company. Provides "welfare" to Grameen Bank staff and clients in the area of education, health and disaster relief, as well as credit to employees.
Grameen Shamogree [Rural Products]	A for-profit company. Finances rural industries and markets their products, including labor-intensive crafts products.
Grameen Telecom	Dedicated to bringing the information revolution to the rural people of Bangladesh. Provide mobile phone service to approximately 100 million rural inhabitants by financing 93,000 Grameen borrowers to provide village pay phone service.

Grameen Shakti [Energy]	A not-for-profit rural power company. Develops non-polluting renewable energy including solar, bio-gas and wind turbine, for non-electrified villages of Bangladesh.
Grameen Cybernet Limited	A for-profit company dedicated to bringing the latest in information technology including Internet to the cities and villages of Bangladesh.
Grameen Communications	A not-for-profit company promoting the use of Internet for improving education, health, sanitation, and research.
Grameen Trust	A not-for-profit Trust. Provides finance, training, and technical assistance to people all over the world, who wish to "replicate" the Grameen Bank model. At present, there are some 500 "Grameen Bank replications" in 75 countries.

Source: Grameen Bank.

Conclusions

The Grameen Bank is dedicated to organizing the poorest of the poor for productive self-employment in an innovative theoretical framework. Central to this framework is the belief that credit is a fundamental human right and that development should be measured according to the per capita income of the bottom 50 percent of the population. The Grameen Bank demonstrates that development is an organized process of (*a*) education, (*b*) environmentally sound productivity, and (*c*) improvement in the quality of life for the poorest of the poor.

In this chapter, we analyzed the communicative practices and organizational patterns of the Grameen Bank from the theory of concertive control giving us a unique and informative perspective on the bank's operations. Although communication and control among workers is partly responsible for the success of Grameen's loan programs, it sustains an oppressive environment for the workers. The workers have socially constructed a system of concertive control in which they compete with one another to maintain the bank's high loan recovery rate. The pressure created by this system of concertive control is overwhelming at times as the fieldworkers work overtime and closely involve themselves in the day-to-day business operations of the members.

There is also a concertive control system operative among the members. This control system is clearest in terms of socially constructed norms regarding loan repayment. Members pressure one another to repay loans because failure to do so can jeopardize the loans of other center members. Also, our interviews indicated that some members so strongly identify with the bank that they may fail to recognize which aspects of the bank's programs are in their best interests.

As discussed in this chapter, concertive control systems are simultaneously restrictive and empowering (Table 2.4). The dialectic that is present in this system is one in which being embedded in control systems is a requirement for emancipation from oppression. In the case of the Grameen Bank, the workers have created a control system that is largely responsible for their success in transforming the lives of millions of poor Bangladeshis. They not only emancipate others from oppression, they are also emancipated from a likely fate of meaningless employment in a struggling national economy that generates relatively few rewarding jobs. Also, the members sustain a system of control that guarantees them continued access to credit for economic and social development. Without the Grameen Bank emancipation from oppression is an unlikely possibility.

Returning to the opening example of Tasmiah it becomes clear how central the dialectic of control and emancipation is to the

Table 2.4
Dimensions of control and emancipation

Dimensions of Control	*Dimensions of Emancipation*
Subject to Socioeconomic Oppression	Relief from Socioeconomic Oppression
Employed by Others	Self-Employment
Competing against Others	Cooperation with Others
Hopelessness	Restoration of Hope
No Access to Financial Resources	Access to Credit as a Human Right
Criticism, Insults, and Threats	Praise and Encouragement
Responding to Orders	Engagement in Democratic Practices
Peer Pressure	Peer Support

experiences of Grameen Bank members. Tasmiah's continued participation in the bank alleviates her suffering and provides hope for her and her children. Such an outcome is clearly emancipatory. At the same time, however, she must internalize control systems that require her to work long hours and subject herself to the scrutiny of center members who will pressure her to repay loans even under difficult circumstances. When Tasmiah expresses her feelings, is offered affection, and is accepted by members, she is potentially emancipated from oppression. At the same time, however, Tasmiah may recognize the need to be protective of self-disclosure, accept that friends view her as a means to an end, and be open to judgment and criticism. These control mechanisms are not separate from the experience of emancipation. Rather, Tasmiah experiences both forces of the dialectic in a dynamic tension that reflects her everyday experience as a Grameen Bank member.

In recent years, the Grameen Bank has increasingly recognized the need to be flexible in responding to the needs of the poor, especially those who face difficult or catastrophic circumstances. Responding to certain criticisms made by Pearl and Phillips (2001) in the *Wall Street Journal*, Yunus (2002, p. 2) explained how the Grameen Bank is making it easier for borrowers to repay overdue loans: "A defaulter can continue to repay overdue loans by converting the overdue amount into a flexible loan. The flexible loan is actually a rescheduled loan. She can negotiate her repayment schedule." The introduction of the flexible, rescheduled loan in the Grameen Bank's lending portfolio represents an important step toward softening some of the control systems that are operative in the organization. Continued scrutiny of the disciplinary mechanisms that operate in the Grameen Bank are necessary to insure that the focus of the bank's programs promote more emancipation than dispassionate control that can further oppress the poor.

In terms of implications for praxis, our observations help to set the stage for debate among development scholars and practitioners. The issue these groups must confront is how to organize for social change without silencing the voices of those receiving assistance. People cannot be organized into collectives without some sort of control system that orients and guides member behavior. However, how can control systems be created in which members retain a voice in establishing their own path to individual and collective empowerment?

Notes

1. This chapter draws upon Auwal and Singhal (1992); Papa, Auwal, and Singhal (1995, 1997); Malaviya, Singhal, Svenkerud, and Srivastava (2004a, 2004b, 2004c); and Singhal, Svenkerud, and Flydal (2002). We especially acknowledge our former Ohio University colleague, Mohammed A. Auwal, presently Associate Professor of Communication Studies at California State University, Los Angeles, for getting us interested in the Grameen Bank, and for co-partnering with us during important parts of this research journey.

2. Prahalad (2005) provides us with additional insights about the empowering impact of these microcredit programs. When loan recipients earn income from their small businesses, they also become consumers. Prahalad (2005) agues: "When the poor are converted into consumers, they get more than access to products and services. They acquire the dignity of attention and choices from the private sector that were previously reserved for the middle class and rich" (p. 20).

3. Burke (1954/1984) also thought dialectically about the experience of identification. As symbol-using creatures Burke believes that humans seek both to identify and to maintain distinctions, mysteries or hierarchies.

4. For an additional example of how and why employees often fail to enact work-family policies because of concertive control see Kirby and Krone (2002).

5. The motivational programs offered to Grameen members are similar in some ways to the post-entry training offered to U.S. Forest Rangers. These training programs instill in the minds of rangers the importance of the Forest Service job to the welfare of the nation, reaffirming the faith of the rangers in the work they perform (Bullis & Tompkins, 1989; Cheney & Tompkins, 1987; Kaufman, 1960).

6. In 2005, there exists one telephone in Bangladesh for every 75 people.

7. Telenor Corporation is the majority owner of Grameen Phone's equity (over 50 percent); Grameen Telecom owns about 35 percent of the equity, and the other partners own the balance.

8. See Richardson et al. (2000) and Bayes et al. (1999).

3 Dialectic of oppression and empowerment in India's dairy cooperatives[1]

The test of a first-rate intelligence is the ability to hold two opposed ideas in mind at the same time and still retain the ability to function.
—F. Scott Fitzgerald, American novelist and writer
(quoted in http://encyclopedia.lockergnome.com/s/b/
F._Scott_Fitzgerald)

To understand the social barriers rural women face in India, let us recount a story that we heard frequently when interviewing women dairy farmers in India's Jaipur District in 1997. The story focused on Sushila Devi of Radhapura village, who was training to become the secretary of the local dairy cooperative society (DCS). Her trainer, Dr. Satsangi, a veterinarian from the Jaipur District Milk Union, was showing the trainees how to test for milk fat. This procedure involved the use of acid. When Sushila Devi poured the liquid mixture in a test tube, a freak chemical reaction caused the glass tube to explode, spraying acid in Sushila's eyes. Satsangi promptly flushed Sushila Devi's eyes with fresh milk (a well-known local remedy) and rushed her in his jeep to the local hospital. Satsangi was worried that Sushila's husband would beat him because he had precipitated the events resulting in Sushila's injury.

After the hospital visit, when Satsangi stopped his jeep in front of Sushila's home, she asked: "Why have you brought me home?" Satsangi responded, "'I have brought you home so you can rest. You are injured and the doctor has asked you to rest." Sushila protested, "Don't leave me here; take me back to the training site." Surprised, Satsangi replied, "Why do you want to go there?" Sushila explained,

"I want to complete the fat testing of milk." Satsangi countered, "Why do you want to complete the testing?" Sushila answered:

> My husband and the other men in this village have told all of us—women DCS members—that women can do nothing. They say that running the DCS is a man's job. Women will get hurt if they try to test the milk. I must complete testing the milk to show that women can do this job, and that we can make this cooperative work. So, please let me complete my training.

Sushila Devi's story is one of remarkable courage and resilience, and women dairy farmers in Radhapura recounted it with pride. In fact, word of Sushila's heroic focus on task completion had spread to many neighboring villages. However, what is the likely impact of this story on women? Certainly, some women may become motivated and empowered by Sushila's determination to succeed in spite of her injuries. Unfortunately, some others may sustain their feelings of oppression because the story reaffirms how completely dominated women are by men in rural India. Would a man have felt the same pressure to complete the milk testing before the end of the day if he had been seriously injured? Why should we celebrate the fact that Sushila could not adequately recuperate from the trauma of her injuries? Does not Sushila's story show how high the barriers to empowerment are for women? Women are not allowed to make mistakes. Further, if a woman does make a mistake (as Sushila did), she must put aside the pain of a serious injury, or she will be "rightfully" put back in her place.

Sushila's story illustrates the dialectic of oppression and empowerment in organizing for social change.[2] As an oppressed group attempts to empower themselves they are often torn between the competing and contradictory forces of oppression and empowerment.[3] Actions that empower in some ways oppress in others.

In the present chapter we focus on the dialectic of oppression and empowerment by focusing on the experiences of women dairy farmers in India. We investigate the efforts of India's National Dairy Development Board (NDDB) in empowering women dairy farmers, especially analyzing how empowerment is displayed in human interaction and feminist action, particularly when women unite and organize to accomplish social change within families and communities. We also analyze how the empowerment of women dairy farmers in India is embedded in democratic practices. We end by explaining the integral role of paradox and contradiction in the process of organizing for change, especially as women dairy farmers negotiate the dialectic tension between oppression and empowerment.

Social Change through Dairy Cooperatives in India

India is the land of the "holy" cow—a country where cattle and milk are highly revered (Kurien, 1997a). Unlike cows in the U.S. or in the Netherlands, Indian cattle do not live in fenced-off ranches, and rarely have access to high-quality fodder. Indian cattle mostly live off crop residue and scrubby forage, and milk production is relatively small scale. Three-quarters of all Indian dairy farmers have an average milch herd of 1.5 animals.

Amidst this seemingly bleak scenario, India boasts of one of the largest webs of dairy cooperatives in the world (Heredia, 1997; Kamath, 1989; Papa, Singhal, Ghanekar, & Papa, 2000). In 2005, some 12.1 million dairy farmers, of which 2.9 million are women, are organized in 112,590 village-level dairy cooperatives, of which 18,500 are all-women dairy cooperatives, where women are not just members but also its elected leaders (Figure 3.1).[4] The 112,590 village-level DCSs are networked in mutually supportive networks with 170 district-level milk unions and state and national level dairy cooperative federations. Together, this cooperative enterprise markets 15 million liters of milk daily, providing steady incomes to 12.1 million farm families and sustenance to 70 million people. Nearly $3 million (U.S.) is paid out daily to dairy cooperative members, of whom 21 percent are landless, and 66 percent represent small and marginal farmers (Kurien, 1997a). A supplemental annual income of about $100 per dairying family means a lot in India where the per capita income is $450 per year.

The visionary architect of India's dairy cooperative movement is Dr. Verghese Kurien, who, for over five decades, led India's journey to achieving what is commonly referred to as the White Revolution —a state of self-sufficiency in milk. Championing the cause of small-scale milk farmers, and advocating the role of dairy cooperatives as engines of social change, Kurien brought modern science and

Figure 3.1

The growth of farmer members in India's dairy cooperative societies
After the formation of the NDDB in 1965, the number of farmer members
organized in village-level dairy cooperative societies climbed rapidly. In
2005, 12.1 million dairy farmers are members of dairy cooperative societies
in India, of which 21 percent are landless, and 66 percent represent small
and marginal farmers. The dairy cooperative enterprise in India directly
contributes to the livelihood of an estimated 70 million people in India.

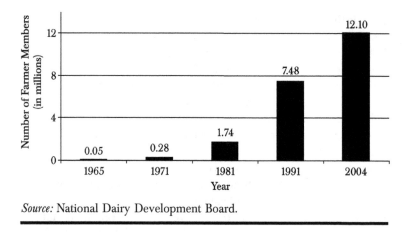

Source: National Dairy Development Board.

technology to enhance the small production base of India's dairy
farmers, as well as professional management skills to collect, store,
process, market, and distribute milk to urban consumers. Starting in
the 1950s with a small cluster of dairy cooperatives in Kaira District
of India's Gujarat State, the DCS network expanded nationally to
encompass 112,590 village-level DCSs (Figure 3.2). Milk production in India increased from a dismal 20 million tons in the 1950s to
a whopping 90 million tons in 2004, making India a milk exporting
country. Per capita milk availability went up from about 100 grams
in the 1950s, to about 231 grams in 2004.

Twice a day, 12.1 million dairy farmers in India pour milk at the
village DCSs. Each pourer's milk is instantly tested for fat content,
and a chain of trucks, chilling plants, refrigerated vans, railway
wagons, and dairy processing plants—all owned by the dairy cooperative network—links the village-based producers to city-based

Figure 3.2
The growth in the number of village-level dairy cooperative societies in India
In the past two decades, the number of all-women dairy cooperatives has risen significantly in India (18,500 out of a total of 112,590), pointing to NDDB's emphasis on the empowerment of women dairy farmers.

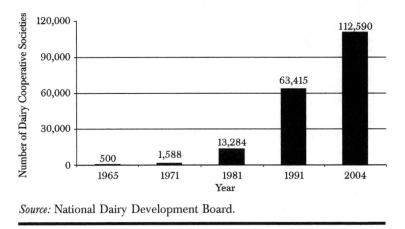

Source: National Dairy Development Board.

consumers (Kurien, 1997a, 1997b). Twice a day, the milk producer receives payment. The cooperative network also provides members with access to enriched cattle feed, artificial insemination services to improve dairy progeny, and veterinary services. Further, the 112,590 DCSs have catalyzed road building (allowing the dairy truck to pass through) and various village development activities in India, including the formation of health clinics, women's thrift groups, and youth clubs.

When author Singhal met Dr. Kurien the first time at NDDB headquarters in Anand, India in 1990, Kurien emphasized: "The dairy cooperatives are less about the development of cows, but more about human development" (personal conversation, July 16, 1990). He noted that the DCS milk collection center which is disinfected twice a day is usually the community's first lesson in modern sanitation. Similarly, the visit of a trained veterinary doctor to deliver a breached calf in the village square is often the community's first introduction to scientific health care. Similarly, farmer visits to cattle-feed plants represent the villagers' first lessons in nutrition.

Plate 3.1
Women dairy farmers in Mamtori-Kalan village, Rajasthan line up to pour milk at an all-women dairy cooperative society
Twice a day, 12.1 million dairy farmers in India line up to pour milk, regardless of caste, religion, or economic differences. It is not unusual for a higher caste member to stand behind a lower caste member just because he/she arrived later. Is this just orderly milk collection? Is it not a blow at the caste system?
Source: Personal Files of the Authors.

Author Singhal also vividly remembers a conversation with Dr. Kurien in New Delhi in 1992, when the NDDB chairman emphasized the daily significance of millions of people lining up at the DCSs to pour milk twice a day (Plate 3.1), regardless of caste, religion, or economic differences:

"What happens to the psyche of a lower caste pourer who stands ahead in line of the high caste *brahmin*, just because he arrived earlier? What happens to the psyche of the high caste *brahmin* who stands behind a lower caste *dalit* just because he came later? Is it just orderly milk collection? Is it not a blow at the caste system?" After a pause, Dr. Kurien continued:

"What happens to the psyche of both the *brahmin* and the *dalit* when they see the milk they separately poured go into a common collection pot? Is this just orderly milk collection? Is it not a blow at the caste system?" Then after another pause, Dr. Kurien asked:

"What happens to the psyche of the *brahmin* and the *dalit* when they come to purchase milk from a dairy cooperative society? Do their caste differences gradually dissolve in milk?"

Box 3.1: Verghese Kurien, India's *Dudhwalla*

Born in 1921 in Kozhikode, in India's Kerala State, in a family of Syrian Christians, Verghese Kurien earned his bachelor's degree in mechanical engineering from Loyola College in Chennai. Kurien excelled in both academics and sports—notably tennis, badminton, cricket, and boxing. In 1946, Kurien arrived in East Lansing, Michigan, on a Government of India merit scholarship to study mechanical engineering. After finishing his degree in 1948, he underwent practical training with Creamery Package, a Wisconsin-based dairy machinery manufacturer, and with Sheffield Farms, a dairy enterprise on Long Island, New York (Heredia, 1997).

In 1949, when he returned to India, the Government of India assigned him to work at a government creamery in Anand, a small town in Kaira District of India's Gujarat State. A self-described "city-bred lad with metropolitan aspirations," Kurien was bored in Anand—"a sleepy village with nothing more than a railway station" (Kurien, 1997a, p. 111). To bide his time, Kurien began to take an interest in the activities of the dairy co-operative society (DCS) in Kaira District. Frustrated with their antiquated dairy equipment—decrepit boilers, gear boxes, shafts and belts, Kurien told Mr. Tribhuvan Das Patel, the chairman of the Kaira cooperative: "Get rid of this junk and buy new equipment" (quoted in Heredia, 1997, p. 61). Upon Kurien's recommendation, the Kaira cooperative, using farmers' money, purchased an expensive Silkeborg Pasteurizer from Mumbai. However, just before the pasteurizer was delivered, Kurien informed Patel that he was leaving.

"You persuade us to buy expensive equipment...and now you are leaving Anand. Is this fair?" asked Patel. "Stay to help us set up the equipment. We will pay you for the next two months. Then you may go" (quoted in Heredia, 1997, p. 65).

Reluctantly, Kurien agreed to stay for two months, becoming an employee of the Kaira cooperative's dairy farmers. Ironically, Kurien never left Anand. Some 55 years later, he still is based in Anand, and still an employee (though officially retired) of dairy farmers. Under his professional management, the Kaira cooperative (more commonly known as Anand Milk Producers Union [AMUL]) experienced continual success, becoming a model of grassroots-based cooperative organizing.

In 1964, Kurien invited Indian Prime Minister Lal Bahadur Shastri to inaugurate a cattle-feed factory in Kanjari, located eight kilometers from Anand (Plate 3.2). Shastri agreed but requested Kurien to arrange his

Box 3.1: Verghese Kurien, India's *Dudhwalla*
(continued)

Plate 3.2
Prime Minister Lal Bahadur Shastri inaugurating the cattle-feed factory in Kanjari, near Anand in 1964. Verghese Kurien is second from right

During this 1964 visit, Shastri was so impressed by the cooperative dairy enterprise in Kaira District that he asked Kurien to replicate the Anand-pattern cooperative all over India. This momentous Prime Ministerial visit led to the formation of National Dairy Development Board (NDDB) in Anand in 1965 with Kurien as its head.

Source: Gujarat Cooperative Milk Marketing Federation.

stay not at a fancy hotel or guest house, but rather at the home of a farmer. Kurien made arrangements for the Prime Minister (minus his security staff) to stay in Ajarpura (near Anand), a village comprising 600 households and 411 active members of the DCS (Kurien, 1997a).

In Ajarpura, Shastri spent a glorious day (and night) talking to dairy farmers. He was struck by the pride that villagers displayed in their DCS.

	Box 3.1: Verghese Kurien, India's _Dudhwalla_ _(continued)_

It was palpable. Later that evening, he asked Dr. Kurien (personal conversation with Dr. Kurien, August 2, 1993): "Dairy cooperative societies have been failures in most of India. What explains the success of AMUL? I see nothing special in the quality of Kaira District's soil, its crops, or its milch herd."

Dr. Kurien told Prime Minister Shastri that the difference between AMUL and other dairy cooperatives in India was that AMUL's governance was in the hands of farmer members, and it was run through professional managers (like himself). When Shastri left Anand, he asked Kurien to replicate the Anand-pattern cooperative all over India. In 1965, the National Dairy Development Board (NDDB) was established in Anand with Kurien at its helm (Kamath, 1989; Kurien, 1997b).

The rest is history. Operation Flood was the name given to replicate the experience of AMUL across the length and breadth of India. While the replication results have been highly effective in some areas, and somewhat disappointing in other locales, the formation of the NDDB gave wings to the Indian dairy cooperative movement, leading to the White Revolution.[5] Under Kurien's leadership, the experience gained from the expansion of dairy cooperatives was applied to establish cooperative networks for the production and marketing of oilseeds, salt, and tree plantations.

Kurien, known as India's _dudhwalla_ [milkman], stepped down as the chairman of the NDDB in 1998. However, in 2005, at age 84, he still continues to be the most ardent champion of India's cooperative sector.

■ NDDB's Programs for Empowering Women Dairy Farmers

Beginning in the late 1980s, the NDDB launched a series of programmatic initiatives to further strengthen its cooperative network, and also to increase the involvement of women dairy farmers (both as members and elected leaders) in dairy cooperative societies. For instance, in 1988–89, the NDDB launched the Cooperative Development (CD) program (which ran over five years) to create stronger and more viable dairy cooperatives that were responsive to the needs of its farmer members. The CD program strengthened village-level

DCSs in India through member education and leadership training, especially concentrating its educational activities on women dairy farmers. In conjunction with the CD program, the NDDB facilitated the formation of all-women's dairy cooperatives throughout India in cooperation with the Women's Development Program (WDP) of the Ministry of Human Resource Development (HRD). In the mid-1990s, the NDDB dovetailed the efforts of its CD program with a Women's Dairy Cooperative Leadership Program (WDCLP) to improve women's participation in the governance of dairy cooperatives. Through these various efforts, the membership of women dairy farmers in India's dairy cooperatives has increased from about 10 percent of the total in 1990; to 25 percent in 2005. By 2010, NDDB would like to double women's membership in DCSs to 50 percent.

Why the focus on empowering women dairy farmers? Although some 85 percent of the daily dairy tasks associated with dairying are carried out by women (Plate 3.3), they still constitute (in 2005) only about 25 percent of the total membership. Further, the money that dairy farmers receive from milk sales is generally controlled by men, who are usually the official members of the village-level DCS and make up most of the elected officers at the village, district, state, and national levels (Papa, Singhal, Ghanekar, & Papa, 2000). Research suggests that when women dairy farmers control income, it translates more directly into better health, childcare, and shelter (Bhatt, 1996).

While our research on the empowerment of women dairy farmers in India was spread across the various women's empowerment training programs—CD, WDP, and WDCLP, we here provide a generalized description of how these programmatic activities were conducted. For instance, the CD program was carried out by 135 five-member core training teams who worked in 85 district milk union cooperatives in India. Each CD team included two female and three male instructors. A CD team on average spent approximately 50 person days in each village-level DCS conducting a village analysis and offering training sessions for male and female members of the cooperative (Plate 3.4). Women dairy farmers who were not members of the cooperative were offered training and encouraged to enroll. The team usually organized a women's club (*mahila mandal*) and a youth club and performed follow-up activities to ensure that new members officially enrolled in the cooperative, that more milk was poured to the cooperative (rather than to private vendors), and that cattle-feed was purchased and fodder locally grown to increase milk yields.

The CD training team conducted women's empowerment meetings in a way that emphasized group discussion, questions and answers, and group singing. Lectures were also offered in which women dairy farmers were informed that although they represent about 50 percent of the population, they performed 70 percent of the hourly work, earned 10 percent of the national income, and owned only 1 percent of national assets. They were also told that because women are the primary producers of milk, the membership in the DCS should be in their names. They were encouraged to learn how the DCS operates because such knowledge represents power.

Plate 3.3
Women in India carry out 85 percent of the dairying work but constitute only 25 percent of the membership in dairy cooperative societies
The proceeds from the milk sales are also generally controlled by men, who are usually the official members of the dairy cooperative societies, and also its elected officials. Since the late 1980s, the NDDB launched various programs to increase the involvement of women dairy farmers both as members and elected leaders.
Source: Personal Files of the Authors.

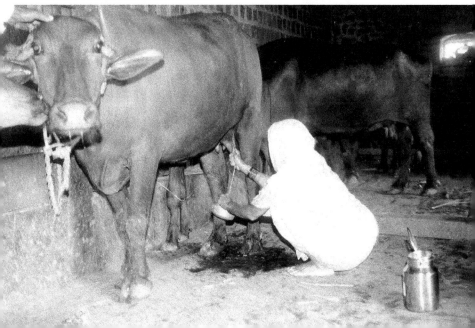

Plate 3.4
NDDB instructors carry out village-based empowerment training programs for women dairy farmers in the Kolhapur Milk Union
These women's empowerment meetings emphasize group discussion, questions and answers, and group singing. In such collective gatherings, women dairy farmers learn about how to increase milk yields, how to run the dairy cooperative society, and how to exercise greater control over the resources they produce. *Source:* Personal Files of the Authors.

Furthermore, CD trainers (as well as trainers of the WDP and WDCLP programs) encouraged women to get elected to the management committees of their DCS, the district milk union, and the state dairy cooperative federation. It was emphasized that these experiences increased their involvement in the decision-making activities of their cooperative and offered opportunities for personal and social empowerment. The CD instructors also persuaded women to support each other in dairying and in other day-to-day activities. As one woman CD trainer illustrated: "Women acting in solidarity (represented by a raised clenched fist) have power that can not be achieved by one woman alone (symbolized by one finger held aloft)" (Papa, Singhal, Ghanekar, & Papa, 2000).

As just explained the CD program helps to promote women's empowerment in a variety of ways. However, as it became clear in the opening story of Sushila, the path from oppression to empowerment, or vice versa, is often a slippery one.

Theoretical Framing of Communicative Empowerment

While a number of communication scholars define and discuss the importance of empowerment, we know relatively little about how the empowerment process unfolds and how it is manifest through specific communicative action (Albrecht, 1988; Buzzanell, 1994; Mumby, 1993; Pacanowsky, 1988; Papa, Singhal, Ghanekar, & Papa, 2000; Trethewey, 1997). In the community psychology literature, empowerment is described as an interactional process that allows people to gain mastery over issues of concern to them through the active engagement of one's community (Rappaport, 1987, 1995; Spreitzer, 1995; Zimmerman, 1990, 1995). In addition, by participating in community organizations and activities, people shape and influence their sociopolitical environment. In this section, we focus on the communicative dimensions of the empowerment process when people attempt to organize for social change.

■ Interaction and Empowerment

We advocate the view that empowerment is a communicative process. When people interact with others to achieve personal and collective goals, empowerment becomes possible (Alvesson & Willmott, 1992; Blau & Alba, 1982; Conger, 1989; Conger & Kanugo, 1988; Pacanowsky, 1988; Shehabuddin, 1992; Singhal & Rogers, 2003; Vogt & Murrell, 1990). Communication is central to coordinating the activities of multiple people, and is also part of negotiating, co-determining, and managing group level power dynamics that pose both opportunities and barriers to empowerment.

The interactive dimension of empowerment has been examined in diverse disciplines, including feminist studies (Young, 1994), urban planning (Wilson, 1996), organizational studies (Cheney, 1995; Mumby, 1997; Papa, Auwal, & Singhal, 1995, 1997), and development communication (Jacobson, 1994; Rahim, 1994; Thomas, 1994; White, 1994). Collective action that emerges from communication increases the potential of overcoming oppression because when people band together they can carry out communal projects, pool or pursue resources, and overcome dependence on outsiders. Further, the process of organizing a collective (talking together, networking,

working together on issues, sharing responsibilities, etc.) enhances psychological empowerment and facilitates community empowerment (Fals Borda, 1968; Jacob, 1991; Young, 1994).

■ Democracy, Cooperatives, and Empowerment

Democratically-organized cooperatives can provide empowerment opportunities for members through communicative actions such as decision-making, negotiation, and dialogue (Cheney, Straub, Speirs-Glebe, Stohl, DeGooyer, Whalen, Garvin-Doxas, & Carlone, 1998). Such communicative actions may empower participants as they share power and work responsibilities and take decisions about the means of distributing surplus capital (Harrison, 1994). Furthermore, the political skills gained in democratic worker-owned and worker-managed cooperatives can be transferred to other spheres, social relationships, and institutions (Bricker-Jenkins, 1992).

For women in India who are socialized to accept directives from men, the opportunity to maintain egalitarian work relationships within a cooperative structure can be a transformative experience (Wayangankar, Rogers, Rao, & Shefner-Rogers, 1995; also see Eisenberg, 1994). For instance, women dairy farmers in Kolhapur, India who belong to thrift groups are "on the one hand, participating in an organization deemed 'acceptable' because it includes only women and is sanctioned by their husbands. On the other hand, they see their thrift group involvement as a giant step outside of women's limitations" (Boyd, 1999, pp. 32–33). In so doing, women limit the control of men in their coordinated economic activity, engaging in an act of resistance. Such local organizations thus represent "principal sites of meaning and identity formation where relations of autonomy and dependence, power and resistance, are continuously negotiated amongst competing interest groups" (Mumby, 1997, p. 345).

■ Power and Resistance

Power and resistance lie at the heart of empowerment (Foucault, 1976; Papa, Singhal, Ghanekar, & Papa, 2000). Mumby (1997) sees power as a productive, disciplinary, and strategic phenomenon with no specific center (e.g., the king, or capitalism). Power is dispersed widely and unevenly; it is neither simply prohibitive nor productive, but simultaneously enables and constrains human thought and action (Mumby, 1997). Resistance to, and the subversion of, the dominant social order is also both an enabling and constraining process (e.g., Bell & Forbes, 1994; Benson, 1992; Burrell, 1993; Collinson, 1994; Jenkins, 1988; Jermier et al., 1994; Lamphere, 1985; Maguire & Mohtar, 1994; Mumby, 1997).

Boyd's (1999) study of women dairy farmers in Kolhapur, India, exemplifies how women resist dominant social forces in ways that are both enabling and constraining. Boyd interviewed women who talked about how their participation in a thrift cooperative provided opportunities for socio-economic progress. Their active participation occurs in spite of their husbands' unstated admonition that they should not "cross the line" by becoming too involved in community activities. However, women also recognize that their progress is tied to men supporting their actions. So, women negotiate their resistance to not upset men. This negotiation embodies the oppression-empowerment dialectic. By limiting their empowerment opportunities due to restrictions placed on them by men, women experience oppression. However, because they willingly accept certain restrictions, they experience empowerment.

■ Empowerment through Dialogue

Dialogue can promote individual and group empowerment through self-reflection, self-knowledge, and liberation from oppressive beliefs (Forester, 1989). Dialogue also leads to mutual learning, acceptance of diversity, interpersonal trust, and understanding (Gronemeyer, 1993; Habermas, 1984). When dialogue is cultivated in democratic organizations, people feel validated in speaking from personal experience because they are valued by their listeners (Eisenberg, 1994).

For Bakhtin (1984), dialogue and empowerment go hand-in-hand:

> The single adequate form for verbally expressing authentic human life is the open-ended dialogue.... To live means to participate in dialogue: to ask questions, to heed, to respond, to agree, and so forth. In this dialogue a person participates wholly and throughout his whole life: with his eyes, lips, hands, soul, spirit, with his whole body and deeds. He invests his entire self in discourse, and this discourse enters into the dialogic fabric of human life. (p. 293)

Box 3.2: India's Women: How Equal?

What is the status of Indian women? The answer depends on what arguments are privileged (Sharan & Bhatt, 1992). On the one hand, India has boasted strong women rulers like *Jhansi ki Rani* (Queen of Jhansi) and the late Prime Minister Indira Gandhi. Indian mythology has wise and strong feminine deities like the Goddess Saraswati and Durga. India was one of the first countries to give women the right to vote. The Indian Constitution guarantees equal rights for men and women (Menon-Sen & Kumar, 2001).

On the other hand, women in India, on average, sleep two hours less per day than men, spend 10 times more time on household work, and only enjoy five minutes of leisure time a day versus two hours for men (Menon-Sen & Kumar, 2001). Women in India, especially in rural areas, often walk miles each day to fetch a pot of drinking water, or a bundle of firewood, while men sit and smoke their *hukkas* (Sharan & Bhatt, 1992; Shiva, 1989) (Plate 3.5).

Plate 3.5
Men in rural India enjoy special privileges in a system steeped in patriarchy
On average, women in India enjoy five minutes of leisure time a day versus two hours for men.
Source: Personal Files of the Authors.

Box 3.2: India's Women: How Equal?
(continued)

In a social system, highly steeped in patriarchy, son preference is widespread. The Jat mother-in-law in India's Haryana State welcomes a new bride by saying "May you be the mother of seven sons" (Jung, 1987). In Bengal and Assam they blow conch shells, and in Maharashtra they beat drums, when a son is born. In Rajasthan, in contrast, when a girl is born, the women withdraw behind their veils and wail. In Punjab it is asserted that girls are conceived on dark nights and boys on moonlit ones (Jung, 1987). A girl's birth is seen as a responsibility and a burden due to the expenses associated with marriage and dowry.

In the desert regions of Rajasthan, a girl becomes marriageable when she is old enough to carry two pitchers of water on her head. Carrying water, gathering firewood, rolling flatbread, and caring for goats, cows, and children are functions that a woman should perform expertly and without question (Jung, 1987; Shiva, 1989).

After marriage, women derive their status from their husbands and power from their sons. Fertility is prized. She is worse than mud if she is barren (Jung, 1987). She is doomed if she has no children. She is doomed if she only produces girls. A woman is born to be a wife and a mother because those two roles constitute her identity, her utility, and her reason to be alive. Much like it is the dharma of the breeze to blow, and the rain to fall, it is the dharma of the Indian wife to serve her husband, in-laws, and children (Jung, 1987). Not surprisingly, often the young girls' role model is her mother, one who suppresses her individuality for the sake of her children.

India's 2001 census shows that men outnumber women: For every 1,000 Indian men, there are only 933 women. With the sole exception of the Indian state of Kerala, every other state has fewer women than men. Punjab, India's most prosperous state, has a disgraceful 874 women per 1,000 men. While in most countries, this ratio favors women, the female-to-male ratio in India has become worse over the past several decades: From 955 females per 1,000 in 1921; to 941 in 1961, to 933 in 2001 (India's Census, 2002). Some argue that India, with its present population of over 1 billion, has to account for some 25–50 million "missing" women. Many of these "missing" females are never born—victims of feticide; the rest did not enjoy adequate opportunities to survive.

Baby girls are more likely to die in Indian families where there is an older male sibling. A study in a Bombay clinic found that 7,999 of the 8,000 aborted fetuses were female (UNDP, 2002). While female feticide

---

Box 3.2: India's Women: How Equal?
(continued)

and infanticide represent the grossest forms of sex discrimination, less visible and more pronounced is the daily discrimination that girls face: Fewer months of breast feeding, less nurturing and play, less medical care, and less parental attention (Menon-Sen & Kumar, 2001).

The life expectancy of Indian women has increased from a low of 32 years in 1951 to 63 years in 2001. In neighboring Sri Lanka, women's life expectancy is 76 years. Female literacy has increased in India from 9 percent in 1951 to 54 percent in 2001. Despite progress, some 250 million Indian women cannot read or write. Most Indian women live in nutritional stress—they are anemic and malnourished—and face nutritional discrimination. They are the last to eat; and they get the least. Indian women are also legally discriminated against in land and property rights (Menon-Sen & Kumar, 2001).

Indian women, no different from most other countries, are under-represented in governance and decision-making positions. Less than 10 percent of Indian parliamentarians, cabinet position holders, and High Court and Supreme Court judges are women. Girls are encouraged to play passive roles from childhood: They engage in little decision-making outside family contexts, and are taught to accept decisions of parents, teachers, and brothers (Sharan & Bhatt, 1992; Menon-Sen & Kumar, 2001). Marriage for most Indian women is not a matter of choice, nor do they choose how many children to have. More than 60 percent of rural Indian women are married before the age of 18, the legal age. Less than half of Indian couples of reproductive age use contraception. Of this, sterilization accounts for more than 75 percent of total contraception; and, not surprisingly, 95 percent of them are female sterilizations (Menon-Sen & Kumar, 2001).

Gender inequality is not the only inequality that exists in India. Women are oppressed and unequal, but so are *dalits* and *adivasis*, the poor, the landless, the disabled, and the marginalized. In India's context, the feminist slogan—"all issues are women's issues and women's issues are everyone's issues"—rings true.

Dialogue can also lead to emancipatory knowledge that frees groups from the hegemonic values embedded in language (Healey, 1992; Innes, 1995). For example, the term "homemaker" is often operationalized in a way that isolates women as the exclusive performers of domestic activities in the home. When women participate in perpetuating this meaning of the term they sustain their own oppression. Through dialogue among women, however, this term can be reconstructed and an alternative meaning may be promoted. Specifically, women may assign new meanings to the term homemaker: One who coordinates the equal contribution of all family members in the performance of domestic work.

For Young (1994), empowerment is a process in which relatively powerless persons engage in dialogue with each other and thereby come to understand the social sources of their powerlessness. They see the possibility of acting collectively to change their social environment. In this process, each participant is personally and collectively empowered. Senge (1990) argues that learning starts with dialogue—"the capacity of members of a team to suspend assumptions and enter into a genuine 'thinking together'" (p. 10). Through dialogue a group may "discover insights not attainable individually…. [It] also involves learning how to recognize the patterns of interaction in teams that undermine learning" (Senge, 1990, p. 10). Thus, through dialogue people may learn to confront communication practices that are oppressive and block the path to empowerment.

Feminist Perspectives on Empowerment

By participating in cooperatives, women dairy farmers in India can discover pathways to empowerment. The information that women receive and the discussions that are held during the NDDB's training programs can spark additional ideas and prompt behaviors that increase women's self-efficacy at home and in other social relationships. These changes among women are consistent in many ways with a range of different feminist perspectives (e.g., liberal, Marxist, cultural-dualist, etc.; Buzzanell, 1994; Natalle, Papa, & Graham, 1994). The starting point for most feminist thought is recognizing that patriarchy exists and that men's domination over women must end for women to experience meaningful empowerment (Buzzanell, 1994; Calas & Smircich, 1992). The paths to may empowerment differ, depending on the feminist stance taken (Buzzanell, 1994; Donovan, 1985; Jaggar, 1983; Langston, 1988).

Feminist scholarship includes rich and complex theoretical perspectives that address the intersections of multiple oppressions (such as race, class, gender, and sexuality) in the lives of women (Boyd, 1999).[6] Standpoint feminism (Harstock, 1983; Winant, 1987) directly addresses these concerns by arguing that women, like men, have a variety of experiences and thus have different "standpoints," from which to view the world. Standpoint feminism considers the perspectives of a variety of excluded, marginalized, or oppressed groups, believing that much can be learned about possibilities of societal reform from their multiple viewpoints (Bullis & Bach, 1996; Cheney et al., 1998).

■ Cooperative Enactment, Integrative Thinking, and Connectedness

Three primary themes characterize feminist organizing processes: cooperative enactment, integrative thinking, and connectedness (Buzzanell, 1994). *Cooperative enactment* emphasizes the importance of working together to reach individual and collective goals rather than competing against one another. *Integrative thinking* centers on the importance of considering context in evaluating choices and actions. For example, while a given action (e.g., small business development) can bring about a specific intended effect (e.g., increased income), feminists think in an integrated way by considering how specific actions can produce direct and indirect effects. For example, a woman may consider how a new form of behavior (e.g., assertiveness) will affect her relationship with her husband, in-laws, children, neighbors, and community members. *Connectedness* refers to attempts to integrate the mind, body, and emotions in making sense of the world around us (Buzzanell, 1994). Humans are holistic beings not limited to displays of rationality; rather, there is an emotional side to all of us. Women can thrive in environments where they have opportunities to connect with and nurture others on the path to collective success. This perspective on connectedness is also consistent with the feminist ethic of care. Women display caring through sensitivity to others, self-sacrifice, and peacemaking (Gilligan, 1982). Such behaviors show how caring comes from interpersonal connection (Young, 1994).

Box 3.3: Cabot Creamery in Vermont
Cooperative Enactment beyond Dairying

Each year, authors Wendy and Michael Papa, both avid skiers, travel to the ski slopes of Vermont. Here they regularly meet with other avid skiers, some of whom come from Cabot Creamery, a dairy cooperative comprising a membership of 1,350 farm families in New England and upstate New York. In their conversations, the Papas have realized that Cabot Creamery embodies the principle of cooperative enactment beyond the dairy enterprise. Farmer members look at the cooperative both as a way of doing business and as a way of service to other community members.

As a cooperative, Cabot Creamery farmers emulate the Rochdale cooperative principles: They value local ownership, participatory decision-making and democratic governance. Further, Cabot's cooperative farmers have internalized a belief that a dairy farm family produces more than fresh milk; they produce generations of good people who know one another and help each other in times of need. This means Cabot's members serve on school and county boards, as volunteer firefighters, and as Green-Up Day participants (a day set aside by the community to clean up the environment). Farmer members are committed to revitalizing their town economies and protecting the environment. Accordingly, their dairying practices preserve, respect, and rejuvenate local land and water resources.

Stephen Fleury, a Cabot Cooperative farmer from Berkshire, Vermont, summarized the community's cooperative spirit by noting: "A Vermont farmer is a neighbor who gives more than he receives. Like pulling a car out of a ditch with his tractor. And he doesn't ask for help in return" (cited in http://www.cabotcreamery.com).

■ Hegemony, Domination, and Resistance

Many internal and external impediments can potentially limit women's empowerment. To voice one's aspirations is not so much the removal of an external impediment as it is the beginning of internal empowerment (Held, 1993). Here, Gramsci's (1971) views on hegemony are particularly informative. Gramsci views hegemony as a process of struggle that embodies, simultaneously, processes of domination and resistance. For example, the practice of *purdah* [veiling] in many parts of the world demonstrates how women struggle with enabling and constraining forces in attempts to empower themselves. While the system of *purdah* often reflects a patriarchal code that keeps women within the domestic domain, it also bestows respect and honor in some contexts. Thus, *purdah* can empower women by helping them form a sense of community through the unifying principle of honor, while oppressing them by confining them to their home (Boyd, 1999; Mohanty, 1997).

A more subtle and oblique form of women's oppression is vested in unreciprocated emotional labor.[7] Women can pressure one another to provide emotional care for their family members yet not protest when it is not reciprocated (Bartky, 1991). However, consistent with Gramsci's perspective, women may derive an intense feeling of satisfaction by caring for others. Thus, the key to understanding the dialectic of women's oppression and empowerment requires a careful assessment of the meanings women give to their actions, including the contexts within which these meanings are situated.

Data Collection through Interviews

We interviewed dairy farmers in six villages of the Kolhapur District Milk Union and six villages of the Jaipur District Milk Union who had participated in the NDDB's CD, WDP, or WDCLP training programs for empowering women dairy farmers. In-depth interviews were conducted with 286 women dairy farmers, 142 from Kolhapur, and 144 from Jaipur. Furthermore, a total of 78 women dairy farmers participated in 11 focus group interviews (five groups in Kolhapur and six groups in Jaipur). The size of focus groups ranged from five to nine participants. In addition, 24 in-depth interviews were conducted with male dairy farmers, 12 from Jaipur and 12 from Kolhapur.

In examining the interview transcripts we engaged in both grounded theory and theory-guided analysis. We examined the statements, responses, and narratives of our interviewees for the purpose of developing a unique grounded theory of the oppression-empowerment dialectic. At the same time our insights were guided by feminist perspectives on empowerment that draw our attention to such concepts as cooperative enactment, integrative thinking, connectedness, and an ethic of care.

The Oppression and Empowerment of Women Dairy Farmers in India

In this section, we focus on how the experiences, stories, accounts, and explanations of women dairy farmers in India speak to empowerment processes through communication, women's unity and organizing, and democratic governance practices. And, in so doing, we explicate how women dairy farmers negotiate the dialectic tension between oppression and empowerment.

■ Women Dairy Farmers' Empowerment as a Communication Process

Empowerment was displayed through different types of communication and in different relational contexts: (*a*) improvements in personal and family health care via health care contact, (*b*) changes in family decision-making and task allocation prompted by information received in the CD program, and (*c*) altered communicative dynamics stemming from economic empowerment.

Communication and Health In many individual interviews with women dairy farmers, specific examples were given concerning improved health care. These women described the information they received from CD trainers about health care and offered evidence of how their empowerment was displayed interactively in their increased interaction with physicians. For example, Anjali Patil from Devthane village explained: "I am more careful now about personal hygiene. I do not use stale food and I use more green vegetables. Children are now given enough milk. I keep my surroundings clean. Earlier we tried homemade medical remedies. Now we consult the doctor." Ujwala Chowgule, a dairy farmer from Kavethe-Guland village, offered similar comments: "I now avoid traditional medicines. We know that nutrition is important and we keep our place clean to avoid infection. We now also listen to the doctor's advice."

Family Decision-Making and Task Allocation A number of women dairy farmers reported that participation in the NDDB's empowerment programs has motivated them to make more individual-level personal decisions. One representative comment was offered by Tulsabai Katale of Katalewadi village: "I get the profit and income by pouring milk to the DCS. I can spend that money as I wish. I got this new decision-making power in me by undergoing the training program." Parvati Patil, a dairy farmer from the same village said: "I decided to increase milk production. To achieve this goal, I decided to take my animal for artificial insemination. Simultaneously, I decided to improve the quality of the milk. Also, I decided to begin saving regularly." These examples of personal decision-making are remarkable as, in India's rural villages, men expect obedience from women and make all-important family decisions.

Increasing involvement in family decision-making is another pathway to empowerment. Many women interviewees reported a change from little or no involvement in family decision-making to joint decision-making with their spouse. Anjali Patil from Devthane village explained: "Earlier my husband did not discuss things with me. Now my husband consults with me so I discuss with him. It is always a joint decision. For example, with family planning we decided together that only two children can best be reared and brought up properly."

Several men also indicated that participation in the NDDB's empowerment programs prompted a change in how family decisions were made. Vasant Patil from Devthane village said: "We now discuss more in the family about doing something. Decisions should only be taken after discussion and after knowing each other's opinion." Similarly, Prakash Bhendawade from Kavethe-Guland village stated: "Earlier I used to make all the decisions. Now my wife and I both discuss the matter and take the decision jointly."

Given the heavy workload most rural women bear in India, an increase in family members' participation in performing dairying activities and household tasks is an important dimension of empowerment. Some women dairy farmers indicated that they received more assistance from their children and their husband in performing dairying activities and household work. Ranjana Patil explained: "I am getting more help from other family members in my household work." Bebitai Mane revealed: "My husband and my children now help in household work. I've noticed that our family fights are reduced." Importantly, each of these women has created within her home a commitment to cooperative enactment by encouraging family members to work collectively toward common goals. These comments offer evidence of how empowerment is displayed through interaction.

Communicative Dynamics of Economic Empowerment   In their empowerment training programs, NDDB's trainers provide information to women dairy farmers that could help them increase their milk yields. Women participants in these training programs collaborate with one another to accomplish personal and collective goals (e.g., increased dairy income). Most women dairy farmers reported an increase in dairying income linked to their participation in the CD program and through their membership in the local DCS. Vasanti Shevre, a women dairy farmer from Devthane village noted: "I improved the quality and the quantity of my milk production because of the training program information and the dairying techniques that cooperative members shared with me. All these things ultimately resulted in increasing my dairying income." Vimla Patil, a woman dairy farmer from Kavethe-Guland village reported: "I have improved the quality of my milk, therefore, my income has increased. Now there is regularity in my life because I am able to save money. My standard of living has improved."

While participation in NDDB's training program offers women dairy farmers information pertinent to dairying during a limited time frame (a few days), membership in a dairy cooperative society offers opportunities for continued learning. As Mumtaz from Kirve village noted: "My economic status improved after I joined the DCS. I took a decision to buy more buffaloes and take extra care of hygiene and cleanliness of buffaloes. I learned about saving money from member meetings, including how to deposit and withdraw money from a bank."

A trainer in Jaipur, Dr. Satsangi, recalled a story that showed how women can learn interactively from one another. After participating in NDDB's training program, two women dairy farmers started using cattle feed provided by the district milk union to improve milk yields. When one woman dairy farmer's cow did not readily accept the new feed, she voiced her concerns to her friend. Her friend responded: "I had similar problems too. Then I started mixing a little of the new cattle feed with her regular green fodder. I slowly added a little more of the new feed each day until she was eating the entire recommended amount."

Women's empowerment requires an economic alternative for survival other than marriage (Lerner, 1993). NDDB's training program has helped many women dairy farmers to increase their incomes through increasing milk yields and milk quality. By increasing their income, women have reduced their dependence on men. Teeja Devi, of Ramsinghpura, observed: "Earlier we were dependent on men but now we can do a lot of work ourselves. Women can do a lot if they have money in their hands." Sumitra Devi, also of Ramsinghpura, concurred: "Earlier women were dependent on men, but now they have become independent as they have started earning money. The women who are unemployed are still dependent on men." Sona, of Mamtori-Kalan, also recognized the link between money and control: "Earlier men had complete control, but now the women have money in their hands and men's control has decreased. We can spend money on the education of our children and on medicine." Tara, a dairy farmer from Sardarpura noted: "Now women go out of the house and do work so the control of men has been decreased. The milk payment is in the women's hands, they don't have to ask for it so the economic control has been reduced."

■ Women Dairy Farmers' Unity and Organizing Activities

In this section we describe women dairy farmer's unity and organizing activities by focusing on: (*a*) women connecting with one another, (*b*) women helping one another, (*c*) forming women's clubs, and (*d*) engaging in collective action.

Women Connecting with One Another   Many women dairy farmers recognized the importance of women's unity and organizing as necessary for meaningful empowerment to occur. Empowerment was linked to contact with other women in public places and the opportunity to share personal stories. Nisha, from the village of Tisangi, explained, "All women in our village came together and started the women's club. I now can express my feelings." Mangal, another dairy farmer from Tisangi, noted: "I developed the courage to speak in the women's club meetings. I did not previously dare to speak in front of men. But now I can speak to them." Sarju Devi, from the village of Mamtori-Kalan, remarked, "Earlier we were not able to meet other women. We now meet other ladies at the milk collection

Plate 3.6
None of these women dairy farmers in Rajasthan have undergone the women's empowerment program of the National Dairy Development Board
Source: Personal Files of the Authors.

center and discuss various issues." Banarasi Devi, from the village of Sitarampura, observed: "The DCS is the contact place for village women. When we meet at the DCS we develop a sense of togetherness." Thus, for many women, the starting point for the interactive dimension of empowerment is coming into contact with other women. The local DCSs, women's clubs, and thrift groups provide places of contact where women can initiate organizing processes for their subsequent empowerment (Plates 3.6 and 3.7).

Consistent with the feminist organizing theme of connectedness (Buzzanell, 1994), when women come into contact with one another they display emotions. Dr. Satsangi, a trainer from Jaipur, noted how central emotions are to women's social experiences:

> In my first women's training program, the women instructors met with the women dairy farmers and started the program by focusing first on social and family matters. All of the women exited weeping. I learned that the instructors encouraged the women to talk about their personal problems and they talked about husbands who drank, sick children, and abusive in-laws.

Plate 3.7
Only one of these women dairy farmers in Rajasthan has undergone the women's empowerment program of the National Dairy Development Board
Women dairy farmers who participate in NDDB's programs experience empowerment in multiple intersecting ways. Some women feel "bolder" in peer group situations; some feel more comfortable in sharing their feelings with others, and some others experience empowerment through collective action.
Source: Personal Files of the Authors.

Sampada, another NDDB trainer from Kolhapur, gave us a similar perspective: "Women are very frank when they speak with us in their houses; this is an intimate discussion. They discuss family problems. They find in us a good caring friend."

NDDB's trainers recognize the importance of attending to the emotions of women dairy farmers consistent with feminist beliefs that "the personal is political" (Cheney, Straub, Speirs-Glebe, Stohl, DeGooyer, Whalen, Garvin-Doxas, & Carlone, 1998). Feminist values, applied to the workplace, tend to emphasize working relationships characterized by mutual support, empowering behaviors, caring, cooperation, and fair treatment (Martin, 1990). In addition, Maguire and Mohtar (1994) argue that by recognizing both the private and public lives of workers, an employer can begin to value employees' entire reality.

Women Helping One Another   There were many instances of women dairy farmers helping one another in our interview data. The formation of helping relationships is consistent both with the feminine ethic of care (Abel & Nelson, 1990; Friedman, 1987; Young, 1994) and the feminist theme of cooperative enactment (Buzzanell, 1994; Norsigian & Pincus, 1984). For example, Bimale Devi, from Sitarampura, described the impact of joining the DCS on her life: "I have developed a cooperative feeling toward other women. I often meet other women and offer to help them whenever I can." Shakuntala Devi, from Mamtori-Kalan, noted: "We organizers of the women's club tell other women that now the world is changing and therefore we should remove our veil and speak about our problems." Kanchan Bhonsle, from Adur, noted: "A woman wanted to leave the women's club meeting early because her husband was to come home. Then I talked to her husband and got him to agree to allow her to spend time in the women's meeting. Now the women can help each other out."

When women help one another, they display agency (Bartky, 1988; Deveaux, 1994). Accomplishing goals in mutually helpful relationships leads women to recognize that their perspectives are not based on subjugated or disruptive knowledge. Rather, they realize that through using their own knowledge and abilities, they can alter their oppressive state (Gutierrez, 1990; Parsons, 1991).

Women also helped one another outside the realm of dairying, displaying how democratic principles not only serve the need of economic production, but also distinctively social or people-oriented ends. As Bachrach and Botwinick (1992) argued: Participatory experience generates a desire for more participation. Democracy in the workplace instigates increasing struggles by feminist organizations for equality in all areas of life, including the home.

Forming Women's Clubs   Clear examples of empowerment through communication were also apparent in our interviewees' comments concerning the formation of village-level women's clubs, especially in the face of men's resistance. Hausabai Patil from Devthane village stated: "Men cannot do anything if women come together. Women should show courage and unite. Under any circumstances we will form a women's club." Shalabai Katale, from Katalewadi village, noted: "If we cooperate with each other then it benefits everybody.

I can't do certain things alone, but I can achieve what I need if we work together."

Most of the women recognized the need to work with, or work on, men to realize their empowerment goals. Anjali Patil, from Devthane, stated: "I will call a meeting of all important male leaders in the village. In the presence of women, I will convince the village leaders about the importance of having a women's club in the village." Navsabai Ambi, from Kavethe-Guland, explained: "I will question why the men oppose the women's club. I will explain to them that if women unite it will be beneficial for the village. So, why should men oppose? With their cooperation, we will establish the women's club."

When women give voice to their needs, it represents not so much the removal of an external impediment; it signifies the beginning of an internal empowerment (Held, 1993). Even if women dairy farmers are not immediately successful in forming women's clubs, they recognize that "their dramatic vocal protests register their anger and convey the message that specific injustices will not be tolerated" (Houppert, 1992, p. 74). Such blatant critiques of patriarchy, hierarchy, and controlling practices represent the "graffiti" of organizational crawlspaces—sites of both resistance and pleasure (Bell & Forbes, 1994).

The formation of women's clubs is especially important because these clubs provide space for rural Indian women to engage in "consciousness-raising talk." Such talk allows women to "hear each other into speech" (Hayden, 1997). By speaking unspoken facts and feelings, new webs of meaning may be generated (Frye, 1993). Furthermore, through consciousness-raising talk a woman may identify ways to resist discourses and practices that subordinate her to men (Heckman, 1990), institutions, or social forces (Ferguson, 1984; Oakley, 1991; Oliver, 1991; Sawicki, 1991).

Collective Action   Many instances of empowerment through collective action were enunciated by women dairy farmers. For example, in the village of Adur, women dairy farmers decided to get together to jointly produce snacks as a way of generating additional income. Later they started making chalk sticks for schools. Then they pooled their resources and purchased milch animals. Through collective action, these women of Adur provide us with a clear illustration of the feminist organizing perspective of cooperative enactment (Buzzanell, 1994; Parsons, 1991).

Sampada, a NDDB trainer from the Kolhapur Milk Union, provided us with an example of a collective action undertaken by women that is consistent with the feminist organizing principle of integrative thinking (Buzzanell, 1994). Women dairy farmers of Malwadi village were concerned with both unsanitary drainage in their community and poor quality roads. Sampada noted: "The chairperson of the village DCS decided to construct a drainage system in front of her house. Everybody followed her example and very soon the entire village had a drainage system. Then, the dairy society rewarded them for their efforts by donating money for the re-pavement of village roads."

Collective actions taken by women dairy farmers provide us with evidence of how social capital produces empowerment. Social capital emerges from interpersonal relationships in the form of trust, cooperation, and consensus building (Fukuyama, 1995; Putnam, 1993; Wilson, 1996). Social capital may refer to the features of their social organization (trust, norms, and networks) that may improve the efficiency of the cooperatives by facilitating coordinated action (Putnam, 1993). For the poor, nonmaterial resources (e.g., communication) can produce social energy that can be transformed into cultural, political, or material wealth (Hirschman, 1984).[8]

■ Women Dairy Farmers' Empowerment in Democratic Processes

In this section we show how empowerment is embedded in democratic practices by examining how women dairy farmers (*a*) make decisions in groups and families, and (*b*) engage in hegemonic struggles.

Making Decisions in Groups and Families   A number of women dairy farmers we interviewed provided insights into how empowerment can be embedded in democratic processes. Involvement in the cooperative taught them how to make decisions in groups. Ranjana Patil, from Devthane village, explained: "I learned how to take bold decisions after carefully thinking over matters. I also understand how to listen to others and express my opinion. Thus, I understand the process of making a joint decision." Ujwala Chowgule, from Kavethe-Guland village, provided a more extended description of how participation in NDDB's empowerment training program taught her democratic principles: "We were told in the training program how to participate in a group; how we should be bold and speak out; how everybody's ideas should be heard; and then how the group should decide. There will be differences of opinion but we have to make compromises if necessary."

Democratic decision-making in dairy cooperatives influenced some farmer members to see the need for democratic decision-making in the family. Pandurang More, a male dairy farmer from Devthane, who is the chairman of his local DCS, stated: "In the dairy cooperative society, the management committee makes the decision, not one person. In the family also, the men and women must jointly make decisions in important matters."

The preceding comments provide evidence of how empowerment is embedded in democratic processes (Cheney, 1995; Eisenberg, 1994; Harrison, 1994). Participation in NDDB's empowerment programs has given women dairy farmers the confidence to become active in group decision-making. Voices that were once suppressed can now be heard. Women have accomplished things collectively in democratically run fora that they could never have accomplished acting individually. Furthermore, lessons learned from democratic participation in cooperatives can extend to other spheres. As Bricker-Jenkins (1992) noted: "By participating in the creation of relationships that are open, egalitarian, mutual, and reciprocal, people can begin to formulate a vision of these [relationships] becoming the norm in their families, workplaces, and communities" (p. 298).

Hegemony, Power, and Resistance   As explained earlier, Gramsci's (1971) notion of hegemony embodies simultaneously the dynamics of power and resistance. We encountered a specific example of the process of hegemonic struggle among a group of women dairy farmers in Lutsaan village in India's Uttar Pradesh State. Although this cooperative (on paper) was an all-women's dairy cooperative, it was administered by two men in violation of cooperative by-laws. Women dairy farmers in Lutsaan were participating in their own oppression by allowing the village men to control their rights to administer their cooperative. Conversely, these same women, through their own democratic decision-making, joined hands and established a business to make *ghee* (clarified butter) from surplus milk. They sold this ghee locally and in the neighboring township through private vendors. This example suggests that hegemonic relations involve both processes of domination and resistance—that is, processes that are oppressive and empowering simultaneously.

■ Dialectic of Oppression and Empowerment among Women Dairy Farmers

In this section the dialectic of oppression and empowerment is revealed through focusing on: (a) the simultaneous experience of empowerment and oppression, (b) paradox and contradiction in social change, (c) the compatibility paradox, (d) internalizing a belief in incompetence, and (e) the paradox of design.

The Simultaneous Experience of Empowerment and Oppression

Despite strong evidence of empowerment embedded in communicative processes, we also encountered numerous examples of oppression. Three women from Mamtori-Kalan were members of a successful dairy cooperative. Their empowerment was a product of attending instructional sessions linked to productive dairying practices, taking control of milk production and sales by membership in the DCS, and participating in the governance of their society. Despite the empowerment they experienced, they described reasons for their oppression. Suji Devi explained, "I cannot face my family elders and seek permission for attending the women's club meeting. If they feel it is necessary then they will send me to the program." Kamala Devi speaks of more generalized problems in Mamtori-Kalan: "In our village women are not united, and that is one reason why they are so backward. Women do not cooperate with each other in our village. If women are united, men cannot oppose our ideas." Finally, Prem Devi laments, "Men decide about major important things. Whatever they decide we will agree." Clearly, for these women, dairy cooperative membership has not produced empowering experiences in their family lives. Thus, empowerment may be localized in a single context of a person's experience. Other contexts may offer only oppression. For Suji, Kamala, and Prem Devi empowerment and oppression exist in a dialectic tension that they live out every day.

One interesting facet of our interview data was that some women described how they had experienced some form of empowerment in their lives, but later in the interview they offered a clear statement of oppression. For example, Nisha Deshpande, from Tisangi, spoke with pride of the savings group she helped organize: "We operate a small savings scheme. We have decided that every member, turn by turn, should collect the contribution, and then deposit the total amount in the bank. We want every member to know the system and also banking activity."

Despite her role in organizing the savings scheme, Nisha admitted that women can do little if men oppose them: "If my husband dominated over me, I would nurse a feeling of restlessness. How can a woman act against a man's wishes? It will be insulting to him. In our village a man has to be given due respect. How can she go anywhere without the permission of her husband?"

Raj Kanwar, from Ramsinghpura, offered us numerous examples of her empowerment. For example, she reported: "I am saving money in the milk business. I am able to use these savings for buying items of my own choice. If we women come together, then we need not be dependent on the men." Later in the interview, however, she indicated how village men still control her life: "I will not oppose the men in the village. I will do what men want me to do." Likewise, Sarju Devi from Vinobapuri, offered evidence of empowerment followed by oppression: "I was helpless earlier. Now I make decisions myself. My life has changed after I joined the DCS." Later in the interview, however, she explained how little control she has in her own home: "I must take permission of the family elders to attend the women's club meeting. If they permit, then I will go and attend the meeting." Similarly, Karva Devi, from Vinobapuri, reported: "After my participation in the training program, I feel I can make my own decisions." Several minutes later, however, she noted: "I will talk to my husband about the women's club meeting and then if he permits I will attend the meeting."

The experience reported by each woman speaks to the dialectic process of shifting between the competing poles of oppression and empowerment. Before joining her respective DCS, each woman's life was dominated by oppression. When a person's life is so controlled by others, the first experiences with empowerment may be overwhelming and perhaps even confusing. For these women, it seems difficult to transfer empowering actions from one context to another. So they internalize both empowerment and oppression as a natural part of their daily experience.

Importantly, these competing poles of communicative action are experienced in dynamic tension. As a woman dairy farmer experiences empowerment through participation in cooperative governance, she reflects on the oppression embedded in powerful patriarchal structures and social-cultural practices that restrict her movement and opportunities. Simultaneously, while a woman dairy farmer may be responding to her oppressive in-laws or a domineering husband, she may reflect on the empowerment opportunities that are available to her through the DCS. So experiencing one force of the dialectic propels the woman dairy farmer to consider the opposite force.

Paradox and Contradiction in Social Change How do we explain the contradictory or paradoxical explanations offered by some of our interviewees? A plausible explanation is that paradox and contradiction are part of the process of social change. Since established patterns of thought or behavior are difficult to change, people often engage in contradictory or paradoxical activities as part of an adjustment process until new behavioral patterns are fully internalized. For example, a person may consider a behavior change and even verbally express a commitment to it; however, further pondering may drive that person back to his or her original behavior choice (Ruesch & Bateson, 1951). An oppressed life is neither comfortable nor easy to change. One may also view these paradoxes as evidence of how women are simultaneously victims and agents in systems of domination (Trethewey, 1997). As McLeod (1992) observed, "often women simultaneously attempt to alter their circumstances and to maintain them, to protest and accommodate" (p. 535).

The Compatibility Paradox The compatibility paradox gives us another way to frame these seemingly contradictory statements from women dairy farmers (see Stohl & Cheney, 2001). NDDB's women's empowerment programs encourage women dairy farmers to participate in ways that are seemingly incompatible with their normative and everyday communication behaviors. As Stohl and Cheney (2001) explain, "when participation programs are implemented in national cultures where the central values contrast greatly with the fundamental premises of participation, workers are put in the paradoxical position of being required to act in ways that are incompatible with their 'natural inclinations' (i.e., the normative view of their culture)." This does not mean that women abandon communication activities that are empowering. Rather, they may isolate such actions to contexts that are safe, such as the domain of the DCS.

In NDDB's women empowerment programs, women dairy farmers are encouraged to co-opt family members in performing household tasks. Although some of our interviewees clearly sought and received help from family members, others reported seeking help only from other women. When women exclude men from partaking in household tasks, and request other women to help, do they not perpetuate their own oppression?

Consider the following comments from women dairy farmers who explain what they will do to attend a women's club meeting when they have unfinished household work. Nana Devi, from Oloki-Dhani, said: "I will ask my daughter-in-law to take care of my work and then I will attend the women's club meeting." Suraj Kanwar, of Ramsinghpura, stated: "I will get up early to get my work done and also take help from my mother-in-law and sister-in-law." Although these women may have lightened their own workload, they did so at the expense of another woman. Communicating with others to co-ordinate household work is an action requiring foresight, persuasive communication, and assertiveness. However, these women limit their empowering actions to a safer context—their relationships with other women. Their full empowerment, however, will only occur when they may be able to directly involve men in performing household work. Until that time women will experience both forces of the dialectic in dynamic tension.

Ultimately, women who rely only on other women for accomplishing tasks have internalized a feminine ideal that is oppressive. This feminine ideal views household work as central to the definition of what it means to be a caring, nurturing woman. A woman who does not perform these tasks may feel that she does not adequately love her family. These debilitating ideals represent a more subtle form of oppression that is rooted in deeply interiorized effects of women upon themselves (Bartky, 1991). Women pressure one another to care for their family members, yet they fail to receive care in return by male household members.

Some of our interviewees, in a display of discursive consciousness, recognized the barriers that women create for one another. For example, Phuli Devi, from Oloki-Dhani, explained: "Women are their own enemies in restricting one another's progress." Rameshwari Devi, of Sardarpura, also supports this perspective: "Women are jealous of one another and this restricts our progress." Finally, Prachati Devi, of Sitarampura, stated: "Women pressure one another to follow the old customs." So, a critical part of the empowerment process for women is to cease restricting one another's choices.

When women act in ways that are personally empowering, yet also act to restrict the choices of other women, they reveal the dialectic of oppression and empowerment. In India, as in most countries, women face oppression and domination that is systemic. Social structures and institutions controlled primarily by men limit what is possible for women to do in most contexts. This experience is so embedded in a woman's daily life that women might act on a personal level that is empowering, yet deny empowerment to another woman. Women's empowerment requires both personal action *and* systemic engagement. Women must help one another to expand each other's choices; not limit them by reinforcing cultural practices that are oppressive. Until that time, many women will be torn between the competing poles of oppression and empowerment.

Internalizing a Belief of Incompetence One way to display empowerment is to engage in a goal-driven personal action. An oppressed person internalizes a belief of incompetence so he or she may seek out the assistance of others whom they believe to be more competent to act. In a number of our interviews, women sought the help of "sponsors" to promote a particular cause rather than engage in personal action themselves. Suraj Kanwar, of Ramsinghpura, for example, explained how she would go about trying to form a women's club in her village: "We will first convince ten men in the village about our women's club.... Then we will approach the village chief through these men." In a similar vein, Gauri Devi, of Vinobapuri, stated: "We will consult a few men in the village and through them influence the village chief. Then he will not go against our proposal." Some women talked of bringing outside experts to help out. Panna Devi, of Vinobapuri, remarked: "I will try to explain to the village women about having a women's club. I will then request experts from outside the village for help. They will convince the village men." Finally, Ganga Devi, of Vinobapuri, describes a slightly different approach to sponsorship: "We women will convince our husbands to explain to the village chief about having a women's club. If he approves then only will we establish a women's club."

Although each aforementioned woman has internalized a belief of incompetence (thereby sustaining her oppression), each has also acted politically in ways that are reflective of empowerment. Women seeking the assistance of sponsors to form a women's club are taking a direct action to bring about a positive change in their community. They also display political savvy in recognizing that their direct personal actions might yield little given the power dynamics in their community. So, they seek the assistance of those who can influence the village power brokers.

Paradox of Design   Oppression also occurs through a paradox of design (Stohl & Cheney, 2001). This paradox occurs when the "architecture" for participation is formed largely in a top-down manner, as is the case when NDDB trainers enter a village for the purpose of launching an all-women's dairy cooperative. The trainers educate women dairy farmers to use technical inputs such as cattle feed, artificial insemination, and animal vaccinations. They also conduct training in dairy management and cooperative governance. Once the NDDB instructors complete their training programs, the everyday running of the cooperative is left to the women dairy farmers. These top-down education and training experiences, while useful, do not directly lead to women carving out democratic spaces of control in their lives. However, over time, the democratic practices of governance that the women dairy farmers learn in the cooperatives carry over into the running of the women's clubs, thrift groups, and other collaborative women's activities. So, the participatory climate engendered in the running of the DCSs allows women to creatively transcend the design paradox. Although others may directly control their initial actions, with the passage of time women establish their own collaborative rules of engagement.

Box 3.4: The Mondragon Cooperative Corporation[9]

The largest employer in the Basque region of Spain is a network of charity-minded, employee-owned cooperatives. The Mondragon Cooperative Corporation (MCC) began when a group of young engineers decided to collaborate in building oil stoves and heaters in the 1950s. There was no looking back. In 2005, MCC employs 66,000 people working in 160 companies in 37 countries—some as far away as Latin America and China. With assets exceeding $17 billion, MCC is involved in many diverse businesses such as a refrigerator manufacturer, a prosperous bank, a supermarket chain, a producer of auto parts, and numerous tool and die makers in Spain.

The main offices of MCC are in Mondragon, a modern town of 24,000 inhabitants located in the center of Basque country, a region that is home to 2.5 million people. More than 1,500 people work in the corporate headquarters. MCC has been described by *Forbes* magazine as one of the 10 best European companies to work for. Employee benefits are significant: housing, subsidized health care, and primary and secondary education for employees' children.

Employees within the 160 companies of MCC internalize an egalitarian spirit that sustains their commitment to the organization. There are no bosses or supervisors in each cooperative. Every worker-owner owns an equal share of the cooperative and decisions are made through systems of both direct and representative democracy at collective assemblies. Ten percent of each year's profits go to charity, 40 percent are reinvested in the company, and 50 percent serve as collateral for workers to seek loans from the corporation's savings bank, the Caja Laboral Popular. MCC also owns an insurance company, a supermarket chain, and a travel agency. The most recent addition is Mondragon University which enrolls 4,000 students pursuing degrees in sciences and humanities.

MCC's charitable work is as diverse as the corporation's businesses. Money has been invested in the promotion of the Basque language (*Euskera*) and in spurring numerous local cultural activities across little towns and cities throughout Spain. MCC's philanthropy has promoted sporting and health care activities, provided help for the handicapped, and care for drug addicts and the elderly.

Miren Etxebarria, a 20-year-old engineering student, expressed her views toward the prospect of working for the MCC. "The salaries might be a bit lower than in some other firms, but to work in a co-op is to get a job for life," she says (cited in http://www.torontothebetter.net/2tgbd-APsp-coop.htm).

Conclusions

In this chapter, our analysis of NDDB's efforts in organizing women dairy farmers yielded three key insights about the process of empowerment. First, women's empowerment is displayed through different forms of communication and feminist action, particularly when women unite and organize to accomplish social change within families and communities. Second, empowerment is embedded in democratic practices: Women participate in discussion fora that yield decisions that improve the quality of life for community members. Third, paradox and contradiction are part of both the empowerment process and the process of organizing for social change as women continually negotiate the dialectic tension that exists between oppression and empowerment.

In this chapter, we recognized the centrality of communicative interaction to the empowerment process. In describing the interactive dimension of women's empowerment, our attention was drawn to three themes of feminist organizing: cooperative enactment, integrative thinking, and connectedness. Specifically, women's empowerment is linked to sharing emotions (connectedness), evaluating personal actions for relational and environmental impact (integrative thinking), and helping one another through collective action (cooperative enactment).

While we gained insights on how democratic practices can be empowering, there are oppressive aspects of democratic practice that were not identified by our respondents. Democratic practices can suppress minority opinions in ways that are oppressive, particularly if a person always finds herself on the minority side of an issue. A consensus paradox can also be created when people feel social pressure to adopt the perspective of the majority (Stohl & Cheney, 2001).

Our research on NDDB's efforts at organizing women dairy farmers flagged the dialectic tensions between communicative oppression and empowerment (Table 3.1). To more completely understand how empowerment is produced through communication, we need to also attend to how communication oppresses. Women may engage in empowering cooperation if they help one another complete household tasks. Yet, if men remain excluded from performing these tasks, ultimately women are oppressed through their particular

Table 3.1
Dimensions of oppression and empowerment

Dimensions of Oppression	Dimensions of Empowerment
Competition with Others	Cooperative Enactment
Disconnected Analytic Thinking	Integrative Thinking
Separation from Others	Connectedness
Power Over Others	Sharing Power with Others
Unreciprocated Emotional Labor	Reciprocated Emotional Labor
Superior–Subordinate Work Relationships	Egalitarian Work Relationships
Passive Acceptance of Expert Information	Dialogue
Mutedness	Giving Voice to One's Needs
Internalizing Belief of Incompetence	Asserting Competence

approach to gaining cooperation. However, women need not remain trapped within the dynamic tension of oppression and empowerment. Consciousness-raising talk among women may focus on how actions may be simultaneously oppressive and empowering. When such talk propels action to realize empowerment more fully, the woman may temporarily experience empowerment without the pulls of its opposing force. That moment may occur when a woman and her husband cooperatively complete a domestic task.

Returning back to Sushila Devi's story at the beginning of the chapter, women must critically evaluate the stories they share with one another because of the potentially oppressive impact of certain narratives. For example, stories that establish heroic standards as necessary to bring about social change can demotivate women who doubt their ability to struggle in the face of resistance from powerful community members. We argue that more research is needed to critically examine how narratives impact women's perceptions in ways that are both empowering and oppressive.

Notes

1. The present chapter draws upon Papa, Singhal, Ghanekar, and Papa (2000); Papa and Singhal (1999); Singhal, Law, Kandath, and Ghanekar (1999); and Rogers and Singhal (2003). The research reported here in this chapter was in part supported by the Ford Foundation, New Delhi.

We thank our colleagues Drs. Everett M. Rogers, Corinne Shefner-Rogers, Nagesh Rao, Krishna Kandath, and Sweety Law, who partnered with us in this research in various capacities, and also several NBBD officials, who supported and collaborated with us on the present research in the 1990s: Dr. Verghese Kurien, Dr. Amrita Patel, Dr. S.N. Singh, Dr. N.V. Belavadi, Mr. Tom Carter, Mr. D.V. Ghanekar, Dr. Arun Wayangankar, and several others. We also wish to acknowledge various officials of the Jaipur and Kolhapur District Milk Unions, including various instructors of NDDB's Cooperative Development Program, who helped us conduct the present study.

2. Sushila's story also highlights the element of totality that characterizes dialectics (Rawlins, 1992). Totality draws attention to relational interdependence, that is, a person's actions in a social system impacts others within that system. Sushila's story was widely communicated in neighboring villages, perhaps causing several women to reflect on their own abilities to act while being pulled between the tensions of empowerment and oppression.

3. For some readers, at first glance, there may appear to be similarities between the control-emancipation (discussed in chapter 2) and empowerment-oppression dialectics (discussed in the present chapter). However, we argue that the two dialectics represent unique struggles. The control-emancipation dialectic focuses on control systems that are embedded in the intervention program of social change. Specifically, the Grameen Bank's loan disbursement and collection programs create and sustain the control systems in which workers and loan recipients find themselves. The empowerment-oppression dialectic, on the other hand, examines the oppression that surfaces from the more personal and localized actions of people living out their day-to-day lives. For example, women who have been conditioned to be subordinate to men internalize oppressive perceptions that limit their agency in other contexts. Family members, friends, and neighbors create and reproduce communicative actions that reify power differentials based on gender, caste, age, and socio-economic status. Our examination of the women's empowerment programs of the NDDB did not reveal a system of control that limited empowerment opportunities for women. Rather, we observed a dialectic of empowerment and oppression that was a product of intact social relations in communities. Women struggled for empowerment against forces they either created for themselves or community members sustained for them.

4. These numbers on dairy cooperatives, farmer members, and women's involvement were kindly provided to us by Dr. Arun Wayangankar, Deputy General Manager (Cooperative Services), NDDB, Anand. We thank him and the NDDB management for this information.

5. For additional information about the history, criticisms, and policies of the NDDB, see Alvares (1983); Doornbos, van Dorsten, Mitra, and Terhal (1990); George (1984, 1985); *The Indian Express* (1996); Kamath (1989); Kurien (1990); and Mascarenhas (1988).

6. Indian feminist movements have a rich and complex history (Kumar, 1993). For instance, some Indian feminists do not articulate a consciousness of patriarchal domination (Gandhi & Shah, 1992). This stance may be justified, because women in India struggle not only against men but against class, caste, and ethnic oppression as peasants, tribals, and untouchables. Other Indian feminists articulate a consciousness of patriarchal domination that is wrapped up in oppression perpetuated by modernity (Sangari & Vaid, 1989). For example, the increased availability of new sex-determination techniques such as amniocentesis has encouraged practices such as female feticide (Patel, 1989).

7. The term "emotional labor" was originally developed by Hochschild (1983) to refer to jobs in which workers are supposed to exhibit certain feelings in order to satisfy organizational role expectations (e.g., of a flight attendant, a health care provider, etc.). The term "unreciprocated emotional labor" refers to a specific situation in which one person in a relationship displays supportive emotions without a return display of supportive emotions by the other person. When a supportive emotional display does not elicit a reciprocal display one may assume that the non-responsive person does not care about the efforts of their partner.

8. Reflecting on this section, one may pose the following question: How important is entrepreneurship as a route to empowerment in such resource poor settings? It seems that women dairy farmers gained agency through entrepreneurship because they lacked the traditional corporate or societal mobility (including the human and social capital) that would make possible a different route to empowerment. Within the dairy cooperatives, women have access to resources and interpersonal support structures that are unavailable to them in their personal homebound contexts. As village women, many of these dairy farmers were denied agency by socio-cultural forces that have been operating for centuries. Only within the cooperative structure did possibilities for entrepreneurship surface as a way to gaining agency.

9. For more on the MCC, see http://www.mondragon.mcc.es.

4 Dialectic of dissemination and dialogue in rural India[1]

Without distance there is no dialogue between the two.
—Martin Buber, Jewish philosopher, theologian, story-teller, and teacher (quoted in http://en.wikiquote.org/wiki/Martin_Buber)

To understand the dialectic between dissemination and dialogue, consider the following three events from three different villages in India's Bihar State.

Inspired by the character of Neha, who establishes a school to educate *dalit* (lower caste) children in *Taru* (a radio soap opera broadcast by All India Radio), young male and female listeners of *Taru* in Abirpur village of Bihar established a school for *dalit* children. These young listeners, all members of *Taru* listening clubs in Abirpur, discussed over several weeks the bold actions of Neha in the radio soap opera. Based on these discussions, they decided that disadvantaged children in Abirpur needed a school. Over the next several months in late 2002, they implemented their plan, overcoming opposition from various community members.[2]

Upon listening to an episode of *Taru* in which a young girl's birthday is celebrated, a married couple in Madhopur village of Bihar discussed why they had never celebrated the birthday of their 7-year-old daughter. They realized that while a son's birthday is celebrated with fanfare in Bihar, a daughter's birthday passes without notice. They talked for weeks about why sons and daughters receive differential treatment in Bihar's rural society. Why, for instance, do boys receive better education, nutrition, and care than girls, and are more pampered by parents, grandparents, and community elders? Inspired by the birthday celebration that was role modeled in *Taru*, and energized by their animated discussions about gender inequality, the couple decided to celebrate their daughter's birthday. It was the first time in Madhopur's history that a girl's birthday was publicly celebrated—with balloons, music, sweets, and cakes. Once the logjam was broken, Madhopur and other neighboring villages saw a string of birthday celebrations for girls.

In July 2002, when author Singhal first met Vandana Kumari, a 17-year-old member of a *Taru* listening club in Kamtaul village of India's Bihar State, she noted: "We listen to each episode of *Taru*. We then discuss the episode's content in our listeners' club. After listening to *Taru*, we have taken decisions to wipe out the caste discrimination in our village and to teach *dalit* (lower caste) women and children." By August 2002, within the first five months of *Taru*'s broadcasts, Vandana's family undertook several social actions that were bold and which previously would have been unthinkable.[3] For instance, Vandana's father, Shailendra Singh, a rural health practitioner (RHP), goaded and supported by his family members, directly intervened to stop a child marriage in Kamtaul village. Vandana's mother, Sunita Singh, once again goaded and supported by family members, launched an adult literacy program for over 20 *dalit* village women (Plate 4.1).

However, the boldest action that the Singh family took during the summer of 2002 was to involve the *dalits* in Kamtaul village in the wedding celebrations of Vandana's elder sister. The *dalits* constitute the lowest rung in India's caste system. Working mainly as scavengers, cleaners, or garbage-handlers, or menial farm laborers, the *dalits* are socially ostracized from the mainstream community. Many in Kamtaul perceived the *dalits* as *achuts* (or "untouchables"; that is, they were so impure that you did not wish to be in their physical presence). Through their creative social actions, the Singh family helped integrate Kamtaul's *dalits* more fully into mainstream society—something that decades of emancipatory government-run affirmative action programs had failed to achieve.

How did listening to *Taru* inspire the Singh family to discuss, debate, and decide what actions to take to address caste discrimination in Kamtaul village? The Singh family told us that in *Taru*'s storyline, Shashikant, a member of the lower caste, is ill-treated in the opening episode in Neha's marriage ceremony. Several guests question his presence, taunting and humiliating him. Taru (the protagonist after whom the soap opera is named), a positive role model for promoting

Plate 4.1
Sunita Singh (right), the wife of rural health practitioner Shailendra Singh, facilitating an adult literacy class for lower-caste women in Kamtaul village

Inspired by the modeled behaviors of Neha, a character in *Taru* who starts a school for underprivileged children, Sunita Singh, goaded and supported by her family members, launched an adult literacy program for *dalit* (low-caste) women in Kamtaul village.

Source: Personal Files of the Authors.

gender and caste equality, is disturbed by the guest's parochial caste behaviors, and apologizes to Shashikant. She argues that the caste system belonged to a bygone era, and *dalits* should participate equally in weddings and all other social rituals.

Inspired by *Taru*, numerous discussions occurred over several months in the Singh household about the ill-treatment of *dalits*. The family, who were ardent members of a *Taru* listening group in Kamtaul, discussed what they could do to combat caste discrimination in their village. How could they challenge a social practice that was so firmly ingrained in Kamtaul's social ethos? Some ideas surfaced through discussion and dialogue, leading Sunita Singh to open a school for *dalit* women. Her daughters and husband supported her actions. For the first time in the history of Kamtaul village, a higher caste woman (Sunita) had stepped into Kamtaul's *Harijan Tola*, the locality where the *dalits* lived.

Empowered by their actions, the Singh family began to discuss other ways to make a more public statement about caste discrimination in Kamtaul. They played out various scenarios in their discussions, rehearsing and refining them. They noted that their discussions revolved mostly around how to reframe the issue of untouchability in a way that it would be culturally acceptable. The wedding celebrations of Vandana's elder sister provided an opportunity to enact what they had discussed.

Dalits are involved in almost all wedding celebrations in rural Bihar; however, their roles are limited to cleaning toilets, handling garbage, and doing other menial jobs. So, rarely do *dalits* come in contact with guests, and almost never would they participate in preparing or serving food—for that would represent "contamination." The Singh family decided to break tradition.

A few days before the marriage, when guests began to arrive at the Singh household, Shailendra Singh (Plate 4.2) asked several local *dalits* to help out. One evening, while chatting with other guests, Shailendra Singh asked one of the *dalits* (whom he had asked previously to dress in clean clothes and be properly groomed) to serve him a glass of water. In full view of others, Singh emptied the glass, and asked the *dalit* to serve water to others. Some guests followed Singh's lead, even if somewhat reluctantly. Some relatives said they were not thirsty. Some others, "who were offended but felt that they couldn't say anything, got up from their chairs, gave some banal reason, and left the scene" (personal interview, September 3, 2002).

Once a new social precedent was legitimized, for the next three days, six or seven *dalits* were actively engaged by the Singh family to serve food and drinks to the invited guests. "We gradually increased their involvement…. *Dalits* went from serving water, to serving drinks, to serving both food and drinks…. They went first from serving family members, to serving close relatives, to serving outside guests" (personal interview, September 3, 2002). On the wedding day, some 30 *dalits* participated in the celebrations and half of them served food and drinks to the 600 guests, of which two-thirds comprised the local population of Kamtaul. In essence, the new codes of social behavior about the participation of *dalits* were further legitimized in Kamtaul.

**Plate 4.2
Shailendra Singh, rural health
practitioner in Kamtaul village,
standing next to a *Taru* poster**
Shailendra, an avid listener of *Taru*, intervened in stopping a child marriage in the
village, and worked tirelessly to remove
caste-based inequities in his village.
Source: Personal Files of the Authors.

Shailendra and Sunita Singh jointly summarized for author Singhal
how *Taru* helped spark social change processes in Kamtaul (personal
interview, September 3, 2002):

> Previously, it was just a thought. As a family, we were always good to
> *dalits*, but still the *samajik deewar* [social wall] existed. But after listening
> to *Taru* and dialoguing about this issue on a daily basis, the thought
> began to take on a concrete shape. We always used to talk about the
> beautiful *dosti* [friendship] relationship between Taru, the high caste
> girl, and Shashikant, the low caste but highly accomplished man. We
> were also inspired by the character of Neha, who despite her in-laws
> opposition decides to open a school for low caste children. So we dis-
> cussed that we needed to do something. And then we said, it is *our*
> daughter's marriage; so we can use that event.

In essence, for the Singh family, *Taru* modeled new realities for a
more egalitarian integration of *dalits* into mainstream society.
Produced by All India Radio, the Indian national radio network,
Taru's explicit purpose was to disseminate the idea of gender and
caste equality to millions of listeners in such Indian states as Bihar,
where the Singh family resided. However, this centralized dissemination of educational messages by the mass-media itself has little

Box 4.1: Martin Luther King Jr.'s "I Have a Dream" Speech

On August 28, 1963, Dr. Martin Luther King Jr. delivered the "I Have a Dream" speech on the steps of the Lincoln Memorial in Washington, D.C. Some 300,000 people heard this speech in person. Several millions in America and the world saw it live on television, and hundreds of millions have since seen it on television, heard it on radio, or read the speech in a book. "I Have a Dream" is hailed as one of the most powerful speeches ever given.

In describing his dream of a nation "where a person would be judged not by the color of their skin but by the content of their character," Dr. King's speech mobilized millions of supporters for desegregation in the United States, prompting the signing of the 1964 Civil Rights Act. The same year, at age 34, King was awarded the Nobel Peace Prize.

An examination of the "I Have a Dream" phenomenon shows the inter-relationships that exist between dissemination and dialogue. King's speech represents an exemplar of mass dissemination; it spread the word on racial equality widely—both in the U.S. and overseas. However, this speech was developed over years of intense dialogue—with Southern church leaders, civil rights' activists, and friends and family members. Through these conversations, Dr. King understood the nature, scope, and brutality of indignities suffered by blacks, and honed his strategy of non-violent civil disobedience. Portions of the "I Have a Dream" speech were presented in various other venues, sparking dialogue with audience members, who, in turn, further informed Dr. King's ideas. In essence, dialogue was an integral component in the development of the speech that was finally delivered in Washington, D.C. in 1963.

Once disseminated by the mass media, the speech inspired further dialogue. Dr. King's words inspired dialogue among millions of people—Blacks and Whites, Christians and non-Christians, and Americans and non-Americans. These dialogues shaped the public, mass media, and policy discourses on Civil Rights. Dialogue about freedom and equality, prejudice and discrimination, privilege and opportunity characterized conversations in families, schools, and in churches, mosques, temples, and synagogues. Many were inspired by Dr. King to personally practice racial tolerance. Many others participated in, or helped organize, Civil Rights campaigns for racial equality.

The real power of this widely disseminated speech lies in the dialogue it has sparked over four decades across the world. "I Have a Dream" illustrates that dialogue shapes dissemination; and dissemination prompts dialogue. For social change to occur, both dissemination and dialogue need to dynamically co-exist, each shaping the other, and, in turn, being shaped by the other.

meaning unless these messages create spaces for discussion and dialogue among audience members. The Singh family was carefully attending to the socially ameliorative information that *Taru* was bringing into their homes, while simultaneously dialoguing about it at home. The new social realities disseminated by *Taru* (for example, a school for *dalit* children, a birthday celebration for girls, and fair treatment of *dalits* during a marriage ceremony) sparked dialogue, discussion, decisions, and actions in several communities of Bihar.

In the present chapter, we argue that a dialectical tension exists between information dissemination and dialogue in organizing for social change efforts. By focusing on social change initiatives that incorporate on-air, mass-mediated information dissemination with on-the-ground discussion and dialogue circles, we analyze how the dialectical tensions between dissemination and dialogue can be dynamically managed. Our chapter begins with an explication of the tensions between dissemination and dialogue, including a discussion of Paulo Freire's dialogic approach to social change, followed by an investigation of how these recursive tensions play out in mass-mediated entertainment-education interventions that spark widespread community conversations. The dialectic of dissemination and dialogue is examined in-depth by focusing on the *Taru* radio soap opera project in India's Bihar State.

Dissemination and Dialogue

In this section, we discuss the characteristics of dissemination and dialogue, including how dissemination and dialogue are dialectically intertwined in social change processes, and how these tensions discursively enact themselves in mass-mediated and small group contexts.

■ Characteristics of Dissemination and Dialogue

Dissemination is an intentional process of information transmission from a source to one or many individuals. In this sense, dissemination involves telling: The message is usually invariant and there is limited, if any, role for feedback. Mass-media messages are thus mostly dissemination. Interpersonal messages can also involve dissemination.

A Grameen Bank worker who discusses the bank's policies, procedures, and formalities with a member engages in dissemination. While dissemination may mean uniformity of transmission, in does not imply uniformity in reception. In fact, there is usually quite a bit of diversity in reception. Interestingly, in the economics of communication, messages are worth more in dissemination than they are in reception (Peters, 1999). Teachers are paid to teach, students spend to learn. In essence, society places a high economic value on expert-centered transmission.

Dialogue involves mutuality and reciprocity in information exchange between two or more individuals. In this sense, dialogue involves not just a channel of information-exchange but is also embodied in the relationship between participants. Dialogue, by its very nature, is recurring and iterative. Through dialogue, human relationships are co-created, co-regulated, and co-modified; that is, something new is created in the interaction. Also, unlike mass-mediated dissemination messages, dialogue is oral, live, immediate, and spatially-bound to a physical context (Peters, 1999).

Recent scholarship has highlighted the importance of dialogue in social change processes (Anderson, Baxter, & Cissna, 2003; Gergen, Gergen, & Barrett, 2004; Hammond, Anderson, & Cissna, 2003; Stewart & Zediker, 2000; Zoller, 2000, 2004). Zoller (2000) argues "dialogic relations involve risking one's position in order to arrive at a new understanding" (p. 193). This observation highlights the fact that risk is always part of any substantive change in a community. Dialogue may also focus on the tensions that surface when social changes are debated. For example, how we may balance the need to arrive at consensus for change while still respecting voices of opposition (Stewart & Zediker, 2000). Zoller (2004) extends this position by explaining that "dialogue requires collaboration that does not rule out disagreement and debate but presumes a focus on joint sense making and a willingness to be vulnerable to be changed through interaction" (p. 214). Dialogue thus represents a primary resource for transforming how we understand ourselves and others and the organizational worlds we inhabit.

Peters (1999) distinguished between dissemination and dialogue by invoking Jesus and Socrates, two great teachers, both of whom questioned past practices and were martyrs as a result. While Jesus represented a case of dissemination, spreading his parables among his followers across geographically dispersed audiences, Socrates practiced dialogue—face-to-face, in the here and the now. Jesus disseminated his message to audiences ranging from a few people to a few thousand (e.g., the Sermon on the Mount), while Socrates mostly dialogued one-on-one with his pupils and fellow Greek citizens.

We argue that dissemination and dialogue are dialectically intertwined and the tension between them is a vital ingredient in organizing for social change efforts. Dissemination and dialogue are neither separable, nor is one holier than the other. Peters (1999) questions the "holy" status bestowed on dialogue, noting that uncritical celebration of dialogue is as naïve; as is the uncritical criticism of dissemination. Peters argues that "dialogue can be tyrannical and dissemination can be just" (Peters, 1999, p. 34)—much like dialogue can be just and dissemination can be tyrannical. Peters finds dialogic reciprocity as a moral ideal to be insufficient, asking why should there be implied indignity in information transmission. In social change processes, dissemination and dialogue must necessarily coexist, each shaping the other and being shaped by the other.

One way to illustrate how the dialectic of dissemination and dialogue operates is to consider the "call and response" tradition in African music (also a part of African-American music). Call and response occurs when a singer produces a word or phrase that is repeated by the chorus and/or the audience. In an interesting variation of this technique, singer Chuck Berry used call and response in the 1950s hit song Johnny B. Goode. The call statement was "Go Johnny Go," and the lead guitar riff produced the response. Among African-Africans, call and response occurs in several different interactional contexts, including in Sunday Church services. Smitherman (1977) defines call and response as "spontaneous verbal and nonverbal interaction between speaker and listener in which all of the statements ('calls') are punctuated by expressions ('responses') from the listener" (p. 104). These responses usually function to affirm or agree with the speaker, urge the speaker on, repeat what the speaker has said, or complete the speaker's statement in response to a request from the speaker (Foster, 2005). In this verbal arena, the dialectic between dissemination and dialogue surfaces as the speaker (for instance, a Methodist preacher) disseminates a message to a large audience. The audience then offers a response. Dialogue emerges when the response becomes so enthusiastic that audience members talk among themselves as the performance is occurring. This dialogue among the audience may in turn influence the speaker's message, rhythm, or flow.

■ Dissemination and Dialogue in Mass-Mediated Contexts

Various theories of mass media effects and group dynamics have wrestled with the dialectic of dissemination and dialogue. For instance, in the 1940s, the mass media were perceived as being magic multipliers of invariant messages, leading to direct, immediate, and powerful effects on audience members (Katz & Lazarsfeld, 1955). Such conclusions about the media's omnipotence in disseminating messages were derived from the role played by the Hearst newspapers in arousing public support in the U.S. for the Spanish-American War; and in the powerful impact of Nazi propaganda before and during World War II (Rogers, 2003). This outdated view of media effects, commonly referred to as the hypodermic needle model, viewed the audience as a group of passive, atomized, and disconnected individuals.

However, several studies conducted after World War II showed that the hypodermic needle model of mass media effects was problematic, and that media effects were better explained by the two-step-flow model (Katz & Lazarsfeld, 1955; Rogers, 1962). In the first step, the mass media influenced only a limited number of individuals in a social system (often called opinion leaders), mostly through a process of information transmission (Rogers, 2003). Media effects, however, were more pronounced in a second step—from the opinion leaders to other individuals in the social system, connected through existing social networks. Here interpersonal communication, discussion, and dialogue were the key vehicles of influence. Importantly, these interpersonal contexts of social influence include a simultaneous and concurrent process of both dissemination (e.g., an opinion leader transmitting information among peer group members) and dialogue (e.g., peer group members mutually clarifying their ideas).

This dissemination-dialogue dialectic in a mass-mediated context is illustrated in the radio farm forum experiments. In 1956, India was the site of the famous Pune Radio Farm Forum Project, which was a field experiment to evaluate the effects of radio farm forums, each consisting of several dozen villagers who gathered weekly to listen to a half-hour radio program (broadcast by All India Radio) and then to discuss its contents (Kivlin, Roy, Fliegel, & Sen, 1968). The theme of the radio forums was "Listen, Discuss, Act!" One of the radio broadcasts might deal with rodents as a problem. Following discussion of this topic in a radio forum, villagers would mount a rat-control campaign in their community.

The research evaluation showed that the Pune radio farm forums helped to "unify villagers around common decisions and common actions," widening "the influence of the *gram panchayat* [village government] and broadening the scope of its action" (Mathur & Neurath, 1959, p. 101). The farm forums spurred discussions among villagers, leading to decisions about digging wells, adopting purebred bulls and Leghorn chickens, and establishing *balwadis* [children's enrichment centers] (Singhal & Rogers, 2001). At the village level, the radio forums acted like voluntary organizations "whose members were neither appointed by authority nor elected to represent specific group interests," signifying an important experiment in village democracy (Mathur & Neurath, 1959, p. 101). Members voluntarily engaged in village clean-up drives, planting papaya trees, and building pit latrines.

The primary purpose of the radio farm forums was to disseminate information on new agricultural practices to rural farmers in India. Radio broadcasting allowed information to be disseminated widely to tens of millions of farmers, residing in tens of thousands of Indian villages. As dozens of farmers gathered around a radio set and heard these messages, simultaneous processes of both dissemination and dialogue unfolded on the ground. Farmers, who were opinion leaders, disseminated their ideas among fellow farmers on how to incorporate new agricultural practices. Concurrently, discussion and dialogue among participating farmers shaped the decisions and actions about agricultural and community organizing initiatives.

■ Dissemination and Dialogue in Small Group Contexts

Both dissemination and dialogue occurs concurrently in small group contexts of social change. During World War II, the famed anthropologist Margaret Mead headed the U.S. Department of Agriculture's Committee on Food Habits. Its mission was to promote healthy diets among the U.S. population during a time when high protein foods were in short supply (Pratkanis & Aronson, 2000). One of Mead's projects sought to increase the consumption of animal meat products that were typically thrown away in American homes. These included protein and mineral-rich beef hearts, animal livers, kidneys, and intestines.

The famed social psychologist Kurt Lewin designed a study to untangle the role of dissemination and dialogue in persuading American housewives to cook and serve such foods. Half the housewives received a lecture by a nutritionist on the merits of intestinal meats, the economic advantages of serving them, and the importance of this activity to the war effort (Rogers, 1994). The nutritionist provided an explanation of how to prepare these glandular foods, how to overcome resistances toward them, and the like. Recipes were handed out.

The other half participated in a group discussion, guided by Alex Bavelas, Lewin's protégé at Iowa. Bavelas began the group discussion by briefly stating the importance of maintaining health during the War, and then posed the question: "Do you think housewives like yourselves could be persuaded to participate in the intestinal meat program?" (Pratkanis & Aronson, 2000, p. 168). The ensuing group discussion, which lasted about 45 minutes (the same time as the lecture) covered many topics that were also covered in the lecture, including a discussion of resistances to ingesting such foods, and how might they be overcome.

Follow-up research, several weeks later, suggested that of the housewives who heard the expert lecture, only 3 percent served intestines as meals. In contrast, 32 percent of the housewives who had engaged in the group discussions served these meats (Lewin, 1958). In essence, the housewives who conversed, dialogued, asked questions, and shared experiences were about 11 times more likely to be persuaded about the cause.

Lewin's findings on the importance of small group processes speaks to the dialectic between dissemination and dialogue. Although the media may efficiently disseminate messages, much like the expert nutritionist in Lewin's lecture condition, it is dialogue within and between social networks of neighbors, friends, and relatives that leads to follow-up decisions and actions. More importantly, small group contexts—whether a radio farm forum comprising farmers in rural India or a group of housewives in a U.S. town—embody a mutually recursive space for both dissemination and dialogue: Information is both transmitted and mutually co-created, fostering new possibilities and realities for the participants.

Dialogic Action in Social Change[4]

Paulo Freire—Brazilian social change theorist, practitioner, and activist—is hailed as the father of dialogic action, an approach to social change that is uniquely situated in the midst of participatory theory, method, and praxis. Simply put, Paulo Freire emphasized the role of dialogue and people's participation in social change. *Participation* is defined as a dynamic, interactional, and transformative process of dialogue between people, groups, and institutions that enables people, both individually and collectively, to realize their full potential and be engaged in their own welfare (Singhal, 2001). Participation, in the Frerian sense, meant working *with* and *by* the people, as opposed to working *on* or working *for* the people (Table 4.1).

Table 4.1
Participatory versus non-participatory strategies for social change

Participatory Strategies	*Non-Participatory Strategies*
Horizontal lateral communication between participants	*Vertical* top-down communication from senders to receivers
Process of dialogue and democratic participation	*Campaign* to mobilize in a short-term without building capacity
Long-term process of sustainable change	*Short-term* planning and quick-fix solutions
Collective empowerment and decision-making	*Individual* behavior change
With the community's involvement	*For* the community
Specific in content, language, and culture	*Massive* and broad-based
People's needs are the focus	*Donors' musts* are the focus
Owned by the community	*Access* determined by social, political, and economic factors
Consciousness-raising	*Persuasion* for short-term

Source: Adapted from Gumucio Dagron (2001).

	Box 4.2: Paulo Freire A Believer in Dialogue

Born in 1921 in Recife, in Northeastern Brazil, Paulo Freire (Plate 4.3) learned lessons about hunger and desperation as an 8-year-old, when his father, a state police official, lost his job. The family savings were soon

arquivos paulo freire

Plate 4.3
Brazilian educator Paulo Freire championed a dialogic approach to social change
Freire's dialogic pedagogy emphasizes the role of "teacher as learner" and the "learner as teacher," with each person learning from the other in a mutual, reciprocal, iterative, and transformative process.
Source: Arquivos do Instituto Paulo Freire.

Box 4.2: Paulo Freire
(continued)

gone, and other kinship safety nets were quickly exhausted. Although his father eventually found a job and Freire's middle-class existence was restored, the powerful childhood lesson learned from the trauma of living in poverty stayed with Freire for life.

Freire's most important career lesson came in the early 1950s when he was in charge of establishing adult literacy programs in poverty-stricken Northeastern Brazil. During an introductory seminar for illiterate and semi-illiterate adults, a wage laborer, who had listened to Freire's presentation on the benefits of learning to read and write, challenged Freire to understand the "world" in which members of the audience were living. Speaking in the local vernacular, the illiterate laborer painted a highly evocative word-picture of the grinding poverty that he and his family endured, of his inability to speak like educated people, and his daily struggles with domination and exploitation.

The laborer's moving story, told in his own words, influenced Freire's ideas about what education should and should not be. He realized that an educator's greatest challenge was to understand, appreciate, and respect the knowledge of people's lived experience as expressed in their vernacular. He also realized that politics and pedagogy were inseparable. With experimentation and experience, Freire's pedagogical methods incorporated ideas on critical reflection, dialogue and participation, autonomy, democracy, problematization, and the crucial connection between theory and practice (Freire, 1970).

Freire's empowering approach was deemed politically dangerous by Brazil's rightwing military regime, which seized control in 1964, and he was exiled for over two decades before returning to São Paulo in the mid-1980s to serve as Secretary of Education for the city of São Paulo. He passed away in 1997, but his ideas of humane, dialogic pedagogy live on in hundreds of organizing for social change efforts around the world.

Freire's best known book, *Pedagogy of the Oppressed* (Freire, 1970), argued that most political, educational, and social change interventions fail because they are designed by technocrats based on their personal conception of reality, which is several steps removed from the reality of those for whom they are designed. Freire's dialogic pedagogy emphasized the role of "teacher as learner" and the "learner as teacher," with each person learning from the other in a mutually transformative process (Freire & Faundez, 1989). The role of the outside facilitator is one of working *with*, and not *for*, the oppressed to organize them in their incessant struggle to regain their humanity (Singhal, 2001). True participation, according to Freire, does not involve a subject–object relationship, but rather a subject–subject relationship.

In Freirean dialogic pedagogy, there is no room for teaching "two plus two equals four." Such rote pedagogy, according to Freire, is dehumanizing as it views learners as empty receptacles to be "filled" with expert knowledge. Freire criticized this "banking" mode of education, in which "deposits" are made by experts. The scope of action allowed students (or intended beneficiaries) "extends only as far as receiving, filing, and storing the deposits" (Freire, 1970, p. 58). Instead, Freire advocated problem-posing as a means to re-present to people what they know and think, not as a lecture, but as an involving problem. So a lesson on "two plus two" might proceed in the following dialogic manner (Singhal, 2001):

> *Teacher*: How many chickens do you have?
> *Poor farmer*: Two.
> *Teacher*: How many chickens does your neighbor have?
> *Poor farmer*: Two.
> *Teacher*: How many chickens does the landlord have?
> *Poor farmer*: Oh, hundreds!
> *Teacher*: Why does he have hundreds, and you have only two?

So goes the dialogic conversation that over time stimulates a process of critical reflection and awareness ("conscientization") on the part of the poor farmer. Once the oppressed, both individually and collectively, reflect critically on their social situation, possibilities arise for them to break the "culture of silence" through the articulation of discontent and action. Freire emphasized that the themes underlying dialogic pedagogy should resonate with people's experiences, and not be well-meaning but alienating rhetoric (Freire, 1970).

However, even Freire, a champion of dialogic action, implicitly acknowledges the role of dissemination in dialogue. The teacher, the facilitator, often an outsider, brought new skills and ideas to oppressed communities; even if it was the skill of facilitating a process of dialogue, self-reflection, and self-actualization on the part of the disempowered. In a similar vein, while being a strong proponent of dialogue (like Socrates), Friere's ideas are still disseminated through his writing. And, his writings, in turn, stimulate dialogue among readers and practitioners. Similarly, the Bible disseminates Jesus' parables far and wide. This dissemination of the parables stimulates dialogue in millions of churches, homes, and public forums. This dialogue, in turn, influences the Bible's further dissemination.

Entertainment-Education and Social Change

In this section, we discuss how entertainment-education initiatives disseminate pro-social models of behaviors, sparking community dialogue and collective actions.

Entertainment-education (E-E) is the process of purposely designing and implementing a media message to both entertain and educate, in order to increase audience members' knowledge about an educational issue, create favorable attitudes, shift social norms, and change overt behavior (Singhal & Rogers, 1999, 2002). The general purpose of E-E interventions, such as the radio serial *Taru* (discussed at the beginning of this chapter), is to contribute to the process of directed social change, which can occur at the level of an individual, community, or society.[5]

The E-E strategy contributes to social change in multiple ways. E-E can influence audience members' awareness, attitudes, and behavior toward a socially desirable end. Here the anticipated effects are located in an individual or a collective of which an individual is a part. Often E-E programs spark conversations among audience members about the social issues that are addressed, leading to dialogue, decisions, and individual or collective actions. An illustration is provided by a radio soap opera, *Twende na Wakati* [Let's Go with the Times], in Tanzania that convinced several hundred thousand sexually-active adults to adopt HIV prevention behaviors (like using condoms and reducing their number of sexual partners) (Rogers, Vaughan, Swalehe, Rao, Svenkerud, & Sood, 1999; Singhal & Rogers, 1999). E-E interventions can also influence the audience's external environment to help create the necessary conditions for social change at the system level (Singhal & Rogers, 2002; Singhal, Cody, Rogers, & Sabido, 2004). Here the major effects are located in the social-political sphere of the audiences' external environment. E-E can serve as a social mobilizer, an advocate or agenda-setter, influencing public and policy initiatives in a socially-desirable direction (Wallack, 1990).

■ Disseminating Models, Sparking Community Action

Entertainment-education programs strategically employ media role models to promote socially-desirable behaviors, and to dissuade socially-undesirable behaviors (Bandura, 2004). The principles of media role modeling were distilled over four decades ago by Professor Albert Bandura at Stanford University, who in the early-1960s conducted experiments to analyze the effect of televised violence on children (Bandura, 1973).

In Bandura's famed Bobo doll experiment, young children watched a film of an adult role model beating a plastic Bobo doll, weighted at its base. The model punched, kicked, and hit the Bobo doll with his fists and a mallet. When hit, the Bobo doll falls backward and immediately springs upright as if offering a counter punch (Pratkanis & Aronson, 2000). Then children were let into a play room with several attractive toys including a Bobo doll. Interestingly, children who watched the film imitated the media model's behavior: They punched, kicked, and hit the Bobo doll (Bandura, 1973). Bandura's experiment suggested that when exposed to a violent televised model, children were likely to exhibit the aggressive behavior they had observed. Also, by glamorizing aggressive behavior, children's restraints against the use of aggression were weakened (Bandura, Grusec, & Menlove, 1966; Bandura, 1973). Bandura's experiments also showed that audience members learn models of behavior as effectively from televised models as from ones in real-life (Bandura, 1962, 1965, 1977).

Bandura's principles of role modeling were creatively employed in the mid-1970s by Miguel Sabido, a creative writer-director-producer at Televisa, the Mexican national television network, to produce a series of E-E *telenovelas* (television novels or soap operas) (Singhal & Rogers, 1999; Sabido, 2004). If media models could promote aggression and other anti-social behaviors, why couldn't their power be tapped for pro-social purposes (Singhal & Obregon, 1999)? Between 1975 and 1982, Sabido incorporated Bandura's principles of role modeling in seven E-E *telenovela* productions. Remarkably, each *telenovela* was popular with its audience, made a profit, and met its educational objectives (Nariman, 1993).

Sabido understood the central concept in mass-mediated observational learning is *modeling*, which Bandura contends is broader than imitation and identification. *Imitation* is the process by which one individual matches the actions of another, usually closely in time

(Bandura, 1986). *Identification* is the process through which a psychological relationship develops between an individual and a model, enhancing the possibility of modeling to occur. Bandura defined *modeling* as the psychological processes in which one individual matches the actions of another, not necessarily closely in time (Bandura, 1977). Modeling influences have broader psychological effects than identification, or the simple response mimicry implied by imitation.

In operationalizing the concept of modeling Sabido was well aware that the relationship between a media consumer and a media model goes beyond the cognitive domain to include the emotive and affective domains. Sabido, for instance, knew that audience members engage in *parasocial relationships* with media models, defined as the seemingly face-to-face interpersonal relationships which can develop between a viewer and a mass media personality (Horton & Wohl, 1956). The media consumer forms a relationship with a performer that is analogous to a real interpersonal relationship. Thus, audience members tune in at a pre-appointed hour to welcome the media model into their homes. Incredibly, some audience members even talk to their favorite characters (that is, to their TV or radio set) as if the characters were real people (Papa et al., 2000; Perse & Rubin, 1989; Rubin & Perse, 1987; Sood & Rogers, 2000).

So, Sabido designed his E-E *telenovelas* in ways that viewers could become affectively involved with the role models and learn socially desirable behaviors from them. For example, when a likable character modeled a behavior that was socially desirable, the character was rewarded. If an unlikable character emulated a socially undesirable behavior, he/she was punished. So, when Martha, the central character in Sabido's family planning telenovela, *Acompáñame* (Accompany Me), visited a family planning clinic, she was visibly rewarded. When a role model in *Ven Conmigo* (Come with Me) refused to enroll in an adult literacy class, he was observably punished. Sabido showed his *telenovela* models initiating, refining, and practicing new socially desirable behaviors.

Data gathered by Mexico's Adult Education System showed that between November, 1975 and December, 1976 (the period during which *Ven Conmigo*, the *telenovela* promoting adult literacy was broadcast), 839,943 illiterates enrolled in adult literacy classes in Mexico. This number of new enrollments in Mexico in 1976 was nine times the number of enrollments in the previous year, and twice the number of enrollments the following year, when *Ven Conmigo* was no longer broadcast (Nariman, 1993; Singhal & Rogers, 1999).

The promise of E-E, illustrated in Mexico by Sabido's *telenovelas*, lies in the possibilities the strategy holds for disseminating "new" behavioral models of individual and collective action (Singhal, Cody, Rogers, & Sabido, 2004). E-E programs can question existing patterns of social behavior and model new ways of dealing with past social practices. For instance, in the 1999 *Soul City* E-E television series in South Africa, a new collective behavior was modeled to portray how neighbors might intervene in a spousal abuse situation (Singhal & Rogers, 2003). The prevailing cultural norm in South Africa was for neighbors, even if they wished to help a victim, not to intervene in a spousal abuse situation. Wife (or partner) abuse is seen as a private matter, carried out in a private space, with curtains drawn and behind closed doors. In the *Soul City* series, neighbors collectively decide to break the ongoing cycle of spousal abuse. When the next wife-beating episode occurred, they gathered around the abuser's residence and collectively banged pots and pans, censuring the abuser's actions (Usdin, Singhal, Shongwe, Goldstein, & Shabalala, 2004).

This prime-time E-E episode, which earned one of the highest audience ratings in South Africa in 1999, demonstrated the importance of creatively modeling collective efficacy in order to energize neighbors, who, for social and cultural reasons, felt previously inefficacious. By watching the neighbors collectively act against an abuser on screen, viewers learned new ways to break the cycle of spousal abuse. Several weeks after this episode was broadcast, pot banging to stop partner abuse was reported in several communities in South Africa (Plate 4.4). Clearly, in these communities, the newly modeled behavior was discussed, debated, and decisions made. Interestingly, patrons of a local pub in Thembisa Township in South Africa reinvented the new collective behavior they learned from *Soul City*. They collectively banged bottles in the bar when a man physically abused his girlfriend (Soul City, 2000).

In essence, E-E programs, by their very nature, disseminate or promote certain desired models of behaviors to a set of audience members. However, this dissemination occurs through role models who engage in a dialogue (often conflictual) over a period of time (as soap operas can run for years), which is followed voluntarily by audience members. This modeled dissemination also prompts

Plate 4.4
Inspired by modeled behavior on *Soul City*, women of Khayelitsha Township in Cape Town, South Africa, march down Matthew Goniwe Street, banging pots and pans to demonstrate how they stop domestic violence in their community

In the 1999 *Soul City* entertainment-education television series in South Africa, a new collective behavior was modeled to portray how neighbors might intervene in a domestic violence situation. Prevailing social norms dictated that neighbors should not intervene in a private spousal matter. In the *Soul City* series, neighbors collectively gathered around the abuser's residence and collectively banged pots and pans, censuring the abuser's actions. This modeled behavior was then observed in several South African communities—as illustrated in the present photo which was published on the cover page of *The Cape Times*.

Source: Soul City Institute of Health and Development Communication.

conversations and dialogues among audience members, who may then come together to take collective decisions or actions.

The *Taru* Project in India

We began this chapter by discussing the dialectic between dissemination and dialogue that characterized the reception of the E-E radio soap opera, *Taru* in India's Bihar State. Here we illuminate this dialectic further by providing a historical background on the *Taru* project, and by analyzing how mass-mediated E-E dissemination efforts (such as *Taru*) can spark discussions, dialogues, and conversations in community contexts. We then describe how dialogue reflexively informs the subsequent dissemination of messages.

■ Historical Background: From *Tinka* to *Taru*

The inspiration for the *Taru* Project came from a previous community-based investigation (led by authors Singhal and Papa) on the impacts of *Tinka Tinka Sukh* [Happiness Lies in Small Pleasures], an E-E radio soap opera, in Lutsaan village of north India. *Tinka Tinka Sukh*, broadcast for one year during 1996–1997 by All India Radio (AIR), promoted gender equality, small family size, and communal harmony to audiences in North India. During this time, AIR received a colorful 30 by 24 inch poster-letter from Lutsaan village in India's Uttar Pradesh State, signed by 184 community members, pledging not to give or accept dowry (an illegal but widespread social practice in India). These villagers also pledged to not allow child marriages (also an illegal but common practice), and pledged to educate their daughters equally with their sons (Papa, Singhal, Law, Pant, Sood, Rogers, & Shefner-Rogers, 2000).

The poster-letter stated: "Listeners of our village [to "*Tinka Tinka Sukh*"] now actively oppose the practice of dowry—they neither give nor receive dowry" (Singhal & Rogers, 1999, p. 1). Birendra Singh Khushwaha, a young tailor in the village, was especially influenced by the radio program episodes about dowry, and initiated the process of writing the poster-letter among the people in his tailor shop. As a result of the forces set in motion by the tailor, the villagers formed radio listening clubs, planted trees for reforestation, and built pit latrines for improving village sanitation. Girls' enrollment in Lutsaan's schools increased from 10 percent at the time of the radio broadcasts, to 38 percent two years later. Fewer dowry marriages and child marriages occurred in Lutsaan, although these practices did not disappear completely in the village (Papa et al., 2000).

The Lutsaan study strongly suggested that E-E interventions had their strongest effects on audiences when the disseminated messages stimulated reflection, dialogue, and debate about the educational topic among audience members, and when services can be delivered locally (Papa, Singhal, Law, Pant, Sood, Rogers, & Shefner-Rogers, 2000). These lessons learned from the Lutsaan study, especially the co-existing tensions between mass-mediated dissemination and community-based dialogue, led, a few years later, to the formulation of the *Taru* Project in India.

■ On-Air and On-Ground Interventions

Through a collaborative partnership between various organizations—Population Communications International of New York, Ohio University (where author Singhal was based), All India Radio (AIR), and two India-based NGOs Janani and Brij Lok Madhuri, a new E-E radio drama called *Taru* was designed and then broadcast in four Hindi-speaking North Indian states—Bihar, Jharkhand, Madhya Pradesh, and Chhattisgarh. The year-long (2002–2003) broadcasts of *Taru* were dove-tailed with a series of on-the-ground activities in 25,000 villages through Janani, an NGO that promotes reproductive health care services in these four states (Singhal, Sharma, Papa, & Witte, 2004). These four states have a population of 190 million people; the highest fertility, infant mortality, and maternal death rates in India; and the lowest literacy and contraceptive prevalence rates.[6]

Janani's modus operandi in rural India is noteworthy. It identifies respected village-based rural health providers (RHPs), and trains the RHP and his spouse by providing a crash course in reproductive health care, first-aid, maternal and child health, and diagnosis and treatment of STIs/RTIs (sexually-transmitted infections and reproductive tract infections) (Plate 4.5). Janani knows that most rural women in India are embarrassed to seek reproductive health services from a male RHP. Now with a trained woman in their midst, rural women feel comfortable to seek prenatal and antenatal care services, as well as contraceptives. Once the RHP couple has successfully completed their training, Janani brands their clinic (painting it bright red and yellow) and incorporates it in its franchisee network of Titly [Butterfly] Clinics, enhancing the visibility of the local RHP and his spouse. Furthermore, after registering in Janani's rural health network, the RHPs begin to stock Janani's branded Mithun [Bull] condoms, Apsara [Angel] oral contraceptive pills, pregnancy dipsticks, and a whole host of reproductive health services.

Pre-program publicity for *Taru* was conducted on-the-air by AIR. On-the-ground *Taru* was publicized by Janani's 25,000 strong network of RHPs (in the four Indian states), *Taru* posters, and over 700 strategically-placed wall paintings at major highway inter-sections. Furthermore, in four villages in Bihar, selected carefully to fulfill

Plate 4.5
A Janani-trained husband–wife team of rural health providers
Janani's rural health practitioners (RHPs), who are highly respected in their respective villages, played a key role in promoting listenership to *Taru*, promoting
the establishment of listener clubs, and serving as spark plugs for change in their
communities. Janani brands its clinics, painting them bright red and yellow, thereby enhancing their local visibility. Further, these RHPs provide a spectrum of
reproductive health services locally, including provision of branded condoms,
oral contraceptive pills, and pregnancy dipsticks.
Source: Personal Files of the Authors.

certain criteria, folk performances dramatizing the *Taru* storyline
were carried out a week prior to the radio serial's broadcasts to prime
the message reception environment. The Singh family's Kamtaul
village (referenced at the beginning of the chapter) was one such site
for the folk performances. Here Shailendra Singh, the local rural
health provider, and his wife Sunita spread word-of-mouth messages
about the folk performance, encouraging hundreds of people to
attend, and awarded transistor radios (with a sticker of *Taru*'s logo)
to groups who correctly answered questions based on the folk performance. These groups were then formalized as *Taru* radio listening
clubs (Plate 4.6). Each group received an attractive notebook (with a

Plate 4.6
Young women members of the *Taru* listening group in Abirpur village of India's Bihar State
Notice that these young women are proudly clutching their radio set that has a *Taru* logo on it. Inspired by *Taru*, the protagonist of the radio soap opera, these young women initiated several village development activities in Abirpur.
Source: Personal Files of the Authors.

Taru logo), and were encouraged to discuss the social themes addressed in *Taru*, relate them to their personal circumstances, and record any decisions, or actions, they took as a result of being exposed to *Taru*.

■ *Taru's* Story

Taru, a 52-episode E-E radio soap opera, promoted gender equality, small family size, reproductive health, and caste and communal harmony. One episode was broadcast each week (between February 2002 and February 2003) on Friday at 8:00 p.m., with a repeat broadcast each Sunday at 3:40 p.m. Each episode of *Taru* began with a theme song and a brief summary of the previous episode. The episode ended with an epilogue that posed a reflective question to the listeners, inviting them to discuss the issue, and write-in their response.

The story of the *Taru* serial revolved around Taru, a young, educated woman who works in Suhagpur village's Sheetal Center, an
organization that provided reproductive health services, carried out
village self-help activities, and fought social injustices through collective action. Taru is an idealistic, intelligent, and polite woman who
works with a network of friends to empower rural women. Taru is a
close friend of Shashikant, an educated and intelligent man, who is
a social worker at the Sheetal Center. Shashikant, a *dalit*, faces caste
discrimination in the village. While community members in Suhagpur
deride Taru's friendship with a *dalit*, Taru likes Shashikant, and he,
in turn, likes her. An undercurrent of romance characterizes their relationship, although it is not explicitly expressed (especially as
Shashikant is highly mindful of his lower caste status relative to Taru's
upper caste family). Their friendship represents a call to caste and
communal harmony.

Taru's mother, Yashoda, is highly supportive of her daughter, whom
she sees as an embodiment of her own unfulfilled dreams. However,
Mangla, Taru's rogue brother, derides Taru's social work, and ridicules
her friendship with Shashikant. With the help of Aloni Baba (a village
saint) and Guruji (a local teacher), Taru and Shashikant join hands to
fight multiple social evils in a series of intersecting storylines, including
preventing a child marriage, stopping the killing of a new-born girl
child, encouraging girls to be treated on par with boys, and *dalits* on
par with high-caste *brahmins*.

A subplot involved Naresh, his wife Nirmala, his sister Ranjana,
his mother Ramdulari, and his four daughters. Ramdulari insists on
a fifth child, arguing for the importance of having a grandson. Nirmala
uses contraception to avoid an unwanted pregnancy. As the story
evolved, Ramdulari undergoes a change of heart and starts valuing
her granddaughters. Taru and Shashikant work with this family
to celebrate the birthday of one of the granddaughters. For the first
time in Suhagpur's history, a girl's birthday is celebrated.

Another subplot involved Neha, a close friend of Taru, who is
married to Kapileshwar, the son of the local *zamindar* (landlord).
Kapileshwar starts out as a dominating husband, restricting Neha's
mobility outside the home. However, with support from Taru and
Shashikant, Neha begins a school for *dalit* children.

Taru's characters modeled several new behaviors, challenging
existing social norms: a friendship between a high-caste girl and a
dalit social worker; the stopping of a child marriage; a high-caste

bahu (daughter-in-law) stepping out of the home to start a school for *dalit* children; a first-time celebration of a girl's birthday, and others. These modeled messsages were reinforced repeatedly over the one year of *Taru*'s broadcasts.

■ **Researching *Taru***

Our research on the *Taru* project was guided by methodological triangulation, the use of multiple research methods (both quantitative and qualitative) to investigate the same phenomenon. The present chapter draws mostly on various types of qualitative data collected over a period of 30 months from four villages in Bihar: Abirpur village in Vaishali District and Kamtaul, Madhopur, and Chandrahatti villages in Muzaffarpur District. In each of these four villages, the local rural health practitioners publicized *Taru*. In addition, folk performances dramatizing the *Taru* storyline were carried out, *Taru* radio listening clubs were formalized, and listener club diaries were maintained.

Our data-sources from these four villages included: (1) some 75 transcripts of in-depth and focus group interviews with listeners of *Taru*, conducted at four points in time—September 2002 (six months after *Taru*'s initial broadcast), March 2003 (after *Taru* had finished its broadcasts), and then in July 2003; and July 2004 (to gauge the over-time nature of these effects); (2) transcripts of 18 *Taru* listeners' club diaries (each with weekly entries); (3) 22 transcripts of audio-taped listeners' club discussions in village Abirpur (post-listening to *Taru*); (4) some 14 hours of video testimony provided by listeners of *Taru* and their community members; and (5) extensive field notes of authors Singhal and Papa (who made a total of five visits to these villages between 2002 and 2004) and of the other half-dozen colleagues and field researchers involved in collecting data.

The Dialectic of Dissemination and Dialogue in *Taru*

Our study of *Tinka Tinka Sukh* in Lutsaan village had suggested that an E-E program can spark the process of social change by portraying (or disseminating) pro-social models of behaviors (Papa et al., 2000). When listeners are attracted to certain role models in an E-E program, and develop parasocial relationships with them, they may be motivated to consider changes in their own behavior. E-E programs may also stimulate dialogue and peer conversations among listeners, which can create opportunities for collective efficacy to emerge as people consider new patterns of thought and behavior. However, existing power structures often resist the process of social change, and people's own thinking is frequently fraught with paradoxes and contradictions as they "negotiate" their actions with their intentions. Was there evidence for these processes in the villages of Bihar, where our present investigation of *Taru* was based?

■ Parasocial Interaction and Modeling in *Taru*

As noted previously, parasocial relationships are the seemingly face-to-face interpersonal relationships which can develop between a viewer and a mass media personality (Horton & Wohl, 1956). Media consumers treat such mediated relationships as non-mediated interpersonal relationships (Papa et al., 2000; Perse & Rubin, 1989; Rubin & Perse, 1987; Sood & Rogers, 2000). Horton and Wohl (1956) argued that when a parasocial relationship is established, the media consumer appreciates the values and motives of the media character, often viewing him or her as a counselor, comforter, and model. Rubin and Perse (1987) argued that parasocial interaction consists of three audience dimensions: cognitive, affective, and behavioral.

Cognitively-oriented parasocial interaction is the degree to which audience members pay careful attention to the characters in a media message and think about its educational content after their exposure (Papa et al., 2000; Sood & Rogers, 2000). Such reflection on the educational themes can help media consumers recognize that they could make different behavioral choices in their personal lives. Bandura's concept of self-efficacy (Bandura, 1997) is linked to behavior change that a person considers and/or enacts. *Self-efficacy* is an individual's perceptions of his/her capacity to deal effectively with a situation, and to control this situation (Bandura, 1995). For example, after watching a role model in an E-E program, is a person persuaded that they have the ability to change their behavior in a socially-desirable way?

In Kamtaul village, RHP Shailendra Singh noted how listening to *Taru* motivated him to intervene in a delicate situation: "We have applied the learnings of *Taru* in real life. Just as Taru and Shashikant prevent a girl child marriage in the radio serial, we also stopped a child marriage from occurring in Kamtaul. We politely said that this was wrong, and concerned people came around and changed their decision" (personal interview, August 19, 2002).

Sunita, Singh's wife, greatly admired Neha, a friend of Taru in the radio serial, who establishes a school to educate *dalit* (low-caste) children. Sunita launched adult literacy classes for 20 lower caste women in Kamtaul's *Harijan Tola* (the lower caste settlement). It is highly uncommon in an Indian rural setting for a high-caste woman to interact with women of lower castes. "If Neha could do it, so could I," Sunita noted.

Ratneshwar, the younger brother of the RHP in Madhopur village, also wished to start a school but did not feel efficacious to do so. After listening to *Taru* and particularly being influenced by characters like Shashikant, Taru, and Neha, he was able to realize his dreams: "I really enjoy teaching children. After listening to *Taru*, I turned this dream into reality." Ratneshwar's School, which meets in front of the Titly Center, is attended by 25–30 children aged 10–12 years. Ratneshwar charges a minimum admission fee.

Affectively-oriented parasocial interaction is the degree to which an audience member identifies with a particular media character, and believes that his/her interests are joined (Burke, 1945). The stronger the identification, the more likely that character's behavior will affect the audience member. Soni in Abirpur village exemplified this identification: "I love Taru. She is so nice. I also like Shashikant. When Taru is sad, Shashikant makes her laugh. When Taru is sad, I am sad. When Mangla asks her to not see Shashikant, and Taru feels bad, I feel bad." Audience members view their favorite characters as close personal friends, and become emotionally upset when certain characters face difficult personal situations.

The affective identification may be so strong that audience members adjust their daily schedules to listen to the radio program to maintain an ongoing relationship with their favorite characters. As Dhurandhar Maharaj, a male listener in Abirpur village, noted: "Every Friday at 8 p.m. I have to be close to my radio. It's like meeting friends."

For some audience members, the identification with a character is so high that they cannot distinguish the fictional character from the actor. For instance, Kumari Neha, a member of the young women's listener group in Abirpur said: "I wish Taru could come to our village. She is so sweet and polite. If I learn so much from hearing her voice, what will she do to me when I see her in person." Neha identifies so strongly with Taru that she cannot make the distinction between the "reel" Taru and the real Taru.

Behaviorally-oriented parasocial interaction is the degree to which individuals overtly react to media characters, for instance, by "talking" to these characters, or by conversing with other audience members about them. Such conversations may influence audience members' thinking about an educational issue and motivate them to change their behavior in a specific way. The centrality of interpersonal or group interaction to behavior change has been documented by various researchers (Auwal & Singhal, 1992; Papa, Auwal, & Singhal, 1995, 1997; Rogers & Kincaid, 1981; Papa et al., 2000).

Katz, Liebes, and Berko (1992) argued that parasocial interaction can prompt referential involvement on the part of audience members. *Referential involvement* is the degree to which an individual relates a media message to his/her personal experiences (Papa et al., 2000; Sood & Rogers, 2000). Before audience members consider behavior change as a result of observing or listening to a media character, they must be able to relate the experiences of the character to their own personal lives. If a connection cannot be made between the lives of a character and the experiences of an audience member, behavior change would certainly seem less likely for that individual.

Usha Kumari, a college student from Abirpur is indebted to *Taru* for making her strong and inspiring her to implement her dreams: "There are many moments when I feel that Taru is directly talking to me. Usually at night. She is telling me 'Usha you can follow your dreams.' I feel she [Taru] is like my elder sister ... and giving me encouragement. I thank her for being with me" (personal conversation, September 4, 2002). Usha's uncle, Manoj Maharaj, is Abirpur's village RHP. He frequently treats villagers for minor ailments. Usha was fascinated by the sight of her uncle giving injections and dreamed that one day she would be able to serve her people's health needs. However, it was difficult to implement as the movement of young, unmarried women is considered inappropriate in her village. Impressed with the boldness of Taru to fight social obstacles, Usha went through an important change in her personal life: "Previously I lacked in self-confidence, but I have slowly gotten out of my shell. I am learning how to administer medication, including injections and saline drips from my uncle" (personal communication, September 4, 2002). Usha estimated that between June and August, 2002 (a three-month period), she administered over 200 injections.

Many young women listeners of *Taru* say they are "transformed." Meenakshi, a member of a 16-year-old listeners group in Madhopur talked "on camera," in front of her parents, about the importance of using a condom to protect oneself from HIV infection. She also mentioned that she would encourage her partner to use condoms when appropriate. Meenakshi noted: "I learned this information about HIV/AIDS from the episodes of *Taru*. After listening to these episodes, I took a decision that I will discuss how to protect oneself from AIDS with my friends and family members." Meenakshi's desire to openly discuss information on sex-related topics in Madhopur village is remarkable, given such topics are taboo.

In sum, exposure to *Taru*'s disseminated content led to parasocial interaction between certain audience members and characters in the soap opera. Audience members also modeled certain newly-disseminated behaviors in *Taru*, for example, Sunita Singh in Kamtaul village established a school for *dalit* women, modeling her behavior after Neha who implemented a similar practice in the radio serial. Importantly, we must not oversimplify the relationship between information dissemination and listener action that prompts social change. Strategies for social change may be stimulated initially by a disseminated message, but these strategies may be developed and planned as a result of an internal dialogue in the mind of the listener who considers alternative courses of action. Now let's turn to an examination of conversations between and among listeners. Specifically, how does mass-mediated dissemination prompt dialogue and conversations among listeners?

■ **Dialogue and Conversations**

Our data provides numerous examples of how *Taru* stimulated dialogue among listeners, creating an enabling environment for social change. Involvement with characters and the storyline of E-E programs, often prompts discussions among audience members concerning socially-desirable and undesirable societal behaviors

Soni Kumari, a member of the young women's listening club in Kamtaul village noted: "Almost 50 percent of the girls in our high school [out of a total of 300] listen to *Taru*. In fact, we have even painted a wall in our school to promote the listening of *Taru*. Every Monday in school, during the break, we meet to discuss the previously broadcast episode." Vandana Kumari, another listening group member, pointed to a specific result that came out of these discussions: "We discussed in school what to do for our friend.... She was only 16 when her parents got her married. She stopped coming to school. We knew she was staying at home. One day, when we saw her father coming to our school, we spoke to our teacher and asked him to convince her father to not keep his daughter at home. Now she has resumed her classes.... She will continue to study until she goes to her husband's home in a year or two."

Kumari Neha, a listening group member in Abirpur village, noted: "Our discussions of *Taru* have given us strength and confidence. Now I am not shy of speaking in front of my parents. Taru taught us that one should always speak sweetly and politely. When you mean well, who can oppose you? Even the devil will melt. We have all told our parents that we will like to go to college, and we will not marry in a household which demands dowry"(personal communication, September 5, 2002).

As noted at the beginning of the chapter, in Kamtaul village, family-based conversations between RHP Shailendra Singh, his wife Sunita, and their two younger daughters and niece (all members of the young women's listening club) led to a debunking of several traditional practices that humiliated lower-caste villagers.

Through dialogue, audience members share their similar or divergent perceptions of the information presented in an E-E program, and discuss the merits and demerits of adopting or rejecting the modeled behaviors. Furthermore, dialogue leads to mutual learning, acceptance of diversity, interpersonal trust, and understanding (Habermas, 1984). Dialogue cannot be separated entirely from information dissemination, however. In fact, when people engage in dialogue, opportunities for dissemination may surface when one person knows more than another person about a topic and chooses to express his/her viewpoint more persuasively.

Dialogues among audience members, sustained over a period of time, create an environment in which new decisions or actions may be considered, both individually and collectively. Often collective efficacy and collective actions emerge from such dialogic conversations.

■ Collective Efficacy and Actions
Stimulated through Dialogue

Our data provided numerous examples of how dialogue among *Taru* listeners inspired collective efficacy and action to solve social problems. As noted previously, in Abirpur village, young female and male members of *Taru* listeners' groups, after seven months of discussion and deliberation, started a school for underprivileged children, inspired by the character of Neha in the radio serial. Some 50 children attended this school regularly, which met six days a week, from 4 to 6 p.m. by the village well. Young women of 15–20 years of age taught these children. Young men talked to *dalit* parents to convince them to send their children to school. They also had to convince their parents that this was a worthwhile activity to undertake. Establishing the school was a collective act of both young men and women in Abirpur. Such mixed-sex collaboration is highly uncommon in Indian villages. As Sunita Kumari noted: "Before listening to *Taru*, we were shy and uncomfortable in talking to boys. Now that we are in a group, we feel comfortable to talk to them, and we do so on an equal footing."

The rise in collective efficacy among young women listeners of *Taru* was reflected by an incident when one of the research team members (Devendra Sharma) was shooting some video in Bihar in December, 2002. It is not common for young women to interrupt conversations among men, let alone challenge their veracity. During a male group interview, some young men claimed that, inspired by a *Taru* episode which portrayed the ills of substance abuse, they quit the habit of eating *gutka* (chewing tobacco). But the young women, who overheard their conversation, aggressively challenged their claim: "These boys are lying. A few may have left the habit, but most of them are just saying this in order to gain fame on the video." The act of challenging the boys openly reflects the collective efficacy gained by the young women's listeners' group in Abirpur village.

Another example from Abirpur village demonstrates how an individual's rise in self-efficacy can subsequently spur collective action. After listening to *Taru*, Dhurandhar Maharaj, a 17-year-old Hindu male listener, questioned the caste and religion-based discrimination that was prevalent in Abirpur, and decided do something about it: "When I heard Mangla [Taru's rogue brother] insult Shashikant for his low-caste, I was furious. Then I realized I myself did not mix with the Muslim students in my class. It took me two–three days to muster enough courage to sit next to Shakeel Anwar, who is Muslim. Now Shakeel is my best friend and all his friends are my friends" (personal conversation, September 3, 2002). Dhurandhar soon realized that Shakeel's younger sister stopped going to school after the eighth grade. Her parents were reluctant to send her to the neighboring town's school without an escort. Dhurandhar, Shakeel, and a number of their closest friends discussed this problem, and decided to take turns escorting Shakeel's sister. Once this plan was implemented, six other friends of Shakeel's sister, who also had stopped going to school for a similar reason, resumed their schooling. Dhurandhar noted: "Now they go in a group and it does not even matter if we can't escort them on certain days."

Our research indicates that listening to *Taru* stimulated inter-personal discussions about educational issues and motivated some listeners to engage in collective action to solve community problems. However, our data suggests, that social change seldom flows directly and immediately from simple exposure to an E-E media program. Consider the following possible impediments to social change sparked by an E-E program. First, audience individuals who attend to the disseminated messages in an E-E program, and dialogue about it over time, may discover that what works for a media character in the fictional storyline may not work for them in real-life. Second, there are always community members who resist the practice of new be-haviors. Third, after listening to an E-E program, certain community members may develop a sense of collective efficacy in solving a social problem, but the solution they devise may not be effective. Finally, although a listener may say that he/she believes in performing a certain action, these beliefs may not reflect his/her actions. Im-portantly, these impediments to social change may drive listeners back and forth between the competing poles of dissemination and dialogue. Specifically, when an impediment to social change is experienced, a listener may reflect more deeply on the disseminated message and then engage in subsequent dialogue to devise a new solution.

■ The Reflexive Turn from Dialogue to Dissemination

The dialectic of dissemination and dialogue was further illustrated in one of the collectively generated responses that emerged among

Taru's listeners. In July 2003, fifty members of *Taru* listener groups from the four villages of Bihar (Abirpur, Kamtaul, Madhopur, and Chandrahatti) took part in a participatory theater workshop over a three-day period. The workshop was led by professional folk artists who helped the participants develop skills in script writing, character development, costume and set design, voice projection, body movement, acting, and singing (see Harter, Sharma, Pant, Singhal, & Sharma, in press).

At the beginning of the workshop, the participants were asked to introduce themselves to the group by telling a story about their personal lives. These stories were situated in the context of the participants' families and communities. As the stories were told, a rich collage of narratives surfaced that held the potential for public performances focusing on the social issues at the center of the *Taru* storyline. The facilitators then helped the participants to identify common themes among the various stories so they could create a "meta-story" from which a performance script could emerge.

Facilitators encouraged the workshop participants to create performances that addressed important social issues in their communities. These personal stories were told in the participants' own vernacular and were woven together to create a master narrative to be performed publicly. Importantly, every aspect of the production of the performance—from character development, dialogues, and technical aspects of stage preparation—were co-created by the workshop participants. Thus, it was their dialogue with one another in story creation and in problem solving that made the productions possible (Plate 4.7).

The three-day participatory theatre workshop was followed by two days of public performances, which were widely promoted through word-of-mouth. The participants served as cast members, directors, stage managers, and technical staff. Four performaces, each about 90 minutes in length, were staged in each of the four villages for audiences that ranged in size from 300 to 500. Through engaging plots, songs, and poetry, these performances advocated for social justice in rural communities, including gender equality, empowerment of *dalits*, and small family size.

The dialogue between the 50 workshop participants, all avid listeners of *Taru*, shaped the public performances that were directly disseminated to some 1,500 audience members in the four village communities. So, what started as information dissemination in the form of a mass media message (*Taru*) became dialogue as listeners discussed the content of the program among themselves. This dialogue, over a period of time, led to several instances of collective organizing and action at the village level such as the production of theatrical performances in the four villages of Bihar State. Importantly, every aspect of this staged performance required dialogue to negotiate the development of characters, emplotments, and outcomes. Dialogue then became mass dissemination as the plays were performed before large audiences in each of the four villages where the participants lived. The dialectic between dissemination and dialogue will inevitably continue as audience members exposed to the theatrical performances discuss the messages and meanings of these performances with family and community members. Both social

Plate 4.7
Taru **listening club members engage in dialogue to develop the scripts of the participatory theater performances**
In July 2003, some 50 members of *Taru* listener groups took part in a participatory theater workshop in rural Bihar, creating performances that addressed important social problems in their communities. All production aspects of the theater performance—including character strands, emplotments, dialogues, stage settings, and props—were generated by the workshop participants through a dialogic process that lasted over three days.
Source: Personal Files of the Authors.

change, and resistance to change, will simultaneously occur as community members in these four villages continue to shift between the competing poles of dissemination and dialogue.

Interestingly, we observed a form of call and response in all the participatory theater performances in Bihar. During the plays, message dissemination occurred as the actors performed and engaged in interaction with one another in front of the assembled audience. The actors, in this instance, produced the call. The response occurred when audience members responded either by shouting a response toward the stage or by talking to another audience member (Plate 4.8).

Plate 4.8
Audience members "respond" to the performers "call" during a *Taru* participatory theater performance in Chandrahatti village, Bihar
During the performances, actors on stage often produced the call, for instance, "Should a girl child be treated any differently than a boy child?" The response occurred as audience members shouted a "No" response toward the stage. Some audience members would then begin talking to each another about the issue. So performers and audience members simultaneously engaged in both call and response.
Source: Personal Files of the Authors.

Dialogue often emerged when a controversial issue was addressed by the actors and audience members talked among themselves about the message embedded in the play. So performers and audience simultaneously engaged in both call and response as well as dissemination and dialogue.

■ Power, Resistance, and Paradoxical Behaviors

Despite engaging message dissemination through *Taru* (as well as the participatory theater performances) *and* compelling dialogue among audience members, our data provided numerous examples of how existing power structures in villages can serve as a barrier to social change. In fact, individuals or groups who wish to undertake a certain ameliorative action, often face resistance from social structures. For instance, in India, caste, gender, and class mediate the extent to which people can overcome restrictions and barriers to progress.

Both in Abirpur and Kamtaul villages, members of the young women's listeners' club criticized the caste bias of their elders, which prevented them from listening to *Taru* with other friends, who belonged to another caste. Initially, the young girls felt powerless to oppose these parochial traditions; however, soon they devised ways to subvert them. In Kamtaul, the young women agreed to individually hear the *Taru* episodes at home, and then later discuss them during school break. By August 2002, six months after *Taru*'s broadcasts began, they felt efficacious enough to openly gather at the local RHP clinic, or at someone's home, to listen collectively.

Paradox and contradiction are also an integral part of the process of social change (Papa et al., 2000). Since established patterns of thought and behavior are difficult to change, people often engage in an adjustment process until the new behavior patterns are fully internalized. For instance, Manoj Maharaj, RHP of Abirpur village, talked at great length about how caste-based discrimination was on the ebb in Abirpur. However, in a casual conversation, Maharaj strongly supported other kinds of discrimination. When author Singhal asked him if Abirpur village had any people living with AIDS, he said: "There are two AIDS patients in the neighboring village. And he [despite being the sole health provider in the area], will not touch them."

Gender equality was a prominent theme throughout the episodes of *Taru*. One of the most vocal proponents of this theme in Kamtaul village was Vandana Kumari, the daughter of Shailendra and Sunita Singh. During one of her interviews in December, 2002, when asked if she would spend her future life tending to the *chulha* [mud stove] (implying she would be a home-maker); she said: "I will not tend to the *chulha*. I will use a gas burner." Although, at that time, Vandana had internalized perceptions about the importance of women going to college and forging a career, she did not recognize that her views on using the gas burner versus the *chulha* contradicted this professed support for women being more than homemakers. Weick (1979) argued that this type of paradox emerges when a person does not recognize that their ideas within one system (for example, homemaking) contradict his/her ideas within another system, such as gender equality. However, when we met Vandana Kumari later in 2003 and 2004, she was articulating her ideas more clearly and enacting her professed beliefs about gender equality. In 2003, she enrolled for pre-medical studies in a neighboring district town, and in 2004 married a city-bred man of her own choice (with support from her parents).

So, power, resistance, and paradoxical thinking were apparent in our *Taru* research sites, as people struggled with social change. *Taru* played an important role in stimulating conversations and bringing personal and collective struggles to the fore. Conversations that support behavior change are important, even if that talk is not always supported by subsequent action. As Rushton (1975, 1976) observed, words alone can exert influence on the behavior of others. Thus, a mother who talks to her daughter about gender equality may influence her daughter to further her formal education, even though the mother still acts under patriarchal dominance. For instance, Neeraj Kumari, a family listeners' group member in Abirpur village, who plays the role of a traditional *bahu* [daughter-in-law], tending to the needs of her in-laws, husband, and two young children, noted: "My life is the way it is. But my children will marry whom they want ... we will not give or take dowry." Gudiya, a young listener in Madhopur said: "I don't know how life will turn out for me, but I will definitely make my daughter like Taru." Vandana Kumari, after 18 months of being caught in the *Taru* fever, told author Singhal in 2003: "I have become Taru."

Box 4.3: Minga Peru
Dissemination and Dialogue in the Amazonian Rainforest

Minga Peru, a non-governmental organization in the Peruvian Amazon, promotes reproductive health, sexual rights, gender equality, and income-generating activities in a region plagued by geographical isolation, poverty, disease, and patriarchal traditions (Elías, 2002).[7] "Minga" in the local Quechua language means "collaborative community work," and Minga's organizing for social change efforts in the Amazonas illustrate the dialectic between dissemination and dialogue.

Minga empowers Amazonian women, who suffer from poor reproductive health, a repressive home environment, and low self-esteem (Elías & Neira, 2004). In certain riverine communities, especially those inhabited by the Huambisa, Aguajun, and Shipibo-Conibo ethnic groups, women may bear on average 10 children (three times the national average), lose one or two children to disease, perhaps contract a sexually transmitted infection, and die before reaching the age of 50 (22 years less than the national average) (Bustamante, 2004; Farrington, 2003).

Minga's dissemination and dialogic activities in the Peruvian Amazon include the production and broadcast of a popular radio program called *Bienvenida Salud* (Welcome Health); the training of a cadre of community *promotoras* (promoters) who organize group listening and conversation sessions around *Bienvenida Salud*; and the implementation of various environmentally-sustainable, income-generating activities.

Bienvenida Salud is a half-hour entertainment-education radio program broadcast three times a week. It disseminates information on reproductive health, sexual rights, and gender equality with the explicit purpose of creating favorable attitudes, shifting social norms, and changing overt behavior (Singhal & Rogers, 2002; Sypher et al., 2002). By 2004, Minga Perú had broadcast over 900 episodes of *Bienvenida Salud*, earning audience ratings of between 45 and 50 percent among its target audience.

The mainstay of *Bienvenida Salud* is a lively, conflict-laden, intergenerational dialogue between its two hosts—Pashuca, who is a community health *promotora*, and Doña Rosa, her mother-in-law. Pashuca promotes gender equality, preventive health, family planning, and rejects all forms of domestic violence. Doña Rosa, however, resists such changes.

Interestingly, the disseminated social content on *Bienvenida Salud* is presented in dialogic form, which, in turn, encourages further dialogue among the listeners. This dialogue then spurs audience letter-writing to

---

Box 4.3: Minga Peru
(continued)

Minga, thereby influencing the next round of information disseminated on *Bienvenida Salud*. All *Bienvenida Salud* stories are based on real-life events, and sent to Minga by audience members as cards or hand-sewn letters (often painted on bark) using vegetable, stone, and natural colors as ink. In these letters, audience members describe their personal problems, struggles, and dilemmas. Romel Castro wrote: "I suffered psychological abuse from my father.... He often came home drunk and would insult my mother and hit her.... Sometimes I would see blood on her face. It's a big problem for me" (quoted in Farrington, 2003, p. 2). Minga distills stories like the ones provided by Romel into a dialogue between Pashuca and Doña Rosa. Further, in addition to on-air broadcasts, Minga provides *Bienvenida Salud* tapes to various local radio stations, to school teachers, and to community *promotoras* (who play the episodes on audio cassettes to small groups). This act of dissemination further spurs dialogue among group members.

Complementing Minga's broadcasts of *Bienvenida Salud*, are a host of on-the-ground interventions, led by a trained cadre of community *promotoras*. Minga trains young women, using culturally appropriate materials, to work as health promoters and change agents in the communities where they live. This training involves dissemination of information, skills training, and the like. *Promotoras* are taught the basics of male and female anatomy, detection of breast and cervical cancers, and simulation of the birth process (Farrington, 2003). They learn carpentry, sewing, weaving, and crocheting; and how to establish and run a fish farm; how to grow medicinal herbs; and create environmentally sustainable ecosystems through agroforestry and small animal husbandry projects. The *promotoras* represent Minga's partners and field-based change agents, modeling healthy reproductive lifestyles, initiating community discussions and dialogue, and serving as local resource persons for Minga's outreach. So, once trained, *promotoras* become spark-plugs for community discussions and dialogue.

In sum, Minga Peru's work in the Peruvian Amazonas empowers members of riverine communities, especially its women, to experience a higher quality of life; to make better informed choices with respect to their reproductive health; and to improve their self-esteem so they may attain their sexual and human rights. Its organizing for social change strategy dynamically manages multiple, co-existing dialectics of dissemination and dialogue.

Conclusions

In this chapter, we argued that both dissemination and dialogue are vital ingredients in organizing for social change efforts. Dissemination involves information transmission and is characterized by showing, telling, and even directing. Mass media messages, by their very nature, are mostly dissemination. Dissemination also occurs in interpersonal or group situations in which a more knowledgeable source conveys information, or an opinion, to other(s). We argue that dissemination is *necessary* in any organizing for social change effort.

Dialogue involves mutuality and reciprocity in information exchange. Through the iterative practice of dialogue, human relationships are co-created, co-regulated, and co-modified. Dialogue can be transformative as something new (empathy, trust, commonality) is created in the interaction for the co-participants. We argue that dialogue is *necessary* in any organizing for social change effort.

Too often, there is a tendency to dichotomize the dissemination and dialogic aspects of a social change phenomenon. We argue that dissemination and dialogue are inseparable, and agree with Peters (1999) that uncritical celebration of dialogue is as naïve as the uncritical criticism of dissemination.

From our analysis of the *Taru* project in India, we learn that E-E programs can disseminate pro-social models of behavior and spark processes of individual and social change through the formation of parasocial relationships between audience members and media characters. Audience members may consider changes in their own behavior based on what has worked or not worked for media characters. E-E programs can also spark dialogue and conversations among audience members as they consider behavior change at the individual and collective level. Some of these conversations may spark collective decisions and actions.

However, individual and social change is rarely a simple, linear process. Audience members may encounter powerful forces of resistance as they attempt to change power dynamics in a community. In addition, attempts to change behavior are often fraught with paradoxes and contradictions that point to the difficulty of altering entrenched actions within complex communities. Despite these difficulties, our findings suggest that synergistic possibilities for social action emerge when E-E broadcasts disseminate pro-social models of behaviors, and such on-air broadcasts are complemented with on-the-ground dialogue circles (as happens through group-based listening).

As we further reflect on the dialogue and conversations that were sparked by *Taru* it is important to remember that the broadcasts of the radio serial were dove-tailed with a series of on-the-ground activities in the four villages we studied. Posters and wall paintings were placed in strategic locations and folk performances dramatizing the storyline were were implemented a week before *Taru*'s first broadcast. Local rural health practitioners also spread the word about *Taru* and were helpful in the formation of listener's clubs. These activities undoubtedly primed the message reception environment in these four rural communities. Without this priming, they perhaps may not have been so ready to orchestrate the social change activities that were initiated.

Notes

1. The present chapter draws upon Singhal, Sharma, Papa, and Witte (2004); Papa, Singhal, Law, Pant, Sood, Rogers, and Shefner-Rogers (2000); Singhal (2004); Singhal and Rogers (1989, 2002); and Rao, Singhal, and Pant (2004).

2. The story of Abirpur's village school is documented in a film titled *Taru Comes to Abirpur* produced by author Singhal and Devendra Sharma, a member of the *Taru* research team. Interested readers may request a copy by writing to author Singhal at singhal@ohio.edu.

3. The *Taru*-sparked actions of Vandana and her family are documented in a film titled *Taru Has Changed My Life* produced by author Singhal and Devendra Sharma, a member of the *Taru* research team. Interested readers may request a copy by writing to author Singhal at singhal@ohio.edu.

4. For more on Paulo Freire, see the following websites: http://www.paulofreire.org/; http://www.infed.org/thinkers/et-freir.htm; http://wwwvms.utexas.edu/~possible/freire.html; http://nlu.nl.edu/ace/Resources/Documents/FreireIssues.html.

5. Numerous other organizations are involved in utilizing and diffusing the E-E strategy: Population Communications International (PCI), a non-governmental organization headquartered in New York City; Johns Hopkins University's Center for Communication Programs (JHU/CCP); Centers for Disease Control and Prevention (CDC) in Atlanta; The BBC World Service Trust; Population Media Center, an NGO headquartered

in Burlington, Vermont, the Soul City Institute for Health and Development Communication in South Africa, Puentos de Encuentro in Nicaragua, and Minga Peru in Peru. Several communication departments are now particularly oriented to studying or teaching about the E-E strategy, including the University of Southern California, the College of Communication at Ohio University; Johns Hopkins University's Bloomberg School of Public Health; the College of Communication and the Arts, Regent University; University of Natal, Durban, South Africa; and various others.

6. Together, the states of Bihar and Jharkhand have a population of 102 million, an annual per capita income of $101 (the lowest of any state in India), a total fertility rate (TFR) of 3.5, a contraceptive prevalence rate of 24 percent, and only 32 percent literacy.

7. Minga was established in 1998 by Eliana Elias, a graduate of the department of social communications from the University of Lima, and her husband, Luis Gonzalez, an Argentinean, in collaboration with the Amazonian Peoples Resources Initiative of the University of Kansas. Minga Peru now works in the Amazonas independently of APRI.

5 Dialectic of fragmentation and unity in rural Appalachia

Show me a hero, and I will write you a tragedy.
—F. Scott Fitzgerald, American novelist and writer
(quoted in http://encyclopedia.lockergnome.com/s/b/
F._Scott_Fitzgerald)

A few years ago, we met Hazel, a 57-year-old woman, at a Friday night community supper in Athens, Ohio, located in America's Appalachian region. Hazel suspects her weight, some 300 pounds, is one reason why she is diabetic. The good lord was kind to her, she noted, keeping her alive despite chronic health problems. She poured her heart out to us in ways that lonely people often do. She felt we were willing to listen, not judge. Hazel came to the supper directly from the doctor's office. She coughed and apologized instantly saying that she suffers from a "nervous reflux." The Friday night supper made her both nervous and excited.

Hazel lives five miles from Athens toward New Marshfield. The houses in her neighborhood are not tightly packed together like in Athens, but not so far apart that people can't be friendly to each other. Her neighbors, Hazel noted, rarely talked to her, perhaps because they looked down on her for being poorer than they are. This upset her. She couldn't figure these neighbors out for they are Christian people and should know better. The Friday night supper in Athens is her main opportunity to socialize and she never misses it.

One way of interpreting Hazel's story is to focus on the function of storytelling itself. Stories are intimately illustrative of the levels of belonging that individuals feel toward others in a community. A community is characterized by stories "produced by people talking with one another" (Ball-Rokeach, Gibbs, Gutierrez Hoyt, Jung, Kirn,

Matei, Wilson, Yuan, & Zhang, 2000, p. 1). Communities are integrated through structure, ecology, interpersonal networks, civic solidarity, and symbolic communication (Friedland, 2001; Fischer, 1982; Morrison, Howard, Johnson, Navarro, Plachetka, & Bell, 1998; Wellman, Carrington, & Hall, 1988). The connectedness and the sense of community that Hazel feels at the weekly supper is in sharp contrast to the isolation she feels at home. Her participation in the weekly community supper serves as both a reminder of her connection to others and her fragmented existence.

The purpose of the present chapter is to analyze the dialectic of *fragmentation* and *unity* in organizing for social change efforts that address poverty, hunger, and homelessness in the United States. By investigating community suppers that feed the poor, hungry, and homeless in the Appalachian region of the U.S., we analyze how the dialectical tensions between fragmentation and unity undergird social change initiatives.

Poverty, Hunger, and Homelessness in America

In the world, every five seconds, someone dies for lack of food; 25,000 will die of hunger today, and 10 million in one year. Half of sub-Saharan Africa is malnourished today, a figure expected to increase by 70 percent in 2010 (Nicholson, 2004).

In 2005, some 40 million Americans live in poverty, up from 25 million in 1980. Of these 13 million are children. Some 31 million Americans are "food insecure," not knowing where their next meal will come from (Borger, 2003). Of these, 10 million Americans experience *real hunger*, defined as the uneasy or painful sensation caused by lack of food.

■ Hunger in America

Hunger is on the rise in the United States (Clarke & Evans, 1994). In 2003, the need for emergency food rose by 20 percent in 25 major American cities (Borger, 2003). A number of programs exist in the United States to feed the hungry: Community suppers, soup kitchens, food pantries, meals on wheels, and so on (Plate 5.1). Some provide food and groceries once a week or once a month; some others provide hot meals twice a day. In Logan, Ohio, 25 miles away from where one of the present authors (Singhal) lives, one can see fortnightly traffic jams driven by hunger and poverty. Several hundred cars line-up at the drive-through food pantry run by Smith Chapel United Methodist Church to pick up food.

However, what happens in Logan, Ohio or in countless other places in the United States, is fairly invisible to policy-makers in Washington, D.C., the nation's capital. The policy, media, and public discourse on poverty, hunger, and homelessness in the U.S. is apathetically silent (Harter, Berquist, Titsworth, Novak, & Broakaw, in press). Few debates occur on these topics under the rotunda of the U.S. Congress, or on the front pages of the *New York Times*. Policy-driven initiatives to end hunger and poverty, such as Franklin Delano Roosevelt's New Deal in the 1930s (during the height of the Great Depression) and Lyndon Johnson's Great Society programs of the 1960s, are all but faint echoes from a distant past (Borger, 2003).

Plate 5.1
Men line up outside a soup kitchen in Chicago during the Great Depression of the 1930s
Although the Great Depression ended nearly seven decades ago, some 31 million Americans in 2005 are "food insecure," not knowing where their next meal will come from. Hunger and poverty are on the rise in the United States.
Source: U.S. Government Archives.

Box 5.1: Micky Weiss, Two Academics, and Food Recovery Benefiting Millions[1]

In 2005, an estimated 30 million Americans depended on non-profit food distribution charities to supplement their diets, making up for calories they could not afford to buy. A vast network stands at the heart of this charitable effort, starting with approximately 240 food banks (many belonging to a national network, America's Second Harvest) and other food recovery groups in every state. These supply 50,000 community outlets where individuals and families can get food. Most of the food comes from donations by manufacturers, processors, wholesalers, brokers, farmers, and other commercial firms. Government contributions make up a small fraction of the total food surplus, which reached 1.4 billion pounds in 2000 and is closer to 2.0 billion pounds in 2005. Shockingly, more than enough food is discarded in the U.S., between field and table, to feed the hungry.

In 1987, Mickey Weiss, a retired produce wholesaler, was visiting his son's dock at the Los Angeles Wholesale Market. On his way, Weiss' car passed a group of homeless people, who were heating stale bread over an open fire. Minutes later, at the family's vegetable company, Weiss watched a forklift hoist two pallets of raspberries (that had not sold in a timely way) and drop them into a dumpster! Something in Weiss' mind clicked that had remained unappreciated over his decades of business experience. "Why were good fruits and vegetables being thrown away?" he suddenly questioned. "Why could they not be directed to the hungry?" (Sturgulewski, 2001).

Working the phones, Weiss convinced wholesalers to donate produce that was "edible, but not sellable." He rounded up high school students to call church-based pantries, congregate meals programs, missions, battered women's shelters, daycare centers, and other agencies serving the needy throughout Southern California to see which ones could use produce to feed their clients. He worked with agriculture departments and government agencies to cut the red tape that discouraged donations of unsold food. Thanks to Weiss, a novel idea was born.

But Weiss' dream was greater, and for several years it remained stymied. He wanted to see similar programs recovering fresh produce operating in every city in America. But only Houston followed Los Angeles' lead and then not much happened for two years. Food banks had been shunning perishable foods because they are so difficult to handle, or had simply been unaware of the existence or the importance of these surpluses. Then in 1991, Weiss met two academics with a passion for reducing people's risks of chronic illness. Peter Clarke and Susan Evans taught at the University of Southern California's (USC's) Annenberg School for Communication and also conducted research in USC's Department of Preventive Medicine. They understood the importance of nutritious diets for health, realized that fresh produce offered great benefits for primary prevention of many conditions, and grasped that people in poverty cannot afford to eat well. They believed that poor nutrition was an even greater menace than hunger. Evans and Clarke quickly became inspired by Weiss' local achievements and established a project to transplant the essence of produce recovery as widely as possible, calling their undertaking From the Wholesaler to the Hungry. They began visiting as many cities as they could persuade to invite them, talking with food banks, potential sources of donations nearby, recipient agencies, political leaders, and more.

This hands-on experience led Clarke and Evans to develop their own model for disseminating what Weiss had started in Los Angeles (Clarke & Evans, 1994). Slowly, their city-by-city visits began paying off, and Evans and Clarke documented accomplishments and pitfalls so that other places could learn. By 2005, their tireless mentoring had launched nearly 150 fresh produce recovery efforts in 44 states and the District of Columbia. Programs are now offering nearly 300 million pounds of produce to low-income people annually. Along the way, Clarke and Evans began managing a grant making program of Kraft Foods and also forged an agreement with the Soref Foundation. Together, between 1995 and the end of 2005, these sources will have channeled nearly $25 million into charitable, surplus fresh food distribution.

Clarke and Evans's crusade for healthier eating has recently turned from the supply-side to the demand-side of the equation. With colleagues at USC's Information Sciences Institute they are developing message-tailoring tools whereby community pantries can provide each low-income client with just the recipes and food handling tips that match a household's characteristics and that align with the fresh foods available that day (Hovy, Philpot, Evans, Clarke, & Woolsey, 2005). Each recipient takes away a personalized, illustrated flyer, "Quick! Help for Meals," along with the food. Early field trials show that this boosts the use of fresh produce in meals by 50 percent, compared to handing out standardized recipes and tips.

Clarke and Evans took Weiss' dream, mixed it with their passion, to make possible healthy, nutritious meals for millions of Americans who would otherwise go hungry.

In fact, much of the U.S. welfare system built during the New Deal and the Great Society was dismantled in the mid-1990s during President Clinton's welfare reforms, which set a time line on how long the poor or unemployed could draw social security payments. With these safety nets gone, hunger and poverty in the U.S. have risen. To exacerbate, the minimum wage in the U.S., adjusted for inflation, has gone down 22 percent since 1980.

Rising hunger, poverty, and homelessness in the United States has been accompanied by a rise in soup kitchens, food pantries, and homeless shelters. Rural America in particular has been badly hit (Fichten, 1991). The idyllic portraits of rural America in the paintings of Norman Rockwell and Georgia O' Keefe mask a stark reality. Some 20 percent of the American population lives in rural areas, where the population is older, poorer, sicker, and less educated (Duncan, 1999). Compared to urban America, rural poverty rates are double. Further, rural America has fewer hospital beds and physicians per capita, fewer job opportunities, and fewer homeless shelters and soup kitchens.

■ Homelessness in America

A person is *homeless*[2] if he/she lacks a fixed, regular, and adequate night-time residence. The homeless live in emergency or transitional shelters, cars, public parks, abandoned buildings, bus and train stations, and the like (National Coalition for the Homeless, 2002, Fact Sheet 2). The National Law Center on Homelessness and Poverty (2004) reported that during 2003 over 3 million men, women, and children were homeless in the U.S.[3] Half of these are women and children who often experience homelessness to flee domestic violence. Further, half of the homeless are African-Americans, even though they constitute only 12 percent of the U.S. population (Figure 5.1). The number of homeless people in the U.S. greatly exceeds the available shelter space. In rural America, there exist fewer shelters and higher levels of homelessness.

Homelessness is increasing in America because of a growing shortage of affordable rental housing and increasing poverty. Homelessness and poverty are inextricably linked. Poverty rates have risen because of eroding employment opportunities, lower wages, and declining public assistance programs. A whopping 37 percent

Figure 5.1
The racial profile of homeless people in the United States
Half of the homeless in the U.S. in 2004 are African-Americans, even though they constitute only 12 percent of the U.S. population. Homelessness is increasing in America because of a growing shortage of affordable rental housing and increasing poverty.

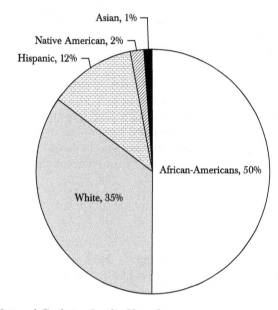

Source: National Coalition for the Homeless.

of the homeless in America had their welfare benefits cut or reduced (Institute for Children and Poverty, 2001). In 2004, people are working more to make the same money. In most U.S. states, a minimum wage worker will have to work 80–90 hours a week to afford a two bedroom apartment at 30 percent of their total income (as per the federal definition of affordable housing [National Coalition for the Homeless, 2002, Fact Sheet 1]). Between 1973 and 1993, some 2.2 million low-rental housing units disappeared from the market in America, abandoned on account of increasing rents. The benefits of economic growth in the U.S. are unequally distributed. The rising tide did not lift all boats; in fact, the most vulnerable boats have either sunk or are barely staying afloat.[4]

Box 5.2: Barbara Ehrenreich
On Not Getting by in America

In 1998, Barbara Ehrenreich, a well-to-do freelance writer, decided to experience the indignities of earning poverty-level wages. Engaging in old-fashioned "immersion journalism," Ehrenreich moved from Florida to Maine to Minnesota living in cheap motels, and taking such jobs as a waitress, a hotel maid, a house cleaner, and a Wal-Mart salesperson (Ehrenreich, 2001). These jobs employ millions of Americans and they typically pay six or seven dollars an hour. Ehrenreich discovered that not only are these jobs physically and mentally exhausting, a person must often work at least two jobs to afford decent housing. Further, when a person works long hours, they are more susceptible to falling sick; yet, few of these back-breaking, low-paying jobs provide health insurance.

Not having health insurance creates significant problems for low wage earners. While working as a waitress in Florida, Ehrenreich befriended Gail, a low wage earner who was supposed to be on her company's health plan. The company claimed, however, that they lost Gail's application and had to start the paperwork all over again. Without the health plan, and without the estrogen supplements that her health plan covered, Gail suffered debilitating migraine headaches. Each visit to the doctor and pharmacy cost her hard-earned dollars. Ehrenreich also discussed the case of a roofer who lost his job because he missed work after he cut his foot. The problem was exacerbated by an infection, but he was unable to pay for the prescribed antibiotic. So, the indignity of poverty goes hand-in-hand with poor health.

Under Clinton's welfare reforms, people in the U.S. who received monetary assistance from government programs, now must work multiple jobs to support themselves. Sadly, many of these workers, who have internalized highly disciplined mechanisms of control to work multiple jobs, cannot afford the security deposits (typically the first and last month's rent "up front") to sign a rental lease. They have little choice but to live in hotel rooms, leased on a weekly or monthly basis. The meager wages they earn rarely allows them to save enough to sign a standard rental lease (Ehrenreich, 2001).

Unlike the Grameen Bank in Bangladesh, the control systems internalized by the working poor in the United States, provide no reasonable opportunities for emancipation from oppression. Ehrenreich (2001) argues that small businesses that earn hundreds of thousands of dollars per year and large corporations such as Wal-Mart that earn billions of dollars each year make their profits on the backs of the working poor. One

---

Box 5.2: Barbara Ehrenreich
(Continued)

---

would think that full-time employment in the U.S., one of the wealthiest countries in the world, should allow a person to have a decent standard of living. Not so. Yet, corporations believe they will not be able to survive in the global economy if they pay workers more money.

In a recent lecture at Ohio University, where author Singhal was in the audience, Ehrenreich posed the following question to the audience: "Aren't you ashamed to live in a country where the largest public housing system is the Federal penitentiary system?"

Fragmentation and Unity in Organizing the Poor

Dialectic theory provided us with a framework to explain the process of organizing for social change within community suppers that feed the poor, hungry, and the homeless. In each of the community suppers we observed, multiple organizing activities took place including setting up the facility where the meal is served, coordinating meal preparation, distribution, and clean up. Participants may also plan for future activities together such as looking for work, sharing an apartment, or seeking medical attention. The organizing activities that are the focus of this chapter are consistent with Mumby's (2001) description of organizing through communicating as "the process of creating collective, coordinated structures of meaning through symbolic practices oriented toward the achievement of organizational goals" (p. 587).

Dialectically-speaking, people who are homeless are often isolated from mainstream society in ways that lead to a *fragmented* existence (Wright, 2005). Rather than feeling connected to others, they see themselves as lonely and separate. In the struggle for survival, they even see other homeless people as competitors rather than allies, further contributing to feelings of fragmentation. Simultaneously, there may be attempts by relatively well-to-do community members to reach out to the homeless in ways that build *unity* in a community setting. The homeless may also band together in ways that connect and temporarily reduce the pain of loneliness.

■ Community

A *community* is characterized by one or more of the following features: defined boundary, close affinity, common interest, and social control (Moemka, 1998). Hillery (1968) defined community as "that unit of social organization or structure which comes into being when inter-actional activities become sufficiently regularized or patterned for us to say that the total complex of them comprise an identifiable entity" (p. 198). This definition of community emphasizes communication, group formation, and formal structure (Berkowitz & Wolff, 2000; Bloom, 2000; Caswell, 2001; Cohen & Phillips, 1998; Constantino-David, 1982; Friedland, 2001; MacIver, 1928). When most people think of community they think of a place in which people connect and interact as they carry on daily activities. These interactions can focus on playful activities or on solving common problems. When people feel a sense of community there are common identifications that unify the group. Members are motivated to continue their asso-ciation with one another, and thrive on it. Also important to note, however, is that people create community life and weave networks of social capital based on competing desires and experiences of both *fragmentation* and *unity*. In order to clarify the dimensions of the frag-mentation and unity dialectic that is present in community, consider the descriptions presented next.

■ Fragmentation

Fragmentation is likely to occur when there exist multiple, competing voices and interpretations in a discursive social setting. This multi-vocality often separates people from one another rather than unifying them (Martin, 1992; Meyerson, 1991; Miller & O'Leary, 1987; Ruud, 1995). Multiple discourses may contribute to fragmentation as dif-ferent dynamics surface in the process of organizing (Putnam & Fairhurst, 2001). For instance, in organizations where there exists a great deal of ambiguity regarding rules and norms, people may find it difficult to interact with others. The result of such fragmentation is that people are disconnected from one another even when they share a common physical space. In essence, fragmentation occurs when there is no form of identification that unifies people to communicate, work, or play with one another in ways that are personally or socially rewarding. People who are fragmented often feel a deep sense of isolation from others. Depression and anger are also common among people who experience fragmentation. If fragmentation continues, a person may lose the ability to connect with others even when others show compassion.

■ Unity

Although a community may be comprised of diverse people, unity within a group implies oneness in spirit, sentiment, aims, purpose, interests and feelings. Even complex groups comprised of many related parts may display unity if the members act as a totality or a whole. Unity holds communities together even when internal and external forces attempt to loosen the ties that bind the collective together. Displays of unity occur when people in a community act together to accomplish a goal that requires the energy and collective effort of all members. Unity may also be exhibited when group members communicate social support for one another. This social support could take the form of emotional support, informational support, and instrumental support (House, 1981; Miller, 2003). Emotional support is exhibited when one person lets another person know they are cared for. Informational support involves providing facts or advice that may help a person solve a problem. Finally, instrumental support offers an individual physical or material assistance in completing a task (e.g., helping someone cook dinner).

Our Research Site and Data

We participated in a total of 30 community suppers sponsored by seven different churches, community groups, and non-profit organizations in the states of Kentucky, Michigan, Ohio, and West Virginia. The total number of hours in participant observation was approximately 450 hours (3 people × 30 suppers × 5 hours per supper). Our involvement in these community suppers ranged from helping to set up tables, chairs, and place settings; cooking the meals to be served; serving the meals; participating in the dinners by sitting among the attendees and engaging in conversation; and cleaning up afterwards.

We would usually arrive at 4:00 in the afternoon and leave at about 9:00 in the evening. Reflective field notes were written immediately following each supper. Importantly, because we were so actively involved in all aspects of the community suppers, our field notes represent the perspective of co-participants.

■ Interviews and Informal Conversations

Both formal interviews and informal conversations were part of the data collected for this project. Formal in-depth interviews were conducted with 33 different workers and volunteers who worked at the community suppers. These interviews (ranging from 30 to 90 minutes) were tape-recorded and transcribed. Questions centered on the experiences of interviewees during the community suppers including types of participation, memorable events, and the meanings the event held for them.

Informal conversations were held with 142 different people who attended the community suppers. With some respondents, three or four separate conversations were conducted across different suppers. All these conversations were with the poor; some were also homeless. Fearing that tape recording equipment would limit participation, we did not record any of these conversations. We concentrated carefully on what was said during these conversations and recreated the text as faithfully as possible in field notes written immediately after the conclusion of the meals. These conversations focused on the meaning that the community suppers held for the attendees and memorable events that had transpired during their attendance.

■ Good Works' Community Suppers

There were many similarities among the different groups sponsoring community suppers. The most participative and complex was the Friday Night Community Supper orchestrated by Good Works, a non-profit organization located in Athens, Ohio, that provides shelter to the poor and homeless in Appalachia along with a variety of other social services (Santee, 2001).

Appalachia is one of the poorest regions in the United States and is the label for a 200,000-square-mile area running along the spine of the Appalachian Mountains from southern New York to northern Mississippi. It includes all of West Virginia and parts of 12 other states: Alabama, Georgia, Kentucky, Maryland, Mississippi, New York, North Carolina, Ohio, Pennsylvania, South Carolina, Tennessee, and Virginia. Among these, Appalachian Ohio, where Good Works is based, has a population of 1.4 million and is one of the poorest regions in the United States. In 2005, nearly one-fifth of the families in Appalachian Ohio lived in poverty, earning $15,000 or less per year for a family of three. Despite the local presence of Ohio University in Athens, Ohio, the college-going rate for Appalachian Ohio is 30 percent, compared to 62 percent for the U.S.

The Friday Night Supper at Good Works has been ongoing since 1992. The idea for this weekly event emerged when Keith Wasserman, the founding director of Good Works (Plate 5.2), realized that they could not always tell what happened to the people who had participated in the organization's programs (as workers, volunteers, and clients). The Friday supper would be a reunion of sorts to allow people to reconnect, and also provide a place for others to meet for the first time. This would be an opportunity to rekindle and sustain friendships and to share in one another's lives. The Friday Night Supper, which attracts from 125 to 140 people, is now an integral part of the Good Works organization (Plate 5.3).

A sponsoring organization shoulders the responsibility of procuring the food and coordinating the cooking, serving, and cleaning. Many of the poor who attend the dinner also help out with cooking, setting up, serving, and cleaning up afterwards. To use Keith's words, "this is a soup kitchen in reverse." The Friday Night Supper does not set up a structure where those with financial means provide handouts to poor people who wait in line to receive food. Keith believes that such structures may work in emergency situations but they make the poor feel worthless, devoid of dignity. By organizing an ongoing event and creating a structure where the poor work alongside their more well-to-do community counterparts, a sense of dignity is fostered. The poor can say with pride, "I worked at the Friday Night Supper and we all had a great time together."

At the Good Works Friday night community supper, the food is served "family style." Each table seats eight people and includes a big salad bowl, along with large dish for the main entree, the vegetables, and the bread. Good Works could more easily serve the food in the style of a soup kitchen by having several big pots and trays of food in a line where people can approach the servers with plates in hand. Such a structure, however, sets up an "us" versus "them" environment with the poor cast as the marginalized other. By serving family style, more work is created for the cooks, the servers, and the cleaners. There are many more serving bowls, pans, and dishes to fill, serve, and clean. The food distribution process is also more complicated. But Good Works believes the additional work is worth it. By sitting at common tables, the well-to-do and the poor share and pass food to each other, signifying a contact between equals.

Community suppers help to spark social change by connecting the disconnected. So many homeless people are disconnected from people around them, particularly from the wealthier people who live in comfortable homes while they live on nearby street corners.

Plate 5.2
Keith Wasserman, founder of Good Works with "Kermit the Frog" during a 2005 Friday Night Community Supper in Appalachian Ohio
Wasserman voluntarily lived as a homeless person in various American cities to first-hand understand poverty, hunger, and homelessness. These street-based experiences shaped the design of Good Works' Friday Night Community Suppers. *Source:* Keith Wasserman.

Plate 5.3
**The Good Works Friday Night Community Supper creates a
comfortable space for the poor and the homeless to connect with
other community members**
The Friday Night Supper, which attracts 125–140 people, serves as a weekly
reunion for the homeless, and also a place for the homeless and well-to-do
community members to connect on an ongoing basis. Unlike in soup kitchens
where people line up for food, the meal in Good Works community suppers is
served "family style" with each table seating eight people. By sitting at common
tables, the well-to-do and the poor pass food to each other, signifying a contact
between equals.
Source: Personal Files of the Authors.

Through these connections, the homeless develop the support networks which may help some of them to move from helplessness to
self-sufficiency. Importantly, these connections are with other
homeless people as well as well-to-do community members. This
inspires social change by building community across different socio-
demographic groups who otherwise may never come in contact with
one another.

Box 5.3: Keith Wasserman and Good Works

After experiencing a tumultuous youth in the city of Cleveland, which included both drug addiction and drug peddling, Keith Wasserman arrived in Athens, Ohio in 1976 to begin his freshman year at Ohio University. Little did he know that Athens, Ohio would become the place of his calling, including his place of service to the poor and the homeless.

Keith founded Good Works, Inc., a Christian non-profit ministry in the early 1980s, building on a senior year internship project at Ohio University. Good Works began with Keith remodeling the basement of his Athens home to open an emergency shelter for homeless people. In 1985, the Good Works shelter moved out of Keith and Darlene's (his wife) basement into its present facility—The Timothy House (named after after Keith and Darlene's son). Timothy House includes four bedrooms with 15 beds, a living room, a kitchen, two bathrooms, two offices, and a large eating/meeting room. In 1994, Good Works purchased another property, The Hannah House. This facility, unlike an emergency shelter, provides a long-term transitional housing opportunity to homeless single men and women, enabling them to move toward independence.

Good Works is more than a homeless shelter. Residents of Timothy House represent a community. Good Works builds trust, teaches responsibility, and strengthens people's faith in themselves and God. Good Works' staff members help the homeless to identify the underlying factors that led to their current situation, moving them from dependence to self-sufficiency.

Good Works' activities were shaped, in part, by Keith's personal and voluntary forays in living as a homeless person. To design a need-based and compassionate program for the poor and the homeless, Keith lived as a homeless person in various American cities, accepting meals at soup kitchens and attending community suppers. Immersed in a voluntary culture of homelessness and poverty, Keith reflected on his experiences, writing extensive field notes and rich diaries (some of these are available on the Good Works website: www.good-works.net/). These experiences informed Good Works' community-building activities among the poor and homeless in rural Appalachia.

Each year, Good Works provides some 200 homeless people a safe, clean, and secure environment to stay. In addition, Good Works provides an estimated 16,000 meals to the poor and homeless each year, including the Friday Night community supper held at The Plains United Methodist Church during winter months and on the Good Works Luhrig Road property (picnic style) the remainder of the year.

Box 5.3: Keith Wasserman and Good Works
(Continued)

Good Works has initiated several other projects to promote employ-ment opportunities for the poor and homeless in Appalachia. One such project is "Good Gifts," a small business venture to help the poor both locally and globally. Working with two international organizations—Ten Thousand Villages and Servv International—Good Works purchases hand-crafted items made by poor people in developing countries and sells them locally (http://www.good-works.net/).

Over lunch in May, 2005, when author Singhal asked Keith Wasserman to reflect on his past three decades of work with the homeless in Appalachia, he noted: "The homeless have a need to connect ... both among themselves and with others in the community. Good Works makes these connections possible."

The Dialectic of Fragmentation and Unity in Community Suppers

The dialectic of fragmentation and unity emerged in the narratives of the organizers, workers, and volunteers, as well as the stories of the poor and the homeless in the community suppers we visited.

■ Communication and Unity

The community suppers that we observed view social change as a process of building unity within community. This unity building pro-cess includes re-connecting the poor and homeless to other people. Some of these connections are with other oppressed people. Other connections are with wealthier members of the community who desire to work alongside the poor.

Community suppers have certain structures in place that foster connections and mutual learning. Participating in meal preparation, serving, and clean-up operations integrates the poor into a setting of organized task completion. Their presence is dignified. They are not being given charity. Rather, they are working with people who all participate in making the meal a success. Their role in the organizing of the community supper is important, no matter how small.

In the community suppers, the poor form connections with others who experience similar problems. Collaborative solutions may then be discovered. For example, two homeless people may pool resources to afford an apartment. Also, connections are made between the poor and the relatively well-to-do community members. When people from different socio-economic groups connect, the poor can access ideas, resources, and possibilities for action that they may have never considered previously. The poor further realize that the poor and the middle class have a common platform of engagement. When more affluent community members work alongside their poor neighbors, hope is restored among the poor. Social change becomes possible when the poor recognize they have a support network.

The integration of the poor and the well-to-do community members prompts social change in other ways too. Help may be given to the homeless in finding shelter. Guidance may be given on job training and employment possibilities. Available medical care services may be identified. Through such assistance, the homeless are able to concentrate less on surviving on a day-to-day basis, and may plan for the future.

At Good Works (GW) a starting point for the process of building unity begins when volunteers who will be cooking the Friday dinner listen to a GW employee describe the history of the meal. This con-textualization is both inspiring and motivational. The compassion that motivates GW staff and the volunteers who work at the Friday Night Suppers is kindled. Some first time volunteers might worry about the daunting task of meal preparation for 125–140 people, but experienced GW volunteers reassure them by saying, "we can do this because we won't be allowed to fail. Our safety net is woven with the threads of our poor neighbors who appreciate all that we do" (field notes, 1999).

When authors Michael and Wendy Papa participated in their first Friday Night Supper, they were part of a group of eight volunteers. While their group prepared the meal, GW staff and community members (including local poor and homeless people) filtered in and out of the kitchen and dining area. Some came in to just smile and say hello. Others helped bring food out to the tables. Some set up the tables; others distributed the place settings. These activities occurred with few words being spoken. As Michael observed in his field notes, "We are involved together in making this dinner happen both because it is the task at hand and because we care about one another" (field notes, 1999).

The Friday Night Supper sponsored by GW reveals some interesting dimensions of building unity within community (Eisenberg, 1998; Jason, 1997; Mandell, 2001; Nalbandian & Oliver, 1999; Naparstek & Dooley, 1998; Warburton, 1998; Warren, 1998). One way to build unity among people is to establish clear boundaries so participants know what to expect in a situation. When boundaries are established, common norms and rules begin to develop making it easy for people to coordinate actions. The boundary of the community suppers is defined by meal preparation and serving, dinnertime conversations, and cleaning up afterwards. Unity is created as people develop close ties with one another through conversations about common interests. Finally, unity is displayed through the establishment of connections, fellowship, and solidarity between and among people (Christenson, Fendley, & Robinson, 1989)

GW's Friday Night Suppers also draw attention to how unity may be created by communication, group formation, and formal structure. In order to orchestrate the suppers for 125–140 people, regular patterned interaction among participants is required, including a formal structure of interlocking activities (McLeod, Daily, Guo, Eveland, Bayer, Yan, & Wang, 1996; Warren, 1978). The relationship among participants, while voluntary and optional, is collectivistic in terms of the interlocking actions that are performed to prepare the dinner, serve it, and clean up afterwards. In the weekly suppers, community members—through informal conversations—form intimate and enduring relationships.

Selfless Service and Unity   Moemeka (1996) explains that there can be no unity within community without individual members who serve selflessly. The sustenance of the community spirit demands that the hungry be fed, that the sick be looked after, and that the community takes care of what the individual does for a living during periods of illness (Ewalt, 1998; Flora, 1992; Moemeka, 1989, 1998; William & Windebank, 2000).

The centrality of selfless service is shown in author Michael Papa's field summary of a community supper sponsored by a Methodist Church in the Appalachian region of Ohio: "After attending this supper, I developed a deeper understanding of the process of building unity within communities. Building unity is a process of doing things together, working toward a common goal, sharing thoughts, disclosing personal information, and giving from the heart." Further, author Papa noted: "As volunteers, we worked collaboratively in a small circle. We were also embedded in a larger circle that contained the members of the church staff, and the community people who attended and worked at the supper. We prepared and cooked together. We served and ate together. We cleaned up together. We shared our thoughts and our histories and we gave of ourselves." Author Wendy Papa noted: "We were embedded in a support structure that would not allow failure. This supper was about people connecting with one another.... When people connect with one another, we end the fragmentation experienced in isolation. Through sharing and listening and doing together we build unity" (field notes, 2000).

The preceding observation clarifies clearly what is possible when people connect with one another and commit to accomplishing something of value together. When the poor and homeless work alongside wealthier members of the community, the differences between them cease to be of importance. Deep identification exists between and among community supper participants. Despite differences in socioeconomic status, participants must recognize that they comprise one community. The task of preparing the dinner and cleaning up requires task identification. People must be willing to share a part of themselves with others. When a strong community is built, structures are put in place that people not only identify with; they work to protect those structures.

The most important dimension of identification that emerged in community suppers was interpersonal identification. Feelings of isolation and humiliation dominate the lives of the homeless. Being able to talk to other human beings lifts some of this isolation. They are accepted by those around them, not judged. While connection and acceptance does not solve all their problems, they derive agency from a safety net of supportive connections.

Spirituality and Unity   Spirituality is often embodied among many of the poor and those who serve the poor. Religious spirituality is often used as a tool for keeping the social order and protecting social norms and communication rules (Mbiti, 1969; Moemeka, 1994). This may not mean forcing religion upon people but rather helping people to recognize the spirituality that is within them.

One person who exemplifies this trait is Keith Wasserman, the founding director of GW. Keith believes that spirituality must emerge from within. When Keith walks through the door to participate in the Friday Night Supper in the basement of Central Avenue United Methodist Church in Athens, Ohio, he brings along his favorite puppet, Kermit the Frog. He does a great imitation and children look up at him with wide eyes and smiles. At the community suppers, Keith jokes with the crowd, getting audience participation, and asking people what they are thankful for. On one occasion, a young girl of about six suddenly spoke up and said that she would like to thank God since he made us all. That comment drew warm laughter from the crowd and a few said "Amen." On that note, food was passed around and the meal started (field notes, 2001).

Keith's facilitation of audience participation helps to build unity among Friday Night Supper participants. He does not preach to those assembled for the supper, rather he asks them to share their thoughts and experiences. Through this approach, he helps community members to both connect and identify with one another through shared experiences of joy and suffering. Importantly, as Chaskin and Abunimah (1999) explain, when individuals in a community feel a sense of connection with one another they feel prepared to participate in the community building process. This sense of connection may not have been realized if Keith presented a more structured religious service. By facilitating an audience-centered approach to spirituality, Keith allows the group to define its own spiritual culture rather than imposing one upon them.

Reconnecting the Isolated   One part of building unity is to reconnect people who have faced separation. Too many of the homeless have been discarded by family, friends, and neighbors. These contacts are usually not renewed when a person is homeless. Eventually, the homeless internalize the belief that they are worthless, not deserving of human contact. If this feeling builds up over a number of years it becomes difficult to reconnect the isolated person with others. This is why so many homeless people shun others and frequently lash out in anger when a person attempts to connect with them. Consider Terry's story.

Terry, a woman in her late 40s and mother of four children, presented one of the most poignant examples of this process to us. Terry first came to a community supper at a Methodist Church in Detroit, Michigan a month after her husband beat her severely, breaking her jaw and slashing her face with a knife. While he was chasing her, he banged his head on a kitchen countertop and passed out. She rushed her children out of the house and never returned. Without the money or insurance to pay for plastic surgery, her face bears the scars she will carry for the rest of her life.

Once released from the hospital's emergency room, Terry and her children had no place to go. When they showed up at the apartment of two of her closest friends, they turned them away saying they had no room. Fortunately, one of her friends agreed to let her (and her children) stay. After a couple of weeks, however, she realized that her family was causing tension in the house. They needed to find another housing option.

When Terry heard about a community supper in the local neighborhood, she decided to attend. It was the first time she had left her house since her face was slashed. She was very self-conscious; she didn't want people to stare. When Terry walked in the door, the man who ran the community supper asked her to sit next to him. He talked to her normally, not staring at her scars. He introduced Terry to several other people. During her second visit, Terry learned that the man directing the community supper program ran a life-in-transition center for people who wished to get back on their feet. Terry stayed at this center for two months until she found a job that paid her enough to rent an apartment. Before coming to the community supper, Terry didn't think there was much hope for the homeless. Now she thinks differently. Even though she has her own apartment, Terry regularly attends the community suppers. As Terry explains, "These people are family to me. Unlike the people who I thought were my friends, the people who go to the supper care about each other" (personal interview, 1999).

Terry came to her first community supper disconnected and lonely. By connecting with the program director and other community members, she rediscovered hope. The path from hopelessness to hope was paved by the social capital embedded in the relationships she developed at the supper. *Social capital* is defined as the building of interpersonal networks between people so as to enhance social trust, foster reciprocity, and facilitate coordination in order to benefit the collective (Preece, 2002; Putnam, 1995, 2000; Wallis, 1998a, 1998b; Woolcock, 1998). Social capital is enacted through patterns of civic engagement, trust, and mutual obligation among persons (Bellah, Madsen, Sullivan Swidler, & Tipton, 1985; Coleman, 1988, 1990; Kawachi, Kennedy, Bruce, & Lochner, 1997; Kawachi, Kennedy, & Lochner, 1997; Portes, 1998; Taylor, 1989; Weitzman & Kawachi, 2000). In terms of the impact of social capital on a community, when people connect with one another; trust grows, improving their lot both as individuals and as a collective.

Building Networks of Support among the Homeless   In the community suppers we attended, well-to-do community members often helped the poor to find affordable housing, pursue possible job opportunities, or locate supportive community organizations. Community suppers also served the purpose of connecting the homeless to one another. A homeless person needn't be helpless. When people connect with one another, synergistic possibilities arise.

Consider the experiences of Sally, a homeless woman from Toledo. When Sally first went to a community supper, she didn't know anyone. She was afraid and embarrassed of what people would think of her. After people started conversations with her, she felt at ease. During her third community supper, Sally befriended Janice. They realized they had much in common, including daughters who were the same age. Janice helped Sally get a job at a local store. Some weeks later, Sally and Janice started talking about moving out of their respective shelters and sharing an apartment. Without each other's support, Sally and Janice were unlikely to afford an apartment on their own. Now they live in a respectable place with dignity. As Sally explained, "It feels like home and we can help each other out by watching the other's child" (personal interview, 2002).

Sally's story highlights the power of building unity, even if it means a connection between two people. Community suppers play an important role in helping people connect with others who experiences common problems. When people connect and identify with others, possibilities for collaborative action arise. Sally's connection with Janice ended homelessness for both of them.

Box 5.4: StreetWise
Empowering the Homeless in Chicago[5]

StreetWise organizes and empowers the homeless of Chicago, providing them an alternative to begging or panhandling. By publishing and distributing the *StreetWise* newspaper, the organization (with the same name) provides employment to men and women in Chicago who are either homeless or at risk of becoming so. The newspaper serves as a vehicle to expand public awareness of the homeless among the homed, and to influence the media, policy, and public discourse on homelessness and poverty (Harter, Edwards, McClanahan, Hopson, & Carson-Stern, 2004).

Begun as a monthly newspaper in 1992, of and by the homeless, *StreetWise* became a bi-monthly publication in 1996, and then a weekly publication a few years later. In 1998, StreetWise launched its Work Empowerment Center (WEC) to assist homeless vendors with job skills, computer access, and a library. WEC provides a safe environment in which homeless people can form networks of cooperative action, a place where they are not judged or stigmatized (Harter et al., 2004).

Since 1992, StreetWise has provided 7,000 homeless men and women in Chicago an opportunity to earn a livelihood, enabling them to secure housing and buy food, clothing and personal necessities (http://www.streetwise.org/). More importantly, StreetWise has provided an opportunity for the homeless to begin their journey to self-sufficiency.

StreetWise vendors, who represent independent entrepreneurs, sell newspapers for one dollar, and keep 65 cents (Plate 5.4). Vendors are encouraged to follow StreetWise's code of conduct which includes respecting the "rules of the street," including using professional language, modeling courteous behavior, and refraining from asking for donations (Harter et al., 2004). By 2004, some 20,000 copies of *StreetWise* were selling every week, totaling a distribution of over a million annual copies.

StreetWise represents an alternative discourse community, privileging voices that are often marginalized, silenced, or rejected by the mainstream media. In its earlier years, it included regular columns titled Labor Beat, Media Watch, and Vendor's Voices. A Labor Beat column, for instance, covered issues of unfair labor practices, rising unemployment, echoing the concerns of immigrant workers, janitorial workers, and the racially underprivileged (Harter et al., 2004). In 2005, it provides space for carefully-selected non-profit organizations to promote their causes and political agendas.

StreetWise relies on the support of Chicago's community businesses, philanthropic organizations, and volunteers to organize the homeless.

Box 5.4: StreetWise
(Continued)

Plate 5.4
***StreetWise* vendors in Chicago proudly holding *their* newspaper while donning their organization's sweatshirts and hats**
By publishing and distributing the *StreetWise* newspaper, StreetWise empowers the homeless of Chicago, providing them an alternative to begging or panhandling. The newspaper expands public awareness of the homeless among the homed.
Source: Suzanne Hanney.

Box 5.4: StreetWise
(Continued)

StreetWise has received numerous recognitions, including awards from the North American Street Newspaper Association (NASNA).

In 2000, StreetWise began offering "Not Your Mama's Bus Tour," an interactive, theatrical and non-traditional bus tour hosted by StreetWise vendors that took tourists through downtown Chicago, showing sites and scenes depicting homeless life (http://www.streetwise.org/ current%20events/bustour.htm). The tour featured five downtown stops in Chicago. At each stop, vendors narrated their personal stories of homelessness, including their path to self-sufficiency. This unconventional tour afforded the vendors a means to earn additional income outside their selling the *StreetWise* newspaper. Vendors earned money for their show performances on the tour bus and additionally pocket $1 for each tour ticket they sold. More importantly, the bus tour raised public awareness on homelessness and poverty.

The bus tour was discontinued[6] in 2003 when StreetWise management took a decision to focus on its core competency, the *StreetWise* newspaper.

■ Communication and Fragmentation

Despite the unity building aspects of community suppers, there is also evidence of fragmentation. Interestingly, these opposing dialectic tensions can be present in a single person's experience. Surrounded by caring people, a homeless person may nonetheless feel alone. Such lonesome feelings can be driven by insecurities or embarrassment. If well-to-do community members are present, a homeless person may feel resentment, jealousy, or disassociation. Consider Bill's story.

Bill, 65 years old when we met him, worked as a miner in his youth. When he was in third-grade, his father said, "You got to come work with me in the mines." With his schooling abruptly over, Bill worked six days a week in the Kentucky mines for the next 10 years. When Bill shares his story with young college student volunteers at community suppers, they often ask him why he did not say *no* to his father. Bill responds: "It's for my parents. They took care of me and fed me. They needed me to help out.... How could I tell them no? Why can't these kids I talk to understand? They come here and cook the dinners but they just don't understand. They're different. They take from their folks. Why don't they want to help their folks? (personal conversation, 2000).

Bill's story exhibits fragmentation. He feels disconnected from the local college students who often volunteer at the community suppers held in a church basement in Athens, Ohio. Bill realizes how different his value system is from theirs. While Bill talks to the students, the talk accentuates these differences further. Rather than making connections, the separation is reinforced (Martin, 1992; Meyerson, 1991; Miller & O'Leary, 1987; Ruud, 1995).

Communication and Disconnection   In all the community suppers we attended, there was evidence of meaningful community building. People laughed and offered support to one another. Sometimes people would burst into tears in recounting a particularly painful experience. Others would then immediately offer consolation. There was not a single community supper where the poor and the homeless did not have an opportunity to forge a connection. There were, however, clear examples of disconnection as well. Often, this disconnection was palpable between groups of people belonging to different socio-economic statuses. At most community suppers, some of the well-to-do people separated themselves from the homeless who were present in the same room. Perhaps being in the same room was being close enough. There was no need to sit with or talk with the poor. Many of the homeless appreciated the work of the well-to-do in preparing and serving meals, but felt slighted by the palpable lack of contact. Carl, a homeless man from Toledo, noted: "Why don't they talk to me? I have things to say. I'm not dumb. I have feelings. If they just sit by themselves, I don't want to talk to them either."

Disconnection and separation was also noticeable within groups. Remember our opening story about Hazel. She was shunned by her poor neighbors because they perceived Hazel as being even poorer. We also saw evidence of disconnection among the poor in community suppers. The homeless often sat in separate areas from the working poor. Those who were unemployed sat separately from those whose jobs barely allowed them to survive. Spatial hierarchy was evident among the poor. This hierarchy is so rigid that one dare not cross over to connect with someone of a higher or lower status.

Disconnection was also experienced by some homeless people during the informal prayers, or the saying of grace, during the community suppers. Sometimes this disconnection was displayed with subtlety. On a number of occasions we observed some of the homeless roll their eyes or shake their heads when others would pray. Other times the disconnection would be verbalized. Tim, a homeless man we spoke to at a community dinner in Detroit told us that he was tired of all the praying: "Why do we have to pray? What's God done for us? It makes me want to yell at these people. Just shut up and eat." Although prayer may connect some people to one another, for Tim it separated him further from others.

Communication and Disconsolation Although the preceding stories highlighted dimensions of fragmentation, the community supper participants were still connected to others, at least in a physical space.

In Charleston, West Virginia we came across a community supper organized by a neighborhood association in which everyone was seated at tables of 8–10 people except for one man who sat alone, hunkering over his plate. He looked like he had slept in his clothes; they were wrinkled and stained. When he glanced upward, he displayed a tense, angry expression. One of the volunteers went across the room to say hello to him. As the volunteer approached, the man moved his face closer to his plate. When the volunteer sat down next to him, the man exploded: "Get the fuck away from me." After a few minutes, he finished his food, stood up, and wiped his hands on his pants. Without making any eye contact with others, he walked to the exit, slamming the door shut as he left (field notes, 2000).

The preceding example highlights some of the intractable problems associated with homelessness and poverty. Despite being surrounded by supportive people, this man felt alone and disconsolate. Although we can only guess, the man probably experienced great pain and abuse in his life. In such cases, defensiveness serves as a protective shell that is difficult to penetrate. As Keith Wasserman of GW explained: "Many of the homeless are like abused puppies who will bite you as you offer human kindness. Are they biting you because they are hurting... or because they have learned to bite in order to survive? The answer is complex. People who are hurting spill their pain onto us when they bump into us. When they walk

---

Box 5.5: Fragmentation and Unity
in Soup Kitchens

Although our investigation focused on community suppers, a more common setting to feed the homeless is through soup kitchens. Keith Wasserman of Good Works and authors Michael and Wendy Papa have visited dozens of soup kitchens throughout the U.S. The dialectic of fragmentation and unity was palpable in soup kitchens as well. Interestingly, the most powerful illustration of the dialectic surfaced when some form of violence was enacted.

Physical violence surfaced in several of the soup kitchens we visited. Consider the following excerpt from author Michael Papa's field notes from a soup kitchen in Charleston, West Virginia: "About an hour after dinner, two men started arguing. One said the other owed him some money. As each became angrier it became clear that the two were going to fight and a crowd started to surround the two men." Author Papa was surprised that the onlookers did nothing to alleviate the tensions: "People were yelling, 'C'mon hit him.' This was obviously considered entertainment for the night. The two men traded blows until one punch snapped back the head of the smaller man and his head hit a light pole. He collapsed to the ground and his attacker just walked away. When a soup kitchen volunteer tried to help the injured man, he yelled, 'Leave me alone.' After ten minutes, he got up and staggered away, alone" (field notes, 2002).

One of the most disturbing acts of violence and intimidation observed by Keith Wasserman was directed at a mentally disabled young man outside of a soup kitchen in Pittsburgh. As Keith documented in his field notes: "The first person I noticed was Martin, a severely mentally disabled young man with a loud voice. He reminded me of the many other 'Martins' who had come to Good Works over the years. It was apparent to me that Martin could not control his speech. Like a two-year-old child, he simply spoke whatever he was thinking at the time." Wasserman noted that Martin's behavior both irritated and amused the other men: "Martin became the center of their attention and he took the brunt of their anger and frustrations. Some of the men clearly enjoyed picking on Martin....Then, the next day Martin started irritating the same group of men....Willie, another homeless man, picked up a garbage can and started to chase Martin into the street. Martin ran and was almost hit by a car. This happened two or three times. The other men applauded Willie for his actions. I got the impression that no one liked Martin and that he had absolutely no friends in the world" (Wasserman, 1999, http://www.good-works.net/).

Box 5.5: Fragmentation and Unity
in Soup Kitchens *(Continued)*

In Martin's example we see how unity existed alongside fragmentation. Martin's tormentors established a spirit of unity among themselves in their coordinated actions of degradation and violence. Simultaneously, their actions served to further fragment Martin's existence. Undoubtedly, Martin felt more alone and isolated after these sad series of events.

Author Michael Papa noted a similar example in a soup kitchen in downtown Atlanta: "A wild-eyed man in his early thirties entered this soup kitchen. His hair was long and matted. He wore a torn shirt without buttons and his pants hung low around his waist. Although everyone else came here for food, he came in clutching a crumpled and stained pizza box. Three or four slices of pizza were on top. When I came within a few feet of him, he grabbed the box more tightly and turned away. He then sat at a corner table." Author Papa further noted: "A group of young men in their twenties began to laugh and then one shouted. 'Hey, it's the pizza man.' 'No it's not,' said another, 'It's pizza man Dan.' After a couple of minutes of huddling together and laughing, the biggest man in the group started singing a rhyming rap song. 'It's Pizza Man Dan from the 404.[7] Got dinner from the trash, he must be poor.' This produced great laughter causing Dan to hunker down more as he ate his pizza." Author Papa realized that the situation was getting tense: "Each time the rapper repeated the lyrics, more laughter occurred. The rapper got closer and closer to Dan. Finally, when he yelled in Dan's ear, Dan jumped up and ran toward the door, clutching his pizza box. He tripped as he exited the door and fell down the steps. The pizza box flew from his arms and he yelped in fear. He got up, grabbed his pizza box, and limped away running. His tormentors rolled around on the floor choking with laughter" (field notes, 2002).

Insidiously, a group of poor men created community by uniting in their torture of another poor man. They enjoyed themselves at the expense of Dan, whose life became more fragmented by this torturous experience. But there is more to this story. At some level, Dan came to this soup kitchen because he wanted to be with other people. Paradoxically, he brought food with him that he wished to devour, and he was fearful of anyone getting close to him. So, he tried to isolate himself. To understand Dan's behavior we must recognize that he was torn between two desires—a desire to be connected and a desire to be separated from others. These opposing forces created great internal turmoil accounting for the panicked look on Dan's face when he entered the soup kitchen.[8]

	Box 5.5: Fragmentation and Unity **in Soup Kitchens** *(Continued)*

One way to understand the violence and degradation observed by Papa and Wasserman is to consider the organizational culture in which the homeless are embedded at a soup kitchen. From the perspective of organizational culture, fragmentation refers to ambiguous cultures where individuals and organizations have fluctuating boundaries and identities (Eisenberg & Riley, 2001). In many organizational cultures consensus is short-lived and issue specific (Kreiner & Schultz, 1993). In such fragmented cultures, members struggle to cope with wide-scale confusion and ambiguity (Eisenberg & Riley, 2001). This fragmentation produces "de-centered" people who constantly restructure their identities (Eisenberg & Riley, 2001). The identities of the poor are constantly fluctuating in a soup kitchen environment: Being a person in need, to a person undeserving of assistance; being a victim, to a perpetrator of violence. Different identities rise to the fore as different situations emerge. The act of survival requires a de-centered person who can constantly restructure his or her identity to meet impending exigencies.

A second way to interpret the violence and degradation is to consider the different forces of identification that operate in soup kitchens. Fragmentation can characterize the interplay between acceptance and rejection of organizational identities, providing space for organizational members to shift among identification, counter-identification, and dis-identification (Holmer-Nadesan, 1996; Phillips & Hardy, 1997; Putnam & Fairhurst, 2001). At one level, the poor and homeless identify with others who have similar experiences. However, so much of the feedback they receive from others (the poor and the wealthy alike) makes them feel worthless. As a result, the homeless both counter-identify and dis-identify with other poor and homeless people. They may reject those who are similar to them by lashing out at them with words, fists, and sometimes weapons. In doing so, they may feel momentary satisfaction, but they also further fragment their own personal identities.

---

away we are often left bruised and stained" (personal con-versation, 2001).

The experiences of separation and fragmentation that we observed in the community suppers can be interpreted in numerous ways. Taylor and Trujillo (2001) provide us with a perspective on the fragmentation of the self when they observe that within every person exists "multiple, de-centered, linguistically constituted and often competing forms of consciousness" (p. 174). In each of our descriptions of fragmentation, the focal individual is clearly de-centered from other individuals. Providing another perspective on fragmentation, Deetz (2001) rejects "the notion of the autonomous, self-determining individual" and in its place suggests a complex, conflictual subject with an emphasis on fundamental dissensus" (p. 32) (see also Garsten & Grey, 1997; Henriques, Holloway, Urwin, Venn, & Walkerdine, 1984; Nukala, 1996). In each of our examples of fragmentation, the poor behave like conflictual subjects fearful or skeptical of connecting with others. Part of this fear or skepticism could be the perception of a fundamental dissension between middle-class attendees and the poor. Finally, as Deetz (2001) observes, identity is a discursive pro- duction. This means that individuals acquire so many simultaneous identities through competing discourses that fragmentation is virtually inevitable (see also Deetz, 1995; Gergen, 1991).

In summary, the dialectic of fragmentation and unity was palpable in our experiences with community suppers. While certain aspects of building unity were apparent in community suppers, so were aspects of fragmentation. In overall terms, however, the unity building aspects of community suppers were more noticeable than fragmentation.

Conclusions

In this chapter, we examined the dialectic tension between *fragment- ation* and *unity* in community suppers. The micro-organizing tech- niques we observed included preparation and distribution of food, orchestration of some sort of religious ritual or ceremony, and fostering of fellowship and solidarity with the poor to offer direction for possible employment, job training, and housing opportunities.

In the organizing approach underlying community suppers, there were clear and powerful instances of building unity within communities. People who participate in these events tend to care deeply about one another. Participants offer a helping hand—whether it be a kind word or help in finding shelter and employment. There are also instances of fragmentation, however. In some instances, people experience dialectic tensions by feeling connected at the supper but simultaneously feeling disconnected upon returning home.

In other instances, people at the supper have been so shaped (even damaged) by their life experiences that they remain fragmented from others despite the community around them.

As we reflect on our experiences at community suppers, the dynamic tension between fragmentation and unity becomes clear (Table 5.1). Our opening example of Hazel at the beginning of the chapter noted her excitement in talking to people and being part of the Friday Night Community Supper. At the same time, however, Hazel reflected on the isolation she feels when she returns to her home where her neighbors ignore her. For Hazel fragmentation and unity are experienced at the same moment. The experience of unity at the community supper is contrasted simultaneously with her reflections of fragmentation at home.

Table 5.1
Dimensions of fragmentation and unity

Dimensions of Fragmentation	Dimensions of Unity
Isolation from Others	Affinity with Others
Focus on Difference from Others	Expression of Common Interests
Anger and Violence toward Others	Love and Concern for Others
Dissension with Others	Consensus with Others
Rejection	Acceptance
Disidentification	Group Identification
Made to Feel Worthless	Made to Feel Worthy
Forced Participation in Activities	Invited Participation in Activities

Transcending the dialectic of fragmentation and unity is a great challenge and not always possible. However, through the continued building of fellowship and community the poor and the homeless can gain in hope. There will always be some people who are so distraught and angry that no help is likely to be accepted, but this does not mean that social change organizers should turn their backs. Lives torn apart can be mended, isolated people can reconnect, hope can be kindled in darkness, and the deepest wounds healed by compassion. As seen through the examples described in this chapter, people can be uplifted despite tragic life experiences. In closing, consider the words of Keith Wasserman, Managing Director of Good Works. His commentary provides some insights about transcending the fragmentation-unity dialectic.

Helping homeless people who have been hurt and abused is impossible outside the context of community. It is in the formation of community that we can bear one another's burdens, share vital information, and hand off to one another the most difficult people who need our assistance and love.... It is in community that we help one another to heal the emotional pain experienced by our homeless neighbors. It is in community that we can do the most loving things toward those who need the most help. It is in community that we can model dignity and responsibility. It is in the context of community that we learn to prevent burn out. What we are suggesting ultimately is that we must intentionally join hands and deliberately attach ourselves to others and organize in a way to maximize our energy so we can all move forward together. (personal interview, 2001)

Keith Wasserman's insights are invaluable, but only if we describe community as a product of forces that both unify and fragment. When we promote only unity among the poor, or between the poor and other social classes, we risk perpetuating the status quo rather than interrogating it. Status quo attitudes have created the problem of homelessness and changes are needed in how we form communities so voices of dissent are not suppressed. Ultimately, we need to transform our cultural conversation about the problem of homelessness through dialogue. Importantly, this dialogue must manage carefully the tension between unity and fragmentation. On the one hand, dialogue helps us to discover the bonds that unify us. Just as important, however, dialogue can fragment us in ways that highlight differences that may be impossible to overcome. These tensions do not deny the existence of community. Rather, the dialectical tensions make for a vibrant community.

Notes

1. We thank Drs. Peter Clarke and Susan Evans for their inputs and insights in finalizing this case.
2. We use the term "homeless" instead of "people without homes." The latter phrase is more accurate as it recognizes that being without a home is only one part of a person's identity. However, it is quite cumbersome to use and we side with simplicity and clarity.
3. Homelessness is a temporary circumstance, not a permanent one. So the "number of homeless" people is not as robust a measure of

homelessness as compared to the "number of homeless people over time" (National Coalition for the Homeless, 2002, Fact Sheet 2).

4. Ironically, the largest federal housing assistance program in the U.S. is the entitlement to deduct mortgage interest from one's income tax. For every dollar that the U.S. government spends on low-income housing programs, the Federal treasury loses $4 to lost revenues from tax breaks. Over 75 percent of this tax benefit is reaped by the top 20 percent of wealthy American in the U.S. In essence, Federal housing policy disproportionately benefits wealthy Americans.

5. We thank Suzanne Hanney, acting editor of *StreetWise,* for providing inputs to this case through a conversation with author Singhal on May 11, 2005.

6. The bus tour was also highly labor intensive, dependent on the vagaries of Chicago weather (including its long winter season), and logistically complicated to implement.

7. 404 is the area code for Atlanta.

8. Although our field notes reflect our subjective experiences, these experiences do guide what we see. Furthermore, given the vast amounts of time that authors Michael and Wendy Papa have spent with the homeless, we believe our interpretations accurately describe the lived experiences and perceptions of those we observed. Of course, we do not wish to generalize our observations to all homeless people in the U.S.

6 A Dialectic Journey of Theory and Praxis

Whatever goes around, comes around.
—Anonymous

In the present book, we focused on *four* dialectic tensions that are central to the process of organizing for social change.

First, we examined the dialectic of *control* and *emancipation.* This dialectic speaks to how disempowered people must embed themselves in control systems to emancipate themselves from oppression. Without some sort of control system it is difficult for the poor to organize themselves for emancipation. These control systems, however, require constant scrutiny, given they may offer emancipation while simultaneously restricting opportunities in other arenas of one's life.

Second, we explored the dialectic of o*ppression* and *empowerment.* This dialectic emphasizes that oppression and empowerment are linked together in a dynamic tension. An act that empowers at one point in time may be oppressive at a later time. Alternatively, an action that appears to be empowering on the surface may actually lead to oppression at a deeper level.

Third, we focused on the dialectic of *dissemination* and *dialogue.* To passively accept information from an expert source is to accept control from another rather than to act independently of one's own free will. However, the path from oppression to self-sufficiency cannot be traversed in a vacuum. The oppressed are often so disconnected from sources of power that outside, expert information may be essential to their well-being. Dialogue among oppressed people is important as well because it provides an opportunity for people to reflect on their present conditions, and take collective decisions and actions.

Finally, we described the dialectic of *fragmentation* and *unity.* The poor and the homeless usually desire unity with others in a community setting that provides a semblance of security. In this community, people view one another as allies in their struggles to become self-sufficient. However, the forces that connect people in community compete with forces that fragment. Diversity in a community often separates people from one another, leading to isolation for some. The organizing struggle then is about sustaining unity despite forces that fragment.

In the present book we concentrated our analysis on four different organizational contexts to examine the process of organizing for social change. In each organizational context, we explored a single dialectic. Because the process of organizing for social change activates each of the four dialectics, an alternative approach might have been to focus on all four dialectics in each of the four organizational environments. To illustrate, let's consider how these four dialectics play out in one of our organizational settings—the Grameen Bank in Bangladesh.

Co-Existing Dialectics in the Grameen Bank

In the Grameen Bank, we focused on the dialectic of *control* and *emancipation.* This dialectic became clear when we recognized that emancipation is possible when one embeds oneself in control mechanisms that allow one to fight forces of oppression. The very control mechanisms that free one from a given type of oppression (money-lenders who charge exorbitant interests rates), however, trap one inside another control framework (working 12–14 hours per day, seven days a week) in order to provide for one's family.

Grameen Bank members also experience the dialectic of *oppression* and *empowerment.* Similar to the experiences of Indian women who are dairy farmers, Grameen Bank women are empowered through the economic activities that bring income to their families. At the same time, however, dominant husbands and in-laws restrict their mobility thereby oppressing many of them. Grameen Bank women are also more likely to seek assistance in performing their work from other women rather than enlist the assistance of men. Asking for assistance from another woman is an empowering action. When men cannot be asked for assistance, women are simultaneously oppressed by gender roles that separate them from men in the economic sphere.

Grameen Bank members also experience the dialectic tension of *dissemination* and *dialgoue.* There is a compelling need for information dissemination. Women receive training and instructions from Grameen fieldworkers so they may understand the dynamics of the Grameen loan system. There are also times when a woman accepts information from another woman who has more expertise on a given topic and/or can offer assistance in solving a problem. Dialogue is also central to the empowerment of Grameen women, however. They share personal stories and experiences of building small businesses. Dialogue also builds trust, camaraderie, and cohesiveness among women members.

Finally, Grameen members experience *fragmentation* and *unity.* Remember the story of Tasmiah. When her husband took her loan money she received no support from her close friend and fellow group members. She was isolated when she needed assistance. After being re-introduced into the group by the Grameen fieldworker, she again enjoyed the benefits of unity with others. The pulls of fragmentation and unity are not isolated, however. In every group there are tensions that pull people apart from one another as well as tensions that link them together.

In essence, we argue that the process of organizing for social change is a dynamic and complex process that produces multiple and simultaneous dialectic tensions that pull people between competing poles of communicative action. The more we understand the dynamics of these multiple forces, the more we will understand how social change processes unfold in complex communities.

Organizing in Complex Social Systems

Our investigation of the four dialectic tensions in four organizational contexts strongly suggests that social change processes are highly complex and non-linear. Mutual causalities and outcomes exist that are often uncertain, emergent, and non-predictable. As we reflect on what we have learned about social changes processes, complexity science emerges as a potentially valuable framework to gain insight into issues of praxis for practitioners of social change initiatives.[1]

What exactly is the value in applying principles of complexity science to understanding complex social change phenomenon? Complexity science is a discipline that is providing new insights into how complex social systems self-organize, evolve, and adapt as a result of emergent and non-linear interactive processes (Glouberman & Zimmerman, 2002). Complexity science is not a single theory; rather it is the study of complex adaptive social systems, including the patterns of relationships within them, how they are sustained, and how outcomes emerge (Zimmerman, Lindberg, & Plsek, 1998). In this sense, complexity science debunks highly-planned blue-print approaches to social change, privileging self-evolving, and adaptive learning approaches (Morgan, 1993, 1997).

Here, using illustrations, we explicate four principles valued by complexity science that hold important implications for scholars and practitioners interested in organizing complex social systems: (1) mutual causality, (2) the butterfly effect, (3) valuing outliers, and (4) celebrating paradoxes. Why the focus on these four principles? We focus on *mutual causality* because in complex social systems outcomes are interdependent, emergent, uncertain, and non-predictable. We focus on *the butterfly effect* because in complex social systems big changes can occur from small interventions. We focus on *valuing outliers* because in complex adaptive systems deviance and anomalies are treated as real phenomenon that provide valuable insight (as opposed to being perceived as useless or undesirable). Finally, we focus on *celebrating paradoxes* because complex adaptive systems are non-linear and embody noise, tension, and fluctuation.

■ Mutual Causality: Negotiating Peace or Eradicating Guinea Worm Disease

In 2004, author Michael Papa started his association with The Carter Center (TCC) in Atlanta, Georgia, serving as a technical advisor to an evaluation plan to document the approaches taken by President Carter in conflict resolution. Papa's efforts centered on the peace negotiations that took place between Uganda and Sudan culminating in the signing of the Nairobi Agreement in Nairobi, Kenya in 1999.

To many outsiders familiar with the Camp David Accords of the late 1970s (in which Carter brokered peace between Egypt and Israel), the Nairobi agreement appears to be a function of President Carter's mediation artistry in negotiating peace between President Al-Bashir of Sudan and President Museveni of Uganda. Although Carter's role was clearly crucial, the peace negotiation process was much more circuitous and complex.

Lasting peace is built from the ground-up as well as from the top-down and middle-outwards. So, President Carter's mediation strategies involved much more than facilitating and mediating negotiation between national leaders. TCC administrators worked simultaneously with state department officials and other key government personnel of Sudan and Uganda "building the ground for peace." They identified all points of agreement between Sudan and Uganda, so Presidents Carter, Al-Bashir and Museveni could focus on only the most divisive issues.

Further, a conflict management training program was implemented for various civil society groups in Sudan and Uganda. Jeffrey Mapendere, Senior Program Officer of TCC, met regularly with different rebel and community groups in both countries to reduce the existing distrust and violence. The goal of these training efforts was to build trust and replace violence with peaceful conflict management strategies.

However, President Carter's views on peace are even broader than negotiating agreements that halt hostilities between adversaries. Carter, for instance, believes there cannot be a lasting peace when people are destitute and suffering from disease. Nor can there be peace when people cannot freely elect their leaders. Not surprisingly, President Carter routinely offers his services to monitor the process of holding free and fair elections in several countries.

So, in the Sudan-Uganda project President Carter and the TCC were closely involved in the eradication of guinea worm disease, common in East Africa. When a person drinks water which has guinea worm eggs, the eggs enter the person's digestive tract, hatch and grow, and then exit the body causing bloody sores and extreme pain. Instances of paralysis and death are common. Thanks to TCC efforts over several years in Sudan and Uganda, guinea worm disease declined from 3.5 million cases to a paltry 33,000—a miraculous feat. Many attribute this progress to TCC's Guinea Worm Eradication Program. Results have been so promising that the World Health Organization has targeted Guinea Worm Disease as only the second disease after small pox to be completely eradicated.

Some interesting observations may be made concerning the inter-relationship between TCC's health and peace initiatives. Although some may say that peace between Sudan and Uganda allowed the guinea worm eradication program to reach its goals, others may argue that the guinea worm eradication program was essential to help promote peace. Because of the ongoing program of eradicating guinea worm disease, TCC and President Carter had sustained relationships with government leaders and key members of civil society in both Sudan and Uganda for over a decade. This long-term building of trust made President Carter and TCC the clear choice in mediating peace between the two countries. Recognizing this reality, President Carter called for a guinea worm cease-fire to end hostilities in Sudan so the health initiative could operate without fear of violence. The cease fire not only helped the health program accomplish its goals, the temporary cessation of hostilities paved the road to peace.

Did the guinea worm eradication program play a role in initiating peace or did the peace agreement play a role in allowing the health program to continue? The answer to this question is not simple. What this example does show is that the path to social change, whether it is the cessation of hostilities, or the adoption of filtration devices to provide potable water, is not clear-cut. There exist competing mutual conditions, complexities, and causalities.

What do you think?

■ The Butterfly Effect: Hunterdon Medical Center

Complexity theorists value the wisdom embodied in what is known as the butterfly effect. That is, a butterfly may flap its wings in Lima, Peru eventually leading to thunderstorms over the Rocky Mountains in Colorado. The principle here is that small changes in input conditions, when sustained over time, can often cause cascading huge effects. Also, as we have implied previously, in complex, adaptive, non-linear social systems, there are usually no independent or dependent variables. All variables are independent and dependent. So, how might one find the few small changes that might have large effects?

Let's consider the case of The Hunterdon Medical Center in Flemington, New Jersey.[2] Hunterdon, a not-for-profit 176 bed health care facility, is a model for patient and community-centered care, and has consistently topped charts for patient satisfaction with nursing care. At Hunterdon, you are not a patient in Room 23, but Mrs. Bloom, who manages the corner deli on Main Street.

How has Hunterdon achieved its well-deserved reputation? Linda Rusch, Hunterdon's Vice President for Patient Care, encourages her staff to make small positive changes in whatever they do (Zimmerman, Lindberg, & Plsek, 1998). To Rusch, small changes act like drops falling on a still pond, creating a ripple effect; or, they can act as a grain of sand that falls on a sandpile, causing large avalanches of sand. An "insignificant" thing can build over time leading to big results (akin to a variety of bamboo that does not sprout for five years, but in the sixth year grows 80 feet).

Akin to most complex adaptive systems, Hunterdon is a site of rich interactions among its agents, fostering connections and cultivating relationships, exemplifying the "feminine" side in health care. Dubunking the aggressive, competitive, male testosterone model of care, Hunterdon instead emphasizes sensitivity, compassion, and expression. The primary energy of the system is channeled into cultivating positive interactions. Rusch labels her style of leadership as a relationship "cultivator"—one who cultivates an environment where people want to come and work. She also sees herself as a "weaver"— who can work like a spider—ceaselessly spinning new tendrils of connection, while continually strengthening ones that exist (Helgeson, 1995).

At Hunterdon, nurses experience what it is like to be a patient. To build empathy, they are put on wheel chairs, rolling beds, and in restraining harnesses. Hunterdon's culture encourages nurses to work outside the hospital. Nurses hold community blood pressure screenings, cholesterol checks, and health fairs. They work with police and car dealerships to teach young parents how to buckle children in car seats.

These small initiatives cascade through the Hunterdon system, replicating themselves and leading to big changes. What implications does the cascading butterfly effect have for scholars and practitioners of organizing for social change?

■ Valuing Outliers: Positive Deviance in Vietnam[3]

Can a community find solutions to its problems without requiring a lot of outside resources? Positive deviance (PD) is an approach to social change that enables communities to discover the wisdom they already have, and then to act on it (Buscell, 2004; Sternin & Choo, 2000; Pascale & Sternin, 2005).

PD initially gained recognition in the work of Tufts University nutrition professor Marian Zeitlen in the 1980s, when she began focusing on why some children in poor communities were better nourished than others (Zeitlin, Ghassemi, & Mansour, 1990). Zeitlin's work privileged an assets-based approach, identifying what's going right in a community in order to amplify it, as opposed to focusing on what's going wrong in a community and fixing it.

Jerry Sternin, a visiting scholar at Tufts University, and his wife, Monique built on Zeitlin's ideas to organize various PD-centered social change interventions around the world (Plate 6.1). They institutionalized PD as an organizing for social change approach by showing how it could be operationalized in a community-setting (Buscell, 2004).

In 1991, the Sternins faced what seemed like an insurmountable challenge in Vietnam. As director of Save the Children in Vietnam, Jerry was asked by government officials to create an effective, large-scale program to combat child malnutrition and to show results within six months. More than 65 percent of all children living in Vietnamese villages were malnourished at the time. The Vietnamese government realized that the results achieved by traditional supplemental feeding programs were rarely maintained after the programs ended. The Sternins had to come up with an approach that enabled the community to take control of their nutritional status. And quickly!

Building on Zeitlin's ideas of PD, the Sternins sought out poor families that had managed to avoid malnutrition without access to any special resources. These families were the positive deviants. They were "positive" because they were doing things right, and "deviants" because they engaged in behaviors that most others did not. The Sternins helped the community to discover that mothers in the PD families collected tiny shrimps and crabs from paddy fields, and added those with sweet potato greens to their children's meals. These foods were accessible to everyone, but most community members believed they were inappropriate for young children (Sternin & Choo, 2000). Also, these PD mothers were feeding their children three to four times a day, rather than the customary twice a day.

The Sternins created a program whereby community members could emulate the positive deviants in their midst. Mothers, whose children were malnourished, were asked to forage for shrimps, crabs, and sweet potato greens, and in the company of other mothers were taught to cook new recipes that their children ate right there. Within weeks, mothers could see their children becoming healthier (Plate 6.2). After the pilot project, which lasted two years, malnutrition had decreased by an amazing 85 percent in the communities where the PD approach was implemented. Over the next several years, the PD intervention became a nationwide program in Vietnam, helping over 2.2 million people, including over 500,000 children improve their nutritional status (Sternin & Choo, 2000; Sternin, Sternin, & Marsh, 1999).

Positive deviance questions the role of outside expertise, believing that the wisdom to solve the problem lies inside. Social change experts, usually, make a living discerning the deficits in a community,

Plate 6.1
Jerry Sternin with a Vietnamese community elder who strongly supported the Positive Deviance nutrition program in his village
Jerry Sternin and his wife, Monique, have led the implementation of various positive deviance (PD)-centered social change interventions around the world. PD privileges an assets-based approach, identifying what's going right in a community in order to amplify it.
Source: Jerry Sternin.

prioritizing the problems, and then trying to implement outside solutions to change them. In the PD approach, the role of experts is to find positive deviants, identify the uncommon but effective things that positive deviants do, and then to make them visible and actionable (Pascale, Millemann, & Gioja, 2000). PD is led by internal change agents who present the social proof to their peers (Macklis, 2001). In PD, the role of the expert is mainly to facilitate a process that can help amplify this wisdom locally. In so doing, solutions and benefits can be sustained, since the solution resides locally.

The PD approach emphasizes hands-on learning and actionable behaviors.[4] As Jerry Sternin notes: "It is easier to act your way into a new way of thinking than to think your way into a new way of acting"

Plate 6.2
Monique Sternin (center) and health volunteers create a nutritious meal based on foods used by Positive Deviants in Quang Vong, Vietnam, 1995

After identifying the nutritional strategies followed by the positive deviants in the community, the Sternins asked mothers, whose children were malnourished, to forage for shrimps, crabs, and sweet potato greens. These mothers then learned how to cook new tasty recipes with these ingredients which they fed to their children. Within weeks, mothers could see their children becoming healthier. The PD intervention in Vietnam helped over 2.2 million people improve their nutritional status.

Source: Jerry Sternin.

(Sternin quoted in Sparks, 2004). So, the PD approach turns the well-known KAP (knowledge, attitude, practice) framework on its head. As opposed to subscribing to a framework that says increased knowledge changes attitudes, and attitudinal changes change practice; PD believes in changing practice. PD believes that people change when that change is distilled from concrete action steps.

Evaluations of PD initiatives show that PD works because the community owns the problem, as well as its solutions (Buscell, 2004; Dorsey, 2000; Sternin, 2003). Positive deviance is now being used to address such diverse issues as childhood anemia, the eradication of female genital mutilation, curbing the trafficking of girls, increasing school retention rates, and promoting higher levels of condom use among commercial sex workers (Sternin, 2003).

The positive deviance approach to organizing for social change is located at the intersection of theory, method, and praxis. Theoretically, it privileges local knowledge. Methodologically, PD does not treat deviance as an anomaly. In contrast to approaches that favor "regresion to the mean," PD valorizes outliers. PD's praxis is humane. It believes in inside-out social change with the help of outside expertise and facilitation.

When author Singhal visited Jerry and Monique Sternin in their Cambridge home in January, 2005, they were making preparations to travel to Davos, Switzerland to conduct a Positive Deviance workshop at the World Economic Forum. When Singhal noted that PD was "going places," Jerry winked and responded: "Yes, the world could do better with more deviance."

What do you think?

■ Celebrating Paradox: Posing Wicked Questions, Managing Polarity

Consistent with dialectic approaches, complexity science believes that contradictions, paradoxes, and tensions are inherently unavoidable in complex adaptive social systems. For instance, organizations inevitably are characterized by the following tensions: The need for leadership to be conservative to maintain stability *and* be revolutionary to spur change; the need for centralized coordination *and* decentralized initiatives; the need to foster team building *and* reward individual achievement, and so on (Johnson, 1996).

Complexity science holds that these tensions cannot be solved by choosing one polarity, and neglecting the other. The on-going, natural tension represented in the polarity, dilemma, or paradox can either be paralyzing, destructive, or debilitating for an organization or can represent entry points for organizational creativity, innovation, and opportunity (Johnson, 1996; Pascale, 1990; Fletcher & Olwyler, 1997). An organization in which tension is smoothed over and differ-ences are glossed over is neither learning nor adapting efficiently (Zimmerman, Lindberg, & Plsek, 1998). On the other hand, a learning and adaptive organization manages polarities by tapping the power of opposing ideas.

Polarity managers can uncover the power of opposing ideas by posing *wicked questions,* questions that have an embedded paradox or tension in the question (Zimmerman, Lindberg, & Plsek, 1998). Wicked questions have no obvious answers, but help expose people's strait-jacketed assumptions about an issue, context, or situation. For example, how can we set direction when we do not know the future? How can we be both a system and many independent parts? A wicked question is not a trick question. With a trick question, someone knows the answer. The value of wicked questions lies in their capacity to expose our assumptions, and open up new options not considered before. Exposing these assumptions in a question is both uncom-fortable and a relief.

Wicked questions are especially useful to pose (a) when there are polarized positions in a group and there seem to be only either-or answers, (b) to open up possibilities which are not intuitively obvious, and (c) to make the "undiscussable" discussable, that is, to articulate the assumptions held by members in a group (Zimmerman, Lindberg, & Plsek, 1998).

Wicked questions invite participation in both forming the questions and searching for solutions to address them. The embedded tension or paradox, uncovered through a wicked question, provides an oppor-tunity for an organization to pursue creativity and innovation.

In sum, scholars and practitioners of social change should consider the implications that complexity science principles—mutual causality, the butterfly effect, valuing outliers, and celebrating paradoxes—have for their work.

What other implications does our book have for praxis on organizing for social change?

Implications for Praxis

We suggest the following:

■ Re-framing Freire: Viewing Deposits as Investments

When Freire (1970) referred to the banking model of education (discussed in chapter 4) he described how traditional educational practices turn students into "receptacles" to be "filled" by teachers, like making deposits at a bank. The teacher deposits and students are the depositories. The role of the student is to receive, memorize, and repeat. Freire argues that the banking model tries to control thinking and action and inhibits our creative powers.

We argue that Freire's metaphor of "making deposits" minimizes the value of expert information that can genuinely empower the oppressed. We believe organizing for social change programs will be better served if Freire's metaphor of "making deposits" (which has taken on a negative connotation) is reframed as the metaphor of "making investments."

An expert in the specific problem confronting an oppressed group may have access to information that may be beneficial. This expert need not view the oppressed as passive entities but as active receivers of information. The expert offers the information because he or she believes in the human potential of the oppressed group. This belief justifies the investment the expert makes in the hope of sparking meaningful social change. Like all investments it is up to the person receiving the information to "work the capital." In this process the oppressed mold, reform or otherwise make the information theirs.

Although the information that sparks the social change may not emerge through dialogue between the external expert and the oppressed group, dialogue may occur among the oppressed. Through this dialogue they produce social change that they own because it is driven by their conversations and actions. The investment therefore produces a return that exceeds the initial principal. The excess capital (e.g., social capital) that is created could not occur without the efforts of the oppressed working with each other.

If we apply this idea to the Grameen Bank in Bangladesh, we may view the banking model to which women members are introduced as being the investment made by the organization. This model is quite specific in terms of loan disbursement and recovery procedures to be followed. However, the loan recipients produce their own ideas for small businesses. They also devise their own ways of helping each other and moving their communities forward. They are not passive receivers of information rather they are active agents in producing meaningful social change.

In the cooperative societies of the National Dairy Development Board in India, women dairy farmers are presented with very specific information about producing milk under hygienic conditions, caring for their cows, and providing them with balanced cattle-feed and animal vaccinations. They are introduced to systems of cooperative decision-making and governance. Like the Grameen borrowers, they too take this organizational investment and make it their own. They figure out ways to help one another deal with issues of both animal and child care. They collaboratively identify new business opportunities made possible by the profits earned from dairying. In short, their ingenuity and hard work allows the investment to grow over time.

When audience members listen to an entertainment-education radio serial, they are exposed to messages crafted by scriptwriters and subject-matter specialists, often based on formative research. These message designers rarely come in direct contact with the people who receive the investment. However, as we observed in several villages of Bihar, listeners took this investment and sparked social change through their actions. The fire that burns within the Singh family in Kamtaul (discussed in chapter 4) cannot be explained by viewing them as passive receptacles of a deposit. The Singh family, like so many other listeners, put the investment to work to create something of societal value.

Finally, the poor and homeless who attended the Good Works' community suppers in Appalachia (discussed in chapter 5) were also exposed to certain models of building community. They were not manipulated into accepting these models blindly. The poor decide for themselves what alternatives there are to living on the street. They decided that being connected to others is preferable to isolation. And they decided how to seek help to become self-sufficient.

Our metaphorical reframing is not inconsistent with Freire (1970) who acknowledges that no one is liberated entirely through his or her own efforts. This opens the door for people to serve as investors in the oppressed. The goal is not manipulation or re-creation of the status quo. The outside investment represents the spark; the social change that emerges is owned by the people who "work the capital."

■ Amplifying Discourses of Dignity

One of the key lessons that we glean about organizing for social change is to create, sustain, and amplify a discourse of dignity. The poor, for instance, are treated with dignity when they are given loans to start their own businesses rather than handouts that sustain relationships of dependency. The poor are treated with dignity at community suppers when people sit around a table for a family-style meal and share personal stories, rather than serving them in silence as too often happens in soup kitchens.

Creating a discourse of dignity also means opposing public discourses that deny dignity to oppressed groups. Unfortunately, the overwhelming public discourse views the poor as societal sponges, drug addicts, thieves, and prostitutes (a discourse that newspapers like *StreetWise*, discussed in chapter 5, are trying to change). Equally disturbing is the elitist proclivity to push the disempowered out of the common range of vision; so they literally cannot be seen (Harter, Berquist, Titsworth, Novak & Browkaw, in press; Joniak, 2005; Von Mahs, 2005). When you cannot see a population of people it is easy to forget them. For example, the *dalits* in rural India live at the periphery of most villages—almost invisible from the common gaze.

Furthermore, there rages a discourse of hypocrisy that further denies dignity to the poor. For example, the rich executive snorts powder cocaine framing it as "reward" for a hard day's work. Yet, that same executive vilifies the poor man smoking crack cocaine to escape a reality that seems hopeless.

Discourses of dignity must end the separation of viewing us versus them. When we see separation, we extend a helping hand to someone who is different and in some way lesser than we are. Restoring the dignity of the poor also means making the invisible more visible. Wealthier and poorer members of society need to come into more frequent contact with one another. Policy-makers in Washington, D.C. or New Delhi need to attend community suppers in Appalachia to understand the dignity and resilience of the poor and the homeless. The mass media also has an important role to play in amplifying a discourse of dignity. Too many news stories stigmatize the actions of

---

Box 6.1: Rush Limbaugh
Promoting Hypocrisy and Denying Dignity

For several years, Rush Limbaugh has made a lucrative career as a conservative radio talk show host in the United States. A darling of many right-wing republicans, and living the consummate good life in a posh, tree-lined mansion in Palm Beach, Florida, Limbaugh derided gender activists as "feminazis," conservationists as "environmental wackos," and the homeless as "scum bags." All too often, in his radio programs, Limbaugh lambasted the poor who use drugs, arguing that drug use destroys families and societies. He advocated strong prison penalties for convicted drug users (Tucker, 2003).

Now Limbaugh faces charges of illegally obtaining hundreds of thousands of dollars worth of prescription painkillers. Because his wealth allows him to hire Roy Black, one of the best criminal defense attorneys in the U.S., it is unlikely that Limbaugh will spend time behind bars or suffer the indignities of random drug tests or routinely reporting to a probation officer.

When will rich, influential people like Rush Limbaugh—who exercise such strong influence on mass media and public discourses—end the hypocrisy of vilifying the poor for the same choices they make themselves?

---

the poor. This provides justification for viewers to look down on the person who begs or steals in order to fill a hungry stomach, or who sells their body to survive. Indignity anywhere, threatens dignity everywhere. So, we need more alternative discourses such as *StreetWise* newspaper, and more city tours like "Not Your Mama's Tour of Chicago."

■ **Centering Struggle as Necessary to Social Change**

Practitioners dedicated to promoting social change need to recognize that struggle and dialectic tensions will always be present when working with the poor. Instead of becoming frustrated by these struggles, they should view them as essential and productive.

Why is struggle an ongoing and necessary condition of social change? First, social change overturns established habits of individuals. When people have grown accustomed to long-standing ways of thinking and acting it is very difficult to internalize and sustain change. So, at a very basic level, people must struggle against the very natural tendency to revert back to the familiar. Take for example the decision to use condoms as a way to prevent STDs and/or as a method of birth control. An individual may commit to this decision; however, when opportunities for sexual relations surface will the commitment remain if a person does not have access to a condom? For some people, the commitment may remain strong. For most, a personal struggle will surface as different options are considered, including "let's take a chance."

Struggle also exists at the community level. Power brokers and elites (such as money lenders), who are threatened by the change, may actively resist it. Peers may not see eye-to-eye on certain issues. Such struggles enact themselves in conversations, arguments, social ridicule, or even violence. When social change efforts require problem solving at the community level, other struggles may surface. There may be a struggle over solution development, selection, and enactment. Furthermore, just because a solution is thoughtfully designed does not mean that it will work. Solving complex social problems often involves trial and error. Participants in the process must be willing to work through the struggles of group problem solving, devising creative solutions, and repeatedly producing possible solutions until one or more seem to work.

Even when support for social change exists in a community, a critical mass of followers must surface. Developing this critical mass can be a very slow process where advocates will have to struggle with uncertainties, hesitancies, and resistances from community members. Before a critical mass develops, resources in support of social change may be lacking. The struggle involved here includes the willingness among advocates to sustain the efforts necessary to persuade people, even if that support is developed gradually one person at a time.

The dialectical perspective advanced in this book exposes perhaps the most difficult struggle. Initiating and sustaining support for social change produces unanticipated dialectics that surface only when people attempt to enact change at the community level. So empowerment can be oppressive, building unity may cause fragmentation, and so on. These dialectics may be a product of unanticipated community resistance. Importantly, community members rarely notice these dialectic tensions until that struggle reaches a crisis point.

By studying the programs of the Grameen Bank we learned that control systems provide structures that make emancipation possible. There will always be struggles and tensions, however. Grameen members are so interconnected with fellow members that breaches in discipline or loan defaults have potentially frightening consequences. This does not mean that control systems should not be part of social change programs. Rather, control systems should be constantly scrutinized to ensure that the emancipatory benefits of membership override the restrictions of control systems. The call for constant scrutiny is not simple. There will be struggles between program advocates and program members. These struggles are necessary because they eventually help strengthen the programs benefiting the poor.

When we talked with women dairy farmers in India we learned that the path from oppression to empowerment contains many struggles. When a person has experienced oppression for years there will be both internal and external impediments to empowerment. Internally, a person may doubt their ability to accomplish what they have long been told is impossible. There may also be powerful pulls toward old habits that are difficult to change. Externally, a poor person struggling to change may face barriers from other vested interests that try to derail their empowerment. In some cases, the oppressed person may be able to fight these impediments; in other instances, they may have no choice but to give up.

Our conversations with listeners of radio soap operas who enacted changes in their communities drew attention to the dialectic between dissemination and dialogue. Here we learned that the struggle is often over whose voice should be considered when social change options are discussed. There will be times when an outside expert may have a broader field of vision about what may be effective. Although dialogue among the poor who will be affected by social change is vital, that dialogue may yield options that are potentially damaging. But even this observation deserves scrutiny because one may argue that learning from one's mistakes may provide deeper lessons than listening passively to an expert.

The lesson for practitioners concerning dissemination and dialogue is the need to be open about how communication occurs between outsiders and community members and how dialogue is sparked and sustained within communities. There is no one best way to disseminate information or to create dialogue. Many possibilities exist concerning a combination of dissemination and dialogic strategies. What works in one community, may not work in another.

The final struggle we considered is the one between fragmentation and unity. Social change requires communication and cooperative action among people who perceive themselves to be connected in some way. The connections a group of people perceives having with one another may create community. However, communities are not defined only by unity. Fragmentation is not only a reality in every community; it also is an important part of diversity. Too much of an emphasis on unity may suppress fragmentation and silence diverse voices. Too much fragmentation may dissolve the ties that connect people, derailing trust and cohesiveness.

There is no precise formula to determine how much unity or fragmentation is necessary to sustain social change initiatives. What is vitally important for practitioners is to discuss the struggles that will inevitably surface within communities concerning unity and fragmentation. This struggle is not one to be resolved. Rather, the struggle will always be present. Managing the struggle with great care may have the outcome of building stronger community or tearing a community apart.

These observations do not negate the possibility of social change. Rather, we offer these observations to prepare social change practitioners and community activists for the struggles they will inevitably face. There are many social change initiatives that have the potential to empower and emancipate the oppressed. Supporters of change must recognize that struggle is at the very center of social change. There is no emancipation, empowerment, dialogue, or unity without struggle. Remaining resolute in the face of obstacles is what is necessary.

These ongoing struggles for social change also point to the length of time required before substantive social changes are fully internalized within a community. The programs of the Grameen Bank in Bangladesh and the National Dairy Development Board (NDDB) in India took decades before they reached maturity. Further, these organizations continually respond to changing needs and opportunities (as evidenced by the expanding nature of the Grameen social change conglomerate). Likewise, community suppers designed to re-connect the poor and social changes prompted by entertainment-education programs may take years before desired outcomes are produced. Simply stated, social change is slow, requiring continual experimentation, and group involvement over long periods of time.

The message for practitioners is the importance of being humble and modest about what can happen in the short term. There will always be setbacks. When people have been oppressed all their lives, when suffering is such a dominant part of one's experience, moving forward is not a quick, linear march toward self-sufficiency.

■ Creating Spaces and Opportunities for Dialogue

Although there will always be struggles between dissemination and dialogue, there are important lessons for practitioners to learn about the vitality of dialogue in promoting social change. In the Grameen Bank, dialogue within groups sparks new ideas about creating or running small businesses. Women in dairy cooperatives engage in dialogue to solve community problems. After being exposed to the characters and storylines of radio soap operas, listening club members promoted dialogue concerning issues such as gender equality, dowry eradication, and forming schools for *dalit* children. Finally, dialogue in community suppers provides connections for people who are often isolated. Problems such as finding available housing and employment opportunities were also addressed through dialogue between and among the homeless and their wealthier neighbors.

Dialogue does not emerge spontaneously, however. People who are poor, disempowered, and often isolated may be hesitant to voice their opinions. They may be muted. Practitioners hoping to facilitate dialogue must be prepared to encounter hesitancies and resistances to engage in dialogue. One possible recommendation may be to network carefully in a community in order to determine if there are certain people more likely to talk in a group about personal or social problems. By "priming the pump" with more active participants, dialogue may emerge and a group may initiate ideas suggestive of social change.

Creating safe and comfortable spaces for dialogue is critical. In Bangladesh and India, for instance, women would attempt to set aside space for dialogue (such as in a *mahila mandal* or women's club) and often men would attempt to invade that space. A strategic consideration then is to help the disempowered find space that is protected so they may openly discuss issues that are not for the ears of

---

Box 6.2: Safe Comfortable Spaces to Reduce AIDS Stigma[5]

Pink Triangle Malaysia (PTM), a non-governmental organization, operates an innovative outreach program targeted at intravenous drug users (IDUs) in Chow Kit, a poor red-light community in Kuala Lumpur, the nation's capital city (Singhal & Rogers, 2003). PTM creatively uses space to reduce stigma and prejudice (UNAIDS, 1999). A culturally-sensitive research protocol to assess the clients' needs, prior to launching the PTM Program, pointed to the importance of creating an *Ikhlas* [sincere] Community Center (ICC), a "safe space" where the IDUs would feel comfortable about dropping in. The ICC provides meals to IDUs, medical care and treatment, referrals to hospitals and drug treatment centers, counseling and psychological support, access to condoms and other risk-reduction services, and referrals to job placements. Clean bathroom and toilet facilities are also provided so that drug users can bathe, wash their clothes, and maintain their hygiene.

The IDUs participate in running these ICC activities: They cook and clean, serve as outreach workers and volunteer counselors, and carry out administrative work. This involvement helps them take ownership of the *Ikhlas* project, and builds their self-esteem. The IDUs of the ICC now routinely liaise with volunteer groups from hospitals, nursing schools, the corporate sector, and colleges, and thus feel more accepted by the general community. Their active involvement also makes the Pink Triangle Malaysia's *Ikhlas* program highly cost-efficient and effective.

The *Ikhlas* program represents a non-stigmatized, non-judgmental space for IDUs in Malaysia, a country where drug use, according to the local law, is punishable by death. However, the humane environment created by ICC is palpable enough that law enforcement authorities look the other way. As such, the ICC achieves harm reduction, rather than seeking to eliminate intravenous drug use.

The principle of harm reduction is also the basis of several Dutch initiatives that create comfortable spaces for commercial sex work, legalized in the Netherlands in 2000 (Kapila & Pye, 1992). Many local municipalities have established *gedoogzones*, streets where soliciting is allowed during predetermined hours. The city of Utrecht has an *afwerplek*, a special car park with parking bays divided by high-fences, where commercial sex work is transacted. Many Dutch towns established *huiskamers* ("living rooms"), where counseling, care, and assistance are available to CSWs. Utrecht's Huiskamer Aanloop Prostitutes Foundation established a mobile caravan-style *huiskamer*, which is parked in local *gedoogzones*

Box 6.2: Safe Comfortable Spaces to Reduce AIDS Stigma *(Continued)*

during permitted hours. CSWs stop by to rest, take a shower, to buy condoms, receive counseling, and for medical care (Kapila & Pye, 1992). This mobile *huiskamer* is an example of creating a mobile "comfortable space" for those at risk for HIV. The Dutch projects, much like the *Ikhlas* in Malaysia, are respectful of people's lifestyles, non-judgmental, and create comfortable spaces where people can take responsibility (and refuge) for their personal decisions.

PATH (Program for Alternative Technology in Health) created youth-friendly drugstores in Thailand and Cambodia. Studies indicated that 40 percent of young men seeking health products view pharmacies as the access point for buying condoms and STD treatment. Pharmacies in Thailand averaged as many as 50 youthful clients at a drugstore per day (Singhal & Rogers, 2003). PATH's strategy in creating "friendly drugstores" involves training Thai pharmacists to interact with young people in a compassionate, non-judgmental manner, and to refer them, if needed, to appropriate clinical services.

---

their oppressors. This will not always be easy because creating space for the powerless to dialogue with one another may be perceived as threatening to those who have power in the community. Careful networking is necessary in this situation as well to find a supportive person in the community who has sufficient power to reserve a space for private discussion. The disempowered need such a space so they may share their experiences and discuss possibilities for the future.

■ Introducing Counter Narratives

The oppressed are often so overwhelmed with their lives that they focus almost exclusively on the negative. They are often trapped by their experiences and by the stories they tell about these experiences. We saw this play out in particular in the community suppers. Even when a person would experience a small gain in their life such as through a day's employment, the conversation would turn to the likelihood that no work would be available for another day. Part of the reason for this negativity is that the poorest of the poor live day-to-day. Survival means a focus on the here and now. A future of self-determination seems to be a delusional dream.

We came into contact with workers and volunteers in Appalachia who talk with the poor on a daily basis. They spoke about feeling overwhelmed by all the negative stories and experiences. Practitioners can help re-center the focus of the oppressed by drawing attention to the small wins, the positives, and their hopes and dreams. Even being able to talk to another person about one's troubles represents a positive in comparison to being lonely in sorrow.

We argue that counter-narratives are essential to re-center the focus of the oppressed. Exactly how may counter-narratives be developed? In order to develop counter-narratives we need to investigate the conditions described by the oppressed in their true complexity. The knowledge offered by the original narratives may be wrong, over-simplified, or based on missing information. Needed is the co-construction of counter-narratives that present new emancipatory knowledge; that is, narratives that hold the potential to reverse old patterns of thinking and acting (Roe, 1999). For example, a group of oppressed people may develop a counter narrative that reconfigures the disempowering elements of their present social environment. Participants may experience new stories in which the social practice of dowry is opposed, a child marriage is stopped, or a poor woman receives an education.

Scholars and practitioners increasingly realize the emancipatory potential of narratives (Lindemann-Nelson, 2001; Burke, 1945/1969). More than simple vehicles for disseminating information, narratives bring together storytellers and audiences, building bridges that allow alternative ideological meaning formations to be created, maintained, and articulated. The power of counter-narratives is based on the view-point that individual and collective identities are narratively construc-ted and damaged (see Carbaugh, 2001) and as such can be narratively repaired (Lindemann-Nelson, 2001; White & Epston, 1990). So, the voicing of personal and collective counter-narratives can liberate and heal in the same way that dominant stories oppress and marginalize. Counter-narratives can re-construct individual and communal iden-tities, and render credible previously muted voices. Thus, counter-narratives become a way for people to heal their personal and collective past, creating possibilities for new beginnings.[6]

One lesson on counter-narratives that practitioners may draw upon is a practice that occurs in some Christian Churches. Some ministers have found that when prayers are solicited from the congregation, the prayers are dominated by requests for help. In many congregations ministers have countered this focus by encouraging prayers to celebrate joys and triumphs, even if small. Practitioners need to encourage narratives that run counter to stories that dominate the lives of the poor and oppressed.

Entertainment-education programs are also uniquely positioned to bring in new stories, new models of behavior, and new ways of thinking, acting, and being. As discussed in chapter 5, E-E programs can present counter narratives that celebrate a young girl's birthday in Indian villages, encourage a high-caste daughter-in-law to open a school for *dalit* women, and empower neighbors to collectively bang pots and pans to break the cycle of domestic violence.

■ Putting the Last First

Mahatma Gandhi's litmus test for undertaking any social action was predicated on asking and answering the following question: Will my actions help alleviate in any way the suffering of the poorest-of-the-poor, the downtrodden, the most vulnerable, and the most marginalized? If the answer was affirmative, he moved forward. If it was negative, he shelved the idea. Not surprisingly, his life's work centered on fighting colonialism, and caste, gender, and socio-economic inequalities.

Gandhi, for instance, knew that clothing production had once been the premier industry in India, until the British colonists had systematically destroyed the spinning and dying of cotton cloth by Indian businessmen, moving cloth manufacturing to their Manchester mills. The result was massive unemployment and poverty in India, and a ruralization of India as former clothing workers were forced to move back to villages (Singhal & Rogers, 2001).

In response to British interference in the clothing industry, Gandhi made hand-spun, hand-woven cloth (*khadi*) the centerpiece of his program for Indian independence (Bean, 1989, p. 335). He spun his own yarn on a spinning wheel each day (Plate 6.3), and urged his followers to do the same (Shridharani, 1946; Mehta, 1977). Furthermore, he dressed only in *khadi*, including his signature loin cloth. This costume was a communication message, distinctively all-Indian (cutting across caste, religious, region, and social class differences) and strongly anti-British. Gandhi's clothes were a statement of *swadeshi*, the promotion of indigenous products. The Indian National Congress in 1921, at Gandhi's urging, voted to require its officers and workers to spin and wear *khadi* and to boycott foreign cloth. The spinning wheel was adopted as the symbol of the National Congress, and placed in the center of the party's flag. *Khadi* cloth emporia (stores) are still found today throughout India, a lasting symbol of India's Gandhian heritage.

Gandhi's focus on *khadi* signifies his belief in putting the last first. Gandhi's famous Salt March to protest British taxation on salt was also couched as a protest of 350 million poor Indians. Salt is perhaps the only item that poor people—who toil in the fields under the hot sun—needed more than the rich. It was an appropriate symbol for organizing the masses against oppressive British colonial policies.

Plate 6.3
Mahatma Gandhi, wearing his hand-spun *khadi* loin cloth, and sitting behind his spinning wheel
Gandhi made hand-spun cloth, *khadi*, the centerpiece of his program for Indian independence from the British. *Khadi* symbolized *swadeshi* [the promotion of indigenous products] and represented a distinctively all-Indian anti-British message, cutting across caste, religious, and socioeconomic lines.
Source: Government of India Archives.

Box 6.3: Whose Reality Counts in the Mayan Highlands of Guatemala?[7]

In the Mayan Highlands of Guatemala, Dr. Carroll Behrhorst put his heart and soul into alleviating the suffering of the poorest of the poor.

The town of Chimaltenango, located 50 kilometers from the capital Guatemala City in the Mayan Highlands of Guatemala, is home to the Behrhorst Clinic, established in the early 1960s by a U.S.-trained medical doctor, Dr. Carroll Behrhorst (Plate 6.4). Although Dr. Behrhorst

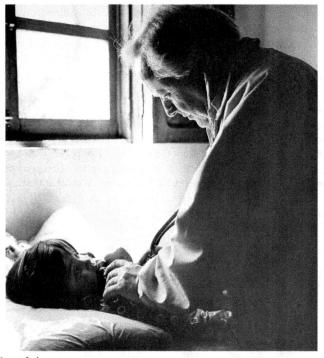

Plate 6.4
Dr. Carroll Behrhorst treating a Mayan Indian child in Chimaltenango, Guatemala
Behrhorst, known as the Albert Schweitzer of Guatemala, realized that good health to the Mayans was not just the absence of disease, but the performance of positive physical and social functions, including a restoration of a person's dignity, self-respect, and pride.
Source: Behrhorst Partners for Development.

	Box 6.3: Whose Reality Counts in the Mayan Highlands of Guatemala? *(Continued)*

(commonly called the "good Doc") passed away in 1990, the clinic in Chimaltenango (that bears his name) symbolizes a model of a people-centered approach to social change worthy of emulation (Luecke, 1993). To Behrhorst, social change could not happen piecemeal; it required holistic, evolving, and multi-pronged approaches, consistent and culturally resonant with people's lived realities (Singhal & Chitnis, 2004).

Known as the Albert Schweitzer of Guatemala, Behrhorst realized within a year or two of practicing medicine among the Cakchikel Mayan Indians that his bio-medical training in the United States, which viewed "body as disease" (in need for a physical cure), was unsuitable for serving local residents (Barton, 1970). The Mayan conception of health was not just the absence of disease, but rather the performance of several positive functions: good appetite, hard work, enjoyment of nature, and participation in social activities (Luecke, 1993). Good health meant a restoration of the patient's dignity, self-respect, and pride (Crawshaw, 1993). Healing was not purely physical (a point of view that his medical training privileged), but also social, spiritual, and psychological.

Behrhorst was disillusioned by his initial focus on just curing patients. Curing the sick in clinics and hospitals was "like trying to empty the Atlantic Ocean with a teaspoon," he noted (cited in Ajquejay, 1993, p. 32). The root cause of illness in Chimaltenango was poverty which resulted in poor sanitation, contaminated water supply, and chronic malnutrition. Having treated over 25,000 patients in his first year alone, Behrhorst's initial work was akin to running an ambulance service at the bottom of a hill where automobiles regularly fell-off. Proper care, Behrhorst realized, involved treatment of causes, not the amelioration of pain. The Clinic's community outreach activities included the training of several hundred village-based health promoters in the Mayan Highlands, who through their presence in the communities where they lived, established home gardens and poultry farms, gravity-based water wells that provided clean potable water, as well as animal husbandry, agro-forestry, literacy, and income-generating projects (Behrhorst, 1993). Community members played an instrumental role in planning and conducting these social development initiatives, mindful of practicality, relevance, and usefulness to local contexts.

The design of the health clinic in Chimaltenango, the centerpiece of the people-centered approach to health care, exemplified a holistic approach to healing (Luecke, 1993). The clinic, constructed by the donated labor of the local residents, had airy rooms and open corridors which opened into a courtyard, much like Mayan dwellings. The rooms were

	Box 6.3: Whose Reality Counts in the Mayan Highlands of Guatemala? *(Continued)*

designed so that families, who often traveled long distances to be in Chimaltenango, could stay with the patients, take care of them, and learn first-hand the basics of health, hygiene, sanitation, first aid, and home-based care. A roomy kitchen, located at the end of the corridor, allowed family members to cook corn tortillas, a local staple food nutritious in carbohydrates, protein, and essential vitamins and minerals. Family members were encouraged to bring their handlooms to the clinics where they could weave cloth while the patients rested. Cooking for loved ones and cloth weaving for income-generation bestowed on patients and their families a sense of home, comfort, self-respect, and dignity. A chicken coop in the clinic provided eggs for consumption, and gravity-based water wells in the courtyard (constructed through the voluntary labor of local residents and patients' family members) brought clean potable water for drinking, washing, and bathing (Behrhorst, 1993).

The nursing staff at the Behrhorst Clinic, consisting of local Mayan women, were chosen for their bi-lingual skills in Spanish and Cakchikel and trained in primary health care (Barton, 1970). These friendly nurses could look at the embroidered fabrics of their patients or their gait, and tell what part of the highlands the patients hailed from. Furthermore, Behrhorst's "healing house" in Chimaltenango never used white sheets as were used in the "white man's hospital" in the capital Guatemala City, 50 kilometers away, where few Mayan Indians would go. Instead, a transparent plastic was used over mattress pads which gave the beds the appearance of the sleeping platforms that the Mayan Indians used in their huts (Barton, 1970). For the "good Doc," attending to such details conveyed respect for his patients (Logan, 1993). To be disrespectful to the cultural traditions of the Mayan Indians, constituted "sin" in Behrhorst's book (Ajquejay, 1993, p. 38).

In sum, the conception of good health in Behrhorst's primary health care project in Chimaltenango was not just based on a physical absence of disease but included a holistic approach to physical, mental, social, and spiritual well-being. The role of the doctor was reframed from a "curer" to "healer." Behrhorst emphasized that the doctor's main responsibility was to leave a bit of his heart with the patient: "First humanity, then technicality," he said (cited in Crawshaw, 1993, p. 10).

For the social change practitioner, Behrhorst had the following advice: "If you wish to serve, go to the people. Live with the people. Learn from them. Love them. Start with what they know. Build on what they have. When the task is finished, the people will say, 'we did it ourselves'" (cited in Luecke, 1993, pp. 183–184).

Further, Gandhi labeled the poor as *daridranarayan* (poor but godly) and the untouchables as *harijans* (children of god). He attributed his effectiveness to a single-minded devotion to work for, and with, the poorest and the most oppressed.

We have mentioned repeatedly that the lives and stories of the poor and oppressed can be overwhelming for even the most dedicated practitioner. Despite this reality, practitioners must focus on the poorest of the poor and the most oppressed community members (Chambers, 1983, 1997). There may be a temptation to look at certain groups of people as beyond help, but those are the people we need to help most.

Muhammad Yunus started the Grameen Bank with the intention of helping the poorest of the poor. In fact, the Grameen Bank has developed a poverty index to make sure that its programs benefit only the neediest. NDDB's dairy cooperatives focus their attention on the marginalized and subsistence farmers who average 1.5 milch animals. Listener's clubs in rural India reached out to create open air schools for the most disadvantaged villagers, and the volunteers and workers at the Friday Night Suppers sponsored by Good Works focus on feeding the poor and the homeless.

The four contexts selected as cases for the present book were selected purposefully because of their focus on the poorest of the poor, the most vulnerable, and the most marginalized. With this group, practitioners will face the greatest challenges in organizing for social change. Because they are relegated to the margins of society, the poorest of the poor are difficult to find. Once they are found, they are likely to be silent and skeptical of any attempt by an outsider to help them. On the path from hopelessness to hope this group will face the greatest setbacks. For these reasons, *practitioners must put the last first.*

Conclusions

Past scholarship and praxis on organizing for social change has privileged binary, either/or, dualistic perspectives. That is, one is empowered or powerless, developed or underdeveloped, educated or illiterate, knowledgeable or ignorant, modern or traditional, and so on. Mainstream approaches to organizing for social change have also embodied such binary distinctions: Top down or bottom-up, centralized or decentralized, expert-centered or people-centered, and so on. The methods employed to understand organizing for social change phenomenon have also been dichotomized into binaries: quantitative versus qualitative, deductive versus inductive, structured versus unstructured, and so on.

We question this dualistic, dichotomized, and binary conception of scholarship and praxis in organizing for social change. We argue instead for a dialectic approach to organizing, acknowledging that contradictory tensions are inevitable and co-present in social change. In fact, contradictions represent the basic drivers of social change. Our analysis shows that control makes emancipation possible. Within the experience of oppression the seeds of empowerment lie. Dissemination may promote dialogue and within fragmentation lies unity.

As our book draws to a close, let's return to a question we posed in the first chapter: Is there a "meta-dialectic" that unifies the struggles we highlight in this book? Clues to this meta-dialectic are found in Baxter and Montgomery's (1996) assertion that the dialectic of *stability* and *change* is ever present in our personal and public lives. A similar dialectic was discussed by Burke (1954/1984) when he described humans' desires for both *permanence* and *change*. Applying this meta-dialectic framework to our four cases it seems possible to argue that control, oppression, dissemination, and fragmentation dominate the lives of the poor. When the poor participate in social change programs, oppositional forces may surface, pulling them toward emancipation, empowerment, dialogue, and unity. This struggle between opposing forces will likely be an ongoing one, even though a person, at any given time, may anchor their lives in forces dominated by stability *or* change.

At a theoretical level, our book suggests that there is tremendous value in examining the lives of people who embody the struggles of change. The poor will always encounter dominant external forces that resist such change and seek to preserve the status quo. Future theorizing in the area of organizing for social change must be mindful of these struggles as they focus on fostering emancipation, empowerment, dialogue, and unity.

Notes

1. Author Singhal thanks Curt Lindberg and Henri Lipmanowicz of the Plexus Institute in New Jersey for introducing him to complexity science principles and insights, and also for the ongoing conversations on the role of complexity science in understanding social phenomenon. Plexus Institute's mission is to foster the health of individuals, families, communities, organizations, and our natural environment by helping people use concepts emerging from the new science of complexity.

2. A story from Linda Rusch, written by Birute Regine, and available from http://www.plexusinstitute.com/services/stories/show.cfm?id=14. Also see Zimmerman, Lindberg, and Plsek (1998).

3. Author Singhal thanks Jerry and Monique Sternin for sharing their PD experiences from all over the world, and for digging up of photos from their PD intervention in Vietnam for use in this section.

4. A positive deviance inquiry focuses on eliminating those client behaviors from the strategy mix that are true but useless (TBU). TBU is a sieve through which a facilitator passes the uncommon qualities of positive deviants to ensure that the identified practices can be practiced by everyone.

5. This case draws upon Singhal and Rogers (2003).

6. We thank Dr. Lynn Harter for her helpful comments in constructing these arguments.

7. This case draws upon Singhal and Chitnis (2004).

References

Abel, E.K., & Nelson, M.K. (1990). *Circles of care: Work and identity in women's lives.* Albany: State University of New York Press.

Ajquejay, F.X. (1993). Gringo doctor—the legend and legacy. In R. Luecke (Ed.), *A new dawn in Guatemala: Toward a worldwide health vision* (pp. 31–42). Prospect Heights, IL: Waveland Press.

Albrecht, T.L. (1988). Communication and control in empowering organizations. In J.A. Anderson (Ed.), *Communication Yearbook 11* (pp. 380–390). Newbury Park, CA: Sage.

Alinsky, S.D. (1971). *Rules for radicals.* New York: Vintage.

Alvares, C. (1983, October). Operation Flood: The white lie. *Illustrated Weekly of India,* 8–14.

Alvesson, M., & Willmott, H. (1992). On the idea of emancipation in management and organization studies. *Academy of Management Review, 17,* 432–464.

Aly, G., Heim, S., & Blunden, A.G. (2003) *Architects of annihilation: Auschwitz and the logic of destruction.* Princeton, NJ: Princeton University Press.

Anderson, R., Baxter, L.A., & Cissna, K. (Eds.) (2003), *Dialogue: Theorizing difference in communication studies.* Thousand Oaks, CA: Sage.

Ashcraft, K.L. (2000). Empowering professional relationships: Organizational communication meets feminist practice. *Management Communication Quarterly, 13,* 347–392.

———. (2001). Feminist organizing and the construction of "alternative" community. In G. Shepherd & E.W. Rothenbuhler (Eds.), *Communication and community* (pp. 79–110). Mahwah, NJ: Lawrence Erlbaum.

Ashcraft, K.L., & Trethewey, A. (2004). Developing tension: An agenda for applied research on the organization of irrationality. *Journal of Applied Communication Research, 32,* 171–181.

Auwal, M.A. (1994a, April). *Problematic of organizing in transmodernity: Representational crisis for non-Western cultures.* Paper presented at the Eighth Annual Communication Research Conference, Ohio University, Athens, OH.

———. (1994b). Reframing subaltern organizational praxis in transmodernity: A study of the Grameen Bank. Unpublished doctoral dissertation, Ohio University, Athens, OH.

Auwal, M.A., & Singhal, A. (1992). The diffusion of Grameen Bank in Bangladesh: Lessons learned about alleviating rural poverty. *Knowledge: Creation, Diffusion, Utilization, 14,* 7–28.

Bachrach, P., & Botwinick, A. (1992). *Power and empowerment: A radical theory of participatory democracy.* Philadelphia: Temple University Press.

Bakhtin, M.M. (1981). *The dialogic imagination: Four essays by M. M. Bakhtin* (M. Holquist, C. Emerson, & M. Holquist, Trans.). Austin, TX: University of Texas Press.

———. (1984). *Problems of Dostoevsky's poetics* (C. Emerson, Ed., and Trans.). Minneapolis, MN: University of Minnesota Press (Original work published in 1929).

Ball-Rokeach, S.J., Gibbs, J., Gutierrez Hoyt, E., Jung, J.Y., Kirn, Y.C., Matei, S., Wilson, M.,Yuan, Y., & Zhang, L. (2000). *The challenge of belonging in the 21st century: The case of Los Angeles* (White Paper). Los Angeles: Annenberg Center for Communication, University of Southern California.

Balkin, S. (1989). *Self-employment for low income people.* London: Praeger.

Bandura, A. (1962). Social learning through imitation. In M.R. Jones (Ed.), *Nebraska Symposium on Motivation* (pp. 231–248). Lincoln: University of Nebraska Press.

———. (1965). Influence of model's reinforcement contingencies on the acquisition of imitative responses. *Journal of Personality and Social Psychology, 1,* 589–595.

———. (1973). *Aggression: A social learning analysis.* Englewood Cliffs, NJ: Prentice-Hall.

———. (1977). *Social learning theory.* Englewood Cliffs, NJ: Prentice-Hall.

———. (1986). *Social foundation of thought.* Englewood Cliffs, NJ: Prentice-Hall.

———. (1995). Exercise of personal and collective efficacy in changing societies. In A. Bandura (Ed.), *Self-efficacy in changing societies* (pp. 1–45). New York: Cambridge University Press.

———. (1997). *Self-efficacy: The exercise of control.* New York: Freeman.

———. (2004). Social cognitive theory for personal and social change by enabling media. In A. Singhal, M. Cody, E.M. Rogers, & M. Sabido (Eds.), *Entertainment-education and social change: History, research, and practice* (pp. 75–96). Mahwah, NJ: Lawrence Erlbaum.

Bandura, A., Grusec, J.A., & Menlove, F.L. (1966). Observational learning as a function of symbolization and incentive set. *Child Development, 37,* 499–506.

Barker, J.R. (1993). Tightening the iron cage: Concertive control in self-managing teams. *Administrative Science Quarterly, 38,* 408–437.

Barker, J.R., & Cheney, G. (1994). The concepts and the practices of discipline in contemporary organizational life. *Communication Monographs, 61,* 19–43.

Barker, J.R., & Tompkins, P.K. (1994). Identification in the self-managing organization: Characteristics of target and tenure. *Human Communication Research, 21,* 223–240.

Barnard, C. (1938). *The functions of the executive.* Cambridge, MA: Harvard University Press.

Bartky, S. (1988). Foucault, femininity, and the modernization of patriarchal power. In I. Diamond & L. Quimby (Eds.), *Feminism and Foucault: Reflections on resistance* (pp. 63–84). Boston: Northeastern University Press.

———. (1991). Shame and gender. In S. Bartky (Ed.), *Femininity and domination: Studies in the phenomenology of oppression* (pp. 63–82). New York: Routledge.

Barton, E. (1970). *Physician to the Mayas.* Philadephia, PA: Fortress Press.

Baxter, L.A. (1988). A dialectical perspective on communication strategies in relational development. In S.W. Duck, D.F. Hay, S.E. Hobfoll, W. Iches, & B. Montgomery (Eds.), *Handbook of personal relationships* (pp. 257–273). London: Wiley.

———. (1990). Dialectical contradictions in relational development. *Journal of Social and Personal Relationships, 7,* 69–88.

———. (1992). Forms and functions of intimate play in personal relationships. *Human Communication Research, 18,* 336–363.

———. (1993). The social side of personal relationships: A dialectical perspective. In S. Duck (Ed.), *Understanding relationship processes, 3: Social context finds relationships* (pp. 139–165). Newbury Park, CA: Sage.

Baxter, L.A., & Montgomery, B.M. (1996). *Relating: Dialogues and dialectics.* New York: The Guilford Press.

Bayes, A., Braun, J., & Akhter, R. (1999). *Village pay phones and poverty reduction.* Bonn, Germany: Center for Development Research.

Bean, S.S. (1989). Gandhi and *khadi,* the fabric of Indian independence. In A.B. Weaver & J. Schneider (Eds.), *Cloth of human experience* (pp. 355–376). Washington, D.C.: Smithsonian Institution Press.

Behrhorst, C. (1993). The Chimaltenango Development Program. In R. Luecke (Ed.), *A new dawn in Guatemala: Toward a worldwide health vision* (pp. 55–76). Prospect Heights, IL: Waveland Press.

Bell, E.L., & Forbes, L.C. (1994). Office folklore in the academic paperwork empire: The institutional space of gendered contexts. *Text and Performance Quarterly, 14,* 181–196.

Bellah, R.N., Madsen, R., Sullivan, W.M., Swidler, A., & Tipton, S.M. (1985). *Habits of the heart.* Berkeley, CA: University of California Press.

Benson, S. (1992). "The clerking sisterhood": Rationalization and the work culture of saleswomen in American department stores, 1890–1960. In A.J. Mills & P. Tancred (Eds.), *Gendering organizational analysis* (pp. 222–234). Newbury Park, CA: Sage.

Berkowitz, W., & Wolff, T. (2000). *The spirit of coalition.* Washington, D.C.: American Public Health Association.

Bernstein, P. (1976). Necessary elements for effective worker participation in decision-making. *Journal of Economic Issues, 10,* 490–522.

Bhatt, E.R. (1996). Women in dairying in India. *Indian Dairymen: Journal of the Indian Dairy Science Association, 48,* 157–158.

Blau, J.R., & Alba, R.D. (1982). Empowering nets of participation. *Administrative Science Quarterly, 27,* 363–379.

Bloom, D. (2000). The civic profile: A case study of community building in New Hampshire. *National Civic Review, 89,* 287–300.

Borger, J. (November 3, 2003). Long queue at drive-in soup kitchen. *The Guardian,* http://www.guardian.co.uk/print/0,3858,4788308110878,00. html (Retrieved on October 23, 2004).

Bornstein, D. (1996). *The price of a dream: The story of the Grameen Bank.* Chicago: University of Chicago Press.

Boyd, C.G. (1999). *"We form a human chain": A third world feminist study of women's engagement with dairy cooperatives in Kolhapur, India.* Unpublished doctoral dissertation, Ohio University, Athens, OH.

Bramly, S. (1991). *Discovering the life of Leonardo da Vinci.* New York: Harper Collins.

Bricker-Jenkins, M. (1992). The propositions and assumptions of feminist social work practice. In M. Bricker-Jenkins, N. R. Hooyman, & N. Gottlieb (Eds.), *Feminist social work practice in clinical settings* (pp. 271–304). Newbury Park, CA: Sage.

Bullis, C., & Bach, B. (1996). Feminism and the disenfranchised: Listening beyond the "other". In E.B. Ray (Ed.), *Communication and disenfranchisement: Social health issues and implications* (pp. 3–28). Mahwah, NJ: Erlbaum.

Bullis, C.A., & Tompkins, P.K. (1989). The forest ranger revisited: A study of control practices and identification. *Communication Monographs, 56,* 287–306.

Burke, K. (1945/1969). *A grammar of motives.* Berkeley: University of California Press.

———. (1950). *A rhetoric of motives.* Berkeley, CA: University of California Press.

———. (1954/1984). *Permanence and change.* Los Altos, CA: Hermes Publications.

Burrell, G. (1993). Eco and the bunnymen. In J. Hassard & M. Parker (Eds.), *Postmodernism and organizations* (pp. 71–82). Newbury Park, CA: Sage.

Buscell, P. (2004). The power of positive deviance. *Emerging,* August–October, 8–20.

Bustamente, C. (2004). Saludes públicas y salud reproductiva en la Amazonía. In E. Elías & E. Neira (Eds.), *Salud reproductiva en la Amazonía: perspectivas desde la cultura, el género y la comunicación* (pp. 269–281). Lima, Peru: Minga Perú.

Buzzanell, P.M. (1994). Gaining a voice: Feminist organizational communication theorizing. *Management Communication Quarterly, 7,* 339–383.

Cabot Creamery Cooperative (2005). Cabot Farmers. Available online at http://www.cabotcreamery.com (Retrieved on January 23, 2005).

Calas, M.B., & Smircich, L. (1992). Re-writing gender into organizational theorizing: Directions from feminist perspectives. In M. Reed & M. Hughes (Eds.), *Rethinking organization: New directions in organizational theory and analysis* (pp. 227–253). London: Sage.

Carbaugh, D. (2001). "The people will come to you": Blackfeet narratives as a resource for contemporary living. In J. Brockmeier & D. Carbaugh (Eds.), *Narrative and identity: Studies in autobiography, self and culture* (pp. 102–128). Amsterdam: John Benjamins.

Caswell, S. (2001). Community capacity building and social policy—what can be achieved? *Social Policy Journal of New England, 18,* 22–36.

Chambers, R. (1983). *Rural development. Putting the last first.* Essex, U.K.: Longman.

———. (1997). *Whose reality counts? Putting the first last.* London, U.K.: Intermediate Technology Development Group.

Chaskin, R., & Abunimah, H. (1999). A view from the city: Local government perspectives on neighborhood based governance in community building initiatives. *Journal of Urban Affairs, 21,* 57–78.

Chen, M., Mitra, M., Athreya, G., Dholakia, A., Law, P., & Rao, A. (1986). *Indian women: A study of their role in the dairy movement.* New Delhi, India: Shakti Books.

Cheney, G. (1995). Democracy in the workplace: Theory and practice from the perspective of communication. *Journal of Applied Communication Research, 23,* 167–200.

———. (1996). *Organizations that work for us: Values, democracy, and communication in the life of a worker-cooperative complex called Mondragon.* Unpublished manuscript, The University of Montana, Missoula, MT.

———. (2000). *Values at work: Employee participation meets market pressure at Mondragon.* New Jersey: Ablex Publishing.

———. (2001). Forms of connection and "severance" in and around the Mondragon worker-cooperative complex. In G. Shepherd & E.W. Rothenbuhler (Eds.), *Communication and community* (pp. 111–134). Mahwah, NJ: Lawrence Erlbaum.

Cheney, G., Straub, J., Speirs-Glebe, Stohl, C., DeGooyer, D., Whalen, S., Garvin-Doxas, K., & Carlone, D. (1998). Democracy, participation, and communication at work: A multidisciplinary review. In M.E. Roloff (Ed.), *Communication Yearbook 21* (pp. 35–91). Thousand Oaks, CA: Sage.

Cheney, G., & Tompkins, P.K. (1987). Coming to terms with organizational identification and commitment. *Central States Speech Journal, 38,* 1–15.

Chiles, A.M., & Zorn, T.E. (1995). Empowerment in organizations: Employees' perceptions of the influences on empowerment. *Journal of Applied Communication Research, 23,* 1–25.

Christenson, J., Fendley, J., & Robinson, J. (1989). Community development. In J. Christenson, & J. Robinson (Eds.), *Community development in
perspective* (pp. 3–13). New York: Holt, Rinehart & Winston.

Clarke, P., & Evans, S.H. 1994. *Orphan innovations: Lessons for improving the
adoption of human services nationwide.* Los Angeles, CA: From the Wholesaler to the Hungry.

Cohen, C., & Phillips, M. (1998). Building community: Principles for social
work practice in housing settings. In P. Ewalt, E. Freeman, & D. Poole
(Eds.), *Community Building* (pp. 239–251). Washington, D.C.: NASW
Press.

Coleman, J. (1988). Social capital in the creation of human capital. *American
Journal of Sociology, 94* (Suppl.), S95–S120.

———. (1990). *Foundations of social theory.* Cambridge, MA: Harvard
University Press.

Collinson, D. (1994). Strategies of resistance: Power, knowledge, and resistance in the workplace. In J.M. Jermier, D. Knights, & W.R. Nord (Eds.),
Resistance and power in organizations (pp. 25–68). London: Routledge.

Conger, J.A. (1989). Leadership: The art of empowering others. *Academy of
Management Review, 13,* 17–24.

Conger, J.A., & Kanugo, R. (1988). The empowerment process: Integrating
theory and practice. *Academy of Management Review, 13,* 471–482.

Constantino-David, K. (1982). Issues in community organizing. *Community
Development Journal, 77*(3), 94–117.

Conville, R.L. (1998). Telling stories: Dialectics of relational transition. In
B.M. Montgomery & L.A. Baxter (Eds.), *Dialectical approaches to studying
personal relationships* (pp. 17–40). Mahwah, NJ: Lawrence Erlbaum
Associates.

Counts, A.M. (1990). *Worm's eye view: Interviews with women of the Grameen
Bank.* Washington, D.C.: Results Educational Fund.

Craig, R.T. (1994, November). *What must be in a communication theory?* Paper
presented at the annual convention of the Speech Communication Association, New Orleans, LA.

Crawshaw, R. (1993). Human being and physician. In R. Luecke (Ed.), *A
new dawn in Guatemala: Toward a worldwide health vision* (pp. 1–16).
Prospect Heights, IL: Waveland Press.

Daley-Harris, S. (2004). *State of the microcredit summit campaign report 2004.*
Washington, D.C.: Microcredit Summit Campaign Secretariat.

Deetz, S.A. (1992). *Democracy in an age of corporate colonization: Developments
in communication and politics of everyday life.* Albany, NY: State University
of New York Press.

———. (1994a). Future of the discipline: The challenges, the research, and
the social contribution. In S.A. Deetz (Ed.), *Communication Yearbook 17*
(pp. 565–600). Thousand Oaks, CA: Sage.

Deetz, S.A. (1994b). Representative practices and the political analysis of corporations. In B. Kovacic (Ed.), *Organizational communication: New perspectives* (pp. 209–242). Albany: State University of New York Press.
———. (1995). *Transforming communication, transforming business: Building responsive and responsible workplaces.* Cresskill, NJ: Hampton.
———. (2001). Conceptual foundations. In F.M. Jablin & L.L. Putnam (Eds.), *The New handbook of organizational communication: Advances in theory, research, and methods* (pp. 3–46). Thousand Oaks, CA: Sage.
Deveaux, M. (1994). Feminism and empowerment: A critical reading of Foucault. *Feminist Studies, 20,* 223–247.
Dindia, K. (1998). "Going into and coming out of the closet": The dialectics of stigma disclosure. In B.M. Montgomery & L.A. Baxter (Eds.), *Dialectical approaches to studying personal relationships* (pp. 83–108). Mahwah, NJ: Lawrence Erlbaum Associates.
Donovan, J. (1985). *Feminist theory: The intellectual traditions of American feminism.* New York: Frederick Unger.
Dorsey, D. (2000). Positive deviant. *Fast Company, 41,* 284–292.
Doornbos, M., van Dorsten, F., Mitra, M., & Terhal, P. (1990). *Dairy aid and development: India's Operation Flood.* New Delhi: Sage.
Duncan, C. (1999). *Worlds apart: Why poverty persists in rural America.* New Haven, CT: Yale University Press.
Dugger, C.W. (January 4, 1999). Calcutta's prostitutes lead the fight on AIDS. *The New York Times.* p. A1.
Ehrenreich, B. (2001). *Nickel and dimed: On (not) getting by in America.* New York: Henry Holt and Company.
Eisenberg, E.M. (1994). Dialogue as democratic discourse: Affirming Harrison. In S.A. Deetz (Ed.), *Communication Yearbook 17* (pp. 275–284). New Brunswick, NJ: Sage.
Eisenberg, E.M., & Goodall, Jr., H.L. (1997). *Organizational communication: Balancing creativity and constraint.* New York: St. Martin's Press.
Eisenberg, E.M., & Riley, P. (2001). Organizational culture. In F.M. Jablin & L.L. Putnam (Eds.), *The new handbook of organizational communication: Advances in theory research, and methods* (pp. 291–322). Thousand Oaks, CA: Sage.
Eisenberg, P. (1998). Philanthropy and community building. *National Civic Review, 87,* 169–176.
Elías, E. (2002, October). *Comunicar para icarar: El modelo Minga de communicación para la salud desde la cultura.* Paper presented to the International Conference on Reproductive Health in the Amazonian Region, Iquitos, Peru.
Elías, E. and Neira, E. (Eds.) (2004), *Salud reproductiva en la Amazonía: perspectivas desde la cultura, el género y la comunicación.* Lima, Peru: Minga Perú

Etzioni, A. (1961). *A comparative analysis of complex organizations.* New York: Free Press.

Ewalt, P. (1998). The revitalization of impoverished communities. In P. Ewalt, E. Freeman, & D. Poole (Eds.), *Community building* (pp. 3–5). Washington, D.C.: NASW Press.

Fairhurst, G.T. (2001). Dualisms in leadership research. In F.M. Jablin & L.L. Putnam (Eds.), *The new handbook of organizational communication: Advances in theory, research, and methods* (pp. 379–439). Thousand Oaks, CA: Sage.

Fals Borda, O.F. (1968). *Subversion y cambio social.* Bogata, Columbia: Ediciones Tercer Mundo.

Farace, R.V., Monge, P.R., & Russell, H.M. (1977). *Communicating and organizing.* New York: Random House.

Farrington, A. (2003). "Family matters" in the Amazon. *Ford Foundation Report, 34*(4), 16–19.

Ferguson, K.E. (1984). *The feminist case against bureaucracy.* Philadelphia: Temple University Press.

Fichten, J. (1991). *Endangered spaces, enduring places: Change, identity and survival in rural America.* Boulder, CO: Westview.

Fischer, C.S. (1982). *To dwell among friends: Personal networks in town and city.* Chicago: University of Chicago Press.

Flora, B. (1992*). Rural communities, legacy, and change.* Boulder, CO: Westview Press.

Forester, J. (1989). *Planning in the face of power.* Berkeley: University of California Press.

Foster, M. (2005). Using call and response to facilitate language mastery and language acquisition among African-American students. http://www.cal.org/resources/digest/0204foster.html (Retrieved April 25, 2005).

Fletcher, J., & Olwyler, K. (1997). *Paradoxical thinking, how to profit from your contradictions.* San Francisco, CA: Berrett-Koehler.

Foucault, M. (1972). *The archaeology of knowledge* (A. Sheridan, Trans.). New York: Vintage.

———. (1976). *Discipline and punish.* New York: Vintage.

———. (1980a). *Power/knowledge* (G. Gordon, L. Marshal, J. Mepham, & K. Soper, Trans.; L. Gordon, Ed.). New York: Pantheon.

———. (1980b). *The history of sexuality: Volume I. An introduction* (R. Harley, Trans.). New York: Vintage.

Freire, P. (1970). *Pedagogy of the oppressed.* New York: Seabury Press.

Freire, P., & Faundez, A. (1989). *Learning to question: A pedagogy of liberation.* New York: Continuum.

Freud, S. (1961). *Leonardo da Vinci: A study in psychosexuality.* New York: Vintage Books.

Friedland, L.A. (2001). Communication, community, and democracy: Toward a theory of the communicatively integrated community. *Communication Research, 28,* 358–391.

Friedman, M. (1987). Beyond caring: The de-moralization of gender. In M. Hanen & K. Nielson (Eds.), *Science, morality, and feminist theory* (pp. 86–110). Calgary, Canada: University of Calgary Press.

Frye, M. (1993). The possibility of feminist theory. In A.M. Jaggar & P.S. Rothenberg (Eds.), *Feminist frameworks: Alternative theoretical accounts of the relationship between women and men* (pp. 103–112). New York: McGraw-Hill.

Fuglesang, A., & Chandler, D. (1988). *Participation as process: What can we learn from the Grameen Bank, Bangladesh.* Dhaka, Bangladesh: Grameen Bank.

———. (1993). *Participation as process: What can we learn from Grameen Bank, Bangladesh* (2nd ed.). Dhaka, Bangladesh: Grameen Bank.

Fukuyama, F. (1995). *Trust: The social virtues and the creation of prosperity.* New York: Free Press.

Gandhi, N., & Shah, N. (1992). *The issues at stake: Theory and practice in the contemporary women's movement in India.* New Delhi: Kali for Women.

Galbraith, J.K. (1967). *The new industrial state.* New York: Signet Books.

Garland, D. (1990). *Modern society: A study in social theory.* Chicago: University of Chicago Press.

Garsten, C., & Grey, C. (1997). How to become oneself: Discourses of subjectivity in post-bureaucratic organizations. *Organization, 4,* 211–228.

Gelb, M.J. (1998). *How to think like Leonardo da Vinci.* New York: Delta Trade Books.

George, S. (1984). Operation Flood and rural India, vested and divested interests. *Economic and Political Weekly, 20,* 2163–2170.

———. (1985). *Operation Flood: An appraisal of current Indian dairy policy.* New Delhi: Oxford University Press.

Gergen, K. (1991). *The saturated self: Dilemmas of identity in contemporary life.* New York: Basic Books.

Gergen, K.J., Gergen, M.M., & Barrett, F.J. (2004). Dialogue: Life and death of the organization. In D. Grant, C. Hsrdy, C. Oswick, & L. Putnam (Eds.), *The Sage handbook of organizational discourse* (pp. 39–60). Thousand Oaks, CA: Sage.

Ghai, D. (1984). *An evaluation of the impact of Grameen Bank project.* Dhaka, Bangladesh: Grameen Bank.

Gilligan, C. (1982). *In a different voice: Psychological theory and women's development.* Cambridge, MA: Harvard University Press.

Glouberman, S., & Zimmerman, B. (2002). *Complicated and complex systems: What would successful reform of medicare look like?* Discussion Paper No. 8. Ottawa, Canada: Commission on the Future of Health Care in Canada.

Grameen Bank (2005, March 15). *Grameen Bank Monthly Update in US $: February, 2005, Statement #1, Issue 32.* Bangladesh: Mirpur, Dhaka.

Gramsci, A. (1971). *Selections from the prison notebooks* (Q. Hoare & G. Nowell Smith, Trans.). New York: International.

Greenberger, D.B., & Strasser, S. (1986). Development and application of a model of personal control in organizations. *Academy of Management Review, 11,* 164–177.

Gronemeyer, M. (1993). Helping. In W. Sachs (Ed.), *The development dictionary: A guide to knowledge as power* (pp. 53–69). London: Zed Books.

Gumucio Dagron, A. (2001). *Making waves: Stories of participatory communication for social change.* New York: Rockefeller Foundation

Gutierrez, L.M. (1990). Working with women of color: An empowerment perspective. *Social Work, 35,* 149–153.

Habermas, J. (1984). *Theory of communicative action.* Boston: Beacon Press.

Hammond, S.C., Anderson, R., & Cissna, K.N. (2003). The problematics of dialogue and power. In P. J. Kabfleisch (Ed.), *Communication Yearbook 27* (pp. 125–158). Mahwah, NJ: Lawrence Erlbaum.

Handy, C. (1994). *The age of paradox.* Cambridge, MA: Harvard Business School Press.

Harrison, T.M. (1994). Communication and interdependence in democratic organizations. In S.A. Deetz (Ed.), *Communication yearbook 17* (pp. 247–274). New Brunswick, NJ: Sage.

Harstock, N. (1983). The feminist standpoint: Developing the ground for a specifically feminist historical materialism. In S. Harding & M. Hintikka (Eds.), *Discovering reality: Feminist perspectives on epistemology, metaphysics, methodology, and philosophy of science* (pp. 283–311). Hingham, MA: Kluwer Boston.

Harter, L.M. (2004). Masculinity(s), the agrarian frontier myth, and cooperative ways of organizing: Contradictions and tensions in the experience and enactment of democracy. *Journal of Applied Communication Research, 32,* 89–118.

Harter, L.M., Berquist, C., Titsworth, B.S., Novak, D., & Broakaw, T. (in press). The structuring of invisibility among the hidden homeless: The politics of space, stigma, and identity construction. *Journal of Applied Communication Research.*

Harter, L.M., Edwards, A., McClanahan, A., Hopson, M.C., & Carson-Stern, E. (2004). Organizing for survival and social change: The case of StreetWise. *Communication Studies, 55*(2), 407–424.

Harter, L.M., & Krone, K.J. (2001). The boundary-spanning role of a cooperative support organization: Managing the paradox of stability and change in non-traditional organizations. *Journal of Applied Communication Research, 29,* 248–277.

Harter, L.M., Sharma, D., Pant, S., Singhal, A., & Sharma, Y. (in press). Catalyzing social reform through participatory folk performances in rural

India. In L. Frey & K. Carragee (Eds.), *Communication and social activism.* Cresskill, NJ: Hampton Press.

Hayden, S. (1997). Re-claiming bodies of knowledge: An exploration of the relationship between feminist theorizing and feminine style in the rhetoric of the Boston Women's health book collective. *Western Journal of Communication, 61,* 127–263.

Healey, P. (1992). Planning through debate: The communicative turn in planning theory. *Town Planning Review, 63,* 143–162.

Heckman, S. (1990). *Gender and knowledge: Elements of a postmodern feminism.* Boston: Northeastern University Press.

Hegel, G.W. F. (1969). *Science of logic* (A.V. Miller, Trans.). New York: George Allen & Unwin.

Held, V. (1993). *Feminist morality: Transforming culture, society, and politics.* Chicago: University of Chicago Press.

Helgeson, S. (1995). *The web of inclusion.* New York: Doubleday.

Henriques, J., Holloway, W., Urwin, C., Venn, C., & Walkerdine, V. (Eds.). (1984*). Changing the subject.* New York: Methuen.

Herald Tribune (2004, October 2–3). Ending the cycle of debt. p. 8.

Heredia, R. (1997). *The AMUL India story.* Anand, Gujarat: Gujarat Cooperative Milk Marketing Federation.

Hillery, G. (1968). *Communal organizations: A study of local societies.* London: University of Chicago Press.

Hirschman, A. (1984). *Getting ahead collectively: Grassroots experiences in Latin America.* Washington, D.C.: Interamerican Foundation.

Hochschild, A. (1983). *The managed heart.* Berkeley, CA: University of California Press.

Holmer-Nadesan, M. (1996). Organizational identity and the space of action. *Organization Studies, 17,* 49–81.

Holton, G.J. (1973). *Thematic origins of scientific thought: Kepler to Einstein.* Cambridge, MA: Harvard University Press.

Horton, D., & Wohl, R.R. (1956). Mass communication and para-social interaction. *Psychiatry, 19,* 215–229.

Hossain, M. (1988). *Credit for alleviation of rural poverty: The Grameen Bank of Bangladesh* (Report No. 6, 5). Washington, D.C.: International Food Policy Research Institute in collaboration with Bangladesh Development Studies.

House, J.S. (1981). *Work stress and social support.* Reading, MA: Addison-Wesley.

Houppert, K. (1992, June 9). Women's action coalition. *Village Voice, 37,* 33–38.

Hovy, E.H., Philpot, A., Evans, S.H., Clarke, P., & Woolsey, S. (2005). Tailored generation of recipes for low-income people. Under review for publication.

Hulme, D. (1990). Can the Grameen Bank be replicated? Recent experiments in Malaysia. *Development Policy Review, 8,* 287–300.

India's Census (2002). www.censusindia.net (Retrieved on January 24, 2005).

Innes, J. (1995). Planning theory's emerging paradigm: Communicative action and interactive practice. *Journal of Planning Education and Research, 14,* 183–190.

Institute for Children and Poverty (2001). *A shelter is not a home: Or is it?* New York: Institute for Children and Poverty.

Jacob, M.K. (1991). The practice of community psychology in Chile. *Applied Psychology: An International Review, 40,* 143–163.

Jacobson, T.L. (1994). Modernization and post-modernization approaches to participatory communication for development. In S.A. White, K.S. Nair, & J. Ascroft (Eds.), *Participatory development communication: Working for change and development* (pp. 60–75). New Delhi: Sage.

Jaggar, A. (1983). Political philosophies of women's liberation. In L. Richardson & V. Taylor (Eds.), *Feminist frontiers: Rethinking sex, gender, and society* (pp. 322–329). New York: Random House.

Jason, L. (1997). *Community building: Values for a sustainable future.* Westport, CT: Praeger.

Jenkins, H. (1988). Star Trek rerun, reread, rewritten: Fan writing as textual poaching. *Critical Studies in Mass Communication, 5,* 85–107.

Jermier, J.M., Knights, D., & Nord, W.R. (1994). *Resistance and power in organizations.* London: Routledge.

Johnson, B. (1996). *Polarity management: Identifying and managing unsolvable problems.* Amherst, MA: HRD Press.

Joniak, E.A. (2005). Exclusionary practices and the delegitimization of client voice: How staff create, sustain, and escalate conflict in a drop-in center for street kids. *American Behavioral Scientist, 48,* 961–988.

Jung, A. (1987). *Unveiling India: A woman's journey.* New Delhi: Penguin Books.

Kamath, M.V. (1989). *Management Kurien style: The story of the white revolution.* New Delhi: Konark Publishers.

Kanter, R.M. (1977). *Men and women of the corporation.* New York: Basic Books.

Kapila, M., & Pye, M.J. (1992). The European response to AIDS. In J. Sepulveda, H. Fineberg, & J. Mann (eds.). *AIDS Prevention through education: A world view* (pp. 199–236). New York: Oxford University Press.

Katz, E., & Lazarsfeld, P.F. (1955). *Personal influence: The part played by people in the flow of mass communications,* New York: Free Press.

Katz, E., Liebes, T., & Berko, L. (1992). On commuting between television fiction and real life. *Quarterly Review of Film and Video, 14,* 157–178.

Kaufman, C. (2003). *Ideas for action: Relevant theory for radical change.* Cambridge, MA: Southend Press.

Kaufman, H. (1960). *The forest ranger: A study in administrative behavior.* Baltimore: Johns Hopkins Press.

Kawachi, I., Kennedy, B.P., Bruce, P., & Lochner, K. (1997). Social capital, income inequality, and mortality. *American Journal of Public Health, 87*, 1491–1498.

Kawachi, I., Kennedy, B.P., & Lochner, K. (1997). Long live community: Social capital as public health. *The American Prospect, 29*, 56–59.

Kirby, E.L., & Krone, K.J. (2002). "The policy exists but you can't really use it": Communication and the structuration of work-family policies. *Journal of Applied Communication Research, 30*, 50–77.

Kivlin, J.E., Roy, P., Fliegel, F.C., & Sen, L.K. (1968). *Communication in India: Experiments in introducing change.* Hyderabad: National Institute of Community Development.

Knoke, D., & Wood, J.R. (1981). *Organized for action: Commitment in voluntary associations.* New Brunswick, NJ: Rutgers University Press.

Kreiner, K., & Schultz, M. (1993). Informal collaboration in R&D: The formation of networks across organizations. *Organization Studies, 14*, 189–209.

Kumar, R. (1993). *The history of doing: An illustrated account of movements for women's rights and feminism in India, 1800–1990.* New Delhi: Kali for Women.

Kurien, V. (1990). *From a drop to a flood.* Anand, India: National Dairy Development Board.

———. (1997a). The AMUL dairy cooperatives: Putting the means of development into the hands of small producers in India. In A. Krishna, N. Uphoff, & M.J. Esman (Eds.), *Reasons for hope: Instructive experiences in rural development* (pp. 105–119). New Delhi: Vistaar Publications.

———. (1997b). *An unfinished dream.* New Delhi: Tata McGraw-Hill Publishing.

Lamphere, L. (1985). Bringing the family to work: Women's culture on the shop floor. *Feminist Studies, 11*, 519–540.

Langston, D. (1988). Feminist theories and the politics of difference. In J.W. Cochran, D. Langston, & C.C. Woodward (Eds.), *Changing our power* (pp. 10–21). Dubuque, IA: Kendall Hunt.

Lao-Tzu (1988). *Tao te Ching* (Stephen Mitchell, Trans.). New York: Harper and Row.

Law, S., & Singhal, A. (1999). Efficacy in letter-writing to an entertainment-education radio serial. *Gazette, 61*(5), 355–372.

Lerner, G. (1993). *The creation of feminist consciousness.* New York: Oxford University Press.

Lewin, K. (1958). Group decision and social change. In E.E. Maccoby, T.M. Newcomb, & E.L. Hartley (Eds.), *Readings in social psychology* (pp. 197–211). Third Edition. New York: Holt, Rinehart, and Winston.

Lindemann-Nelson, H. (2001). *Damaged identities, narrative repair.* Ithaca, NY: Cornell University Press.

Lindlof, T.R. (1995). *Qualitative communication research methods.* Thousand Oaks, CA: Sage.

Logan, M.H. (1993). The 'Ahk'ohn Utz' of Chimaltenango: The medical value of cultural understanding. In R. Luecke (Ed.), *A new dawn in Guatemala: Toward a worldwide health vision* (pp. 125–134). Prospect Heights, IL: Waveland Press.

Luecke, R. (Ed.) (1993). *A new dawn in Guatemala: Toward a worldwide health vision.* Prospect Heights, IL: Waveland Press.

Macklis, R.M. (2001). Successful patient safety initiatives: Driven from within. *Group Practice Journal, 50*(10), 1–5.

MacIver, R.M. (1928). *Community: A sociological study.* New York: Macmillan.

Maguire, M., & Mohtar, L.E. (1994). Performance and the celebration of a subaltern counterpublic. *Text and Performance Quarterly, 14,* 238–252.

Malaviya, P., Singhal, A., Svenkerud, P.J., & Srivastava, S. (2004a). *Telenor in Bangladesh (A): The prospect of doing well and doing good.* Fontainebleau, France: INSEAD—The European Institute of Business Administration.

———. (2004b). *Telenor in Bangladesh (B): Achieving multiple bottom lines at GrameenPhone.* Fontainebleau, France: INSEAD—The European Institute of Business Administration.

———. (2004c). *Telenor in Bangladesh (C): The way forward.* Fontainebleau, France: INSEAD—The European Institute of Business Administration.

Mamet, D. (2005, February 13). Attention must be paid. *The New York Times.* http://www.nytimes.com/2005/02/13/opinion/13Mamet.html? (Retrieved on February 14, 2005).

Mandell, M. (2001). Collaboration through network structures for community building efforts. *National Civic Review, 90,* 279–287.

Martin, J. (1992). *Culture in organizations: Three perspectives.* New York: Oxford University Press.

Martin, P.Y. (1990). Rethinking feminist organizations. *Gender & Society, 4,* 182–206.

Marx, K. (1977). *A contribution to the critique of political economy* (S.W. Ryazaskaya, Trans.). Wappinger Falls, NY: Beekman Publishers.

Mascarenhas, R.C. (1988). *A strategy for rural development: Dairy cooperatives in India.* New Delhi: Sage.

Mathur, J.C., & Neurath, P. (1959). *An Indian experiment in farm radio forums.* Paris: UNESCO.

May, T. (1993). *Between genealogy and epistemology: Psychology, politics and knowledge in the thought of Michel Foucault.* University Park, PA: The Pennsylvania State University Press.

Mbiti, J.S. (1969). *African religions and philosophy.* London: Heineman.

McLeod, A.E. (1992). Hegemonic relations and gender resistance: The new veiling as accommodating protest in Cairo. *Signs, 17*, 533–557.

McLeod, J.M., Daily, K.A., Guo, Z., Eveland, W.P., Bayer, J., Yan, S., & Wang, H. (1996). Community integration, local media use and democratic processes. *Communication Research, 23* (2), 179–209.

Mehta, V. (1977). *Mahatma Gandhi and his apostles.* New York: Viking.

Menon-Sen, K., & Kumar, A.K.S. (2001). *Women in India: How free? How equal?* New Delhi: Office of the United Nations Resident Coordinator in India.

Merton, R.K. (1968). *Social theory and social structure.* New York: Free Press.

Meyerson, D.E. (1991). Acknowledging and uncovering ambiguities in cultures. In P.J. Frost, L.F. Moore, M.R. Louis, C.C. Lundberg, & J. Martin (Eds.), *Reframing organizational culture* (pp. 254–270). Newbury Park, CA: Sage.

Miller, K. (2002). *Communication theories: Perspectives, processes, and contexts.* New York: McGraw-Hill.

———. (2003). *Organizational communication: Approaches and processes* (3rd ed.). Belmont, CA: Wadsworth.

Miller, P., & O'Leary, T. (1987). Accounting and the construction of the governable person. *Accounting, Organizations, and Society, 12*, 235–265.

Moemeka, A.A. (1989). Communication and African culture: A sociological analysis. In S.T.K. Boafo (Ed.), *Communication and culture: African perspectives* (pp. 2–10). Nairobi, Kenya: WACC/ACCE.

———. (1994, April). *Socio-cultural dimensions of leadership in Africa.* Paper presented at the Global Majority Retreat, Rocky Hill, CT.

———. (1996). Communication and culture: Community and self-respect as African values. In C. Christians & M. Traber (Eds.), *Communication ethics and universal values* (pp. 170–193). Thousand Oaks, CA: Sage.

———. (1998). Communalism as a fundamental dimension of culture. *Journal of Communication, 47*, 118–141.

Mohanty, C.T. (1997).Women workers and capitalist scripts: Ideologies of domination, common interests, and the politics of solidarity. In M.J. Alexander & C.T. Mohanty (Eds.), *Feminist genealogies, colonial legacies, democratic futures* (pp. 3–29). New York: Routledge.

Monge, P.R., & Miller, K.I. (1988). Participative processes in organizations. In G.M. Goldhaber & G.A. Barnett (Eds.), *Handbook of organizational communication* (pp. 213–229). Norwood, NJ: Ablex.

Montgomery, B.M., & Baxter, L.A. (Eds.) (1998). *Dialectical approaches to studying personal relationships.* Mahwah, NJ: Lawrence Erlbaum.

Morgan, G. (1993). *Imagination: The art of creative management.* Newbury Park, CA: Sage.

———. (1997). *Images of organization* (2nd ed.). Newbury Park, CA: Sage.

Morrison, J., Howard, J., Johnson, C., Navarro, F., Plachetka, B., & Bell, T. (1998). Strengthening neighborhoods by building community networks. In P. Ewalt, E. Freeman, & D. Poole (Eds.), *Community building* (pp. 107–116). Washington, D.C.: NASW Press.

Morse, J.M. (1994). "Emerging from the data": The cognitive process of analysis in qualitative inquiry. In J.M. Morse (Ed.), *Critical issues in qualitative research methods* (pp. 23–43). Thousand Oaks, CA: Sage.

Mumby, D.K. (1993). Critical organizational communication studies: The next ten years. *Communication Monographs, 60,* 34–46.

———. (1997). The problem of hegemony: Reading Gramsci for organizational communication studies. *Western Journal of Communication, 61,* 343–365.

———. (2001). Power and politics. In F.M. Jablin & L.L. Putnam (Eds.), *The new handbook of organizational communication: Advances in theory, research, and methods* (pp. 585–623). Thousand Oaks, CA: Sage.

Nalbandian, J., & Oliver, J. (1999). City and county management as community building. *Public Management, 81,* 20–22.

Naparstek, A., & Dooley, D. (1998). Countering urban disinvestment through community building initiatives. In P. Ewalt, E. Freeman, & D. Poole (Eds.), *Community building* (pp. 6–16). Washington, D.C.: NASW Press.

Nariman, H. (1993). *Soap operas for social change.* Westport, CT: Praegar.

Natalle, E.J., Papa, M.J., & Graham, E.E. (1994). Feminist philosophy and the transformation of organizational communication. In B. Kovacic (Ed.), *New perspectives in organizational communication* (pp. 258–284). Albany: State University of New York Press.

National Coalition for the Homeless (2002, September). *How many people experience homelessness?* Washington, D.C.

National Law Center on Homelessness and Poverty (2004). On homelessness and poverty. Available online at http://www.nlchp.org/index.cfm (Retrieved on August 17, 2004).

Nicholson, J. (2004, October 2–3). Biotech food for the hungry. *The International Herald Tribune,* p. 8.

Norsigian, J., & Pincus, J. (1984). Organizing for change: U.S.A. In J. Pincus & W. Sanford (Eds.), *The new our bodies, ourselves* (pp. 598–610). New York: Simon &: Schuster.

Nukala, S. (1996). *The discursive construction of Asian-American employees.* Unpublished doctoral dissertation, Rutgers University, New Brunswick, NJ.

O'Connor, E.S. (1995). Paradoxes of participation: Textual analysis and organizational change. *Organization Studies, 16,* 769–803.

Ogilvy, J. (1990, February). This postmodern business. *Marketing and Research Today, 23*(4), 4–20.

Oakley, J. (1991). Defiant moments: Gender, resistance and individuals. *Man, 26,* 3–22.

Oliver, K. (1991). Fractal politics: How to use "the subject". *Praxis International, 11,* 178–194.

Pacanowsky, M. (1988). Communication in the empowering organization. In J.A. Anderson (Ed.), *Communication yearbook 11* (pp. 356–379). Newbury Park, CA: Sage.

Papa, M.J., Auwal, M.A., & Singhal, A. (1995). Dialectic of emancipation and control in organizing for social change: A multitheoretic study of the Grameen Bank in Bangladesh. *Communication Theory, 5,* 189–223.

———. (1997). Organizing for social change within concertive control systems: Member identification, empowerment, and the masking of discipline. *Communication Monographs, 64,* 219–249.

Papa, M.J., & Singhal, A. (1999). The empowering and disempowering dimensions in the communication of women dairy farmers. In National Dairy Development Board, *Women's Empowerment through Dairy Cooperatives in India* (pp. 133–185). Anand, Gujarat, India: National Dairy Development Board.

Papa, M.J., Singhal, A., Ghanekar, D., & Papa, W.H. (2000). Organizing for social change through cooperative action: The [dis]empowering dimensions of women's communication. *Communication Theory, 10,* 90–123.

Papa, M.J., Singhal, A., Law, S., Pant, S., Sood, S., Rogers, E.M., & Shefner-Rogers, C.L. (2000). Entertainment education and social change: An analysis of parasocial interaction, social learning, collective efficacy, and paradoxical communication. *Journal of Communication, 50,* 31–56.

Papa, W.H., Papa, M.J., Kandath, K.P., Worrell, T., & Muthuswamy, N. (in press). Dialectic of unity and fragmentation in feeding the homeless: Promoting social justice through communication. *Atlantic Journal of Communication.*

Parker, M. (1992). Post-modern organizations or postmodern organizational theory? *Organization Studies, 13,* 1–17.

Parsons, R.J. (1991). Empowerment: Purpose and practice principle in social work. *Social Work in Groups, 14*(2), 7–21.

Pascale, R.T. (1990). *Managing on the Edge.* New York: Touchstone.

Pascale, R.T., & Sternin, J. (2005). Your company's secret change agents. *Harvard Business Review,* May, 1–11.

Pascale, R.T., Millemann, M., & Gioja (2000). *Surfing the edge of chaos: The laws of nature and the new laws of business.* New York: Crown Publishing Group.

Patel, V. (1989). Sex-determination and sex pre-selection tests in India: Modern techniques for femicide. *Bulletin of Concerned Asian Scholars, 21,* 2–10.

Pearl, D., & Phillips, M.M. (2001, November 27). Grameen Bank, which pioneered loans for the poor, has hit a repayment snag. *The Wall Street Journal,* A1.

Perse, E.M., & Rubin, R.B. (1989). Attribution in social and parasocial relationships. *Communication Research, 16,* 59–77.

Peters, J.D. (1999). *Speaking into the air: A history of the idea of communication.* Chicago: University of Chicago Press.

Peters, T.J., & Waterman, R.H. (1988). *In search of excellence.* New York: Warner Books.

Philip, R. (1994). *Member participation and cooperative performance.* Rome: Food & Agriculture Organization.

Phillips, N., & Hardy, C. (1997). Managing multiple identities: Discourse, legitimacy and resources in the UK refugee system. *Organization, 4,* 159–185.

Poole, M.S., & Van de Ven, A.H. (1989). Using paradox to build management and organizational theories. *Academy of Management Review, 14,* 562–578.

Portes, A. (1998). Social capital: Its origins and applications in modern sociology. *Annual Review of Sociology, 24,* 1–24.

Prahalad, C.K. (2005). *The fortune at the bottom of the pyramid: Eradicating poverty through profits.* Upper Saddle River, NJ: Wharton School Publishing.

Pratkanis, A., & Aronson, E. (2000). *Age of propaganda: The everyday use and abuse of persuasion.* New York: W.H. Freeman and Company.

Preece, J. (2002). Supporting community and building social capital. *Communications of the ACM, 16,* 36–40.

Presthus, R. (1962). *The organizational society.* New York: Random House.

Putnam, L.L. (1986). Contradictions and paradoxes in organizations. In L. Thayer (Ed.), *Organization and communication: Emerging perspectives* (pp. 151–167). Norwood, NJ: Ablex.

Putnam, L.L., & Fairhurst, G.T. (2001). Discourse analysis in organizations: Issues and concerns. In F.M. Jablin & L.L. Putnam (Eds.), *The new handbook of organizational communication: Advances in theory, research and methods* (pp. 78–136). Thousand Oaks, CA: Sage.

Putnam, R.D. (1993). *Making democracy work: Civic traditions in modern Italy.* Princeton, NJ: Princeton University Press.

———. (1995). Bowling alone: America's declining social capital. *Journal of Democracy, 6,* 238–262.

———. (2000). *Bowling alone: The collapse and revival of American community.* New York: Simon & Schuster.

Quadir, I. (2003). Bottom-up economics. *Harvard Business Review, 81*(8), 18–20.

Rahim, S.A. (1994). Participatory development communication as a dialogical process. In S.A. White, K.S. Nair, & J. Ascroft (Eds.), *Participatory development communication: Working for change and development* (pp. 117–137). New Delhi: Sage.

Rahman, A. (1988). Alleviation of rural poverty: Replicability of the Grameen Bank model. *South Asia Journal, 1*, 475–486.

———. (1989a). *Impact of the Grameen Bank in rural power structure* (Report No. 61). Dhaka, Bangladesh: Bangladesh Institute of Development Studies.

———. (1989b). *Impact of Grameen Bank on the nutritional status of the rural poor* (Report No. 108). Dhaka, Bangladesh: Bangladesh Institute of Development Studies.

Rao, N., Singhal, A., & Pant, S. (2004, September). *Positioning entertainment-education for second-order change.* Paper presented to the Fourth International Conference on Entertainment-Education and Social Change, Cape Town, South Africa.

Rappaport, J. (1987). Terms of empowerment/exemplars of prevention: Toward a theory of community psychology. *American Journal of Community Psychology, 15*, 121–148.

———. (1995). Empowerment meets narrative: Listening to stories and creating settings. *American Journal of Community Psychology, 23*, 795–807.

Rawlins, W.K. (1992). *Friendship matters: Communication, dialectics, and the life course.* New York: Aldine De Gruyer.

———. (1998). Writing about friendship matters: A case study in dialectical and dialogical inquiry. In B.M. Montgomery & L.A. Baxter (Eds.), *Dialectical approaches to studying personal relationships* (pp. 63–81). Mahwah, NJ: Lawrence Erlbaum Associates.

Ray, J.K. (1987). *To chase a miracle: A study of the Grameen Bank of Bangladesh.* Dhaka: University Press Limited.

Reissman, L. (1949). A study of role conceptions in bureaucracy. *Social Forces, 27*, 305–310.

Richardson, D., Ramirez, R., & Haq, M. (2000). *Grameen telecom's village phone programme in rural Bangladesh: A multimedia case study.* Ottawa, Canada: Canadian International Development Agency.

Roe, E. (1999). *Except Africa: Remaking development, rethinking power.* London: Transaction Publishers.

Rogers, E.M. (1962). *Diffusion of innovations* (1st ed.). New York: Free Press.

———. (1994). *A history of communication study: A biographic approach.* New York: Free Press.

———. (2003). *Diffusion of innovations* (5th ed.). New York: Free Press.

Rogers, E.M., & Kincaid, D.L. (1981). *Communication networks: Toward a new paradigm for research.* New York: Free Press.

Rogers, E.M. & Singhal, A. (2003). Empowerment and communication: Lessons learned from organizing for social change. *Communication Yearbook 27*, 67–85.

Rogers, E.M., & Steinfatt, T.M. (1999). *Intercultural Communication.* Prospect Heights, IL: Waveland Press.

Rogers, E.M., Vaughan, P.W., Swalehe, R.M.A., Rao, N., Svenkerud, P., & Sood, S. (1999). Effects of an entertainment-education radio soap opera on family planning in Tanzania. *Studies in Family Planning, 30*(3), 193–211.

Rossi, M. (1989). Hegel and Hegelianism. *The New Encyclopædia Britannica* (vol. 20). Chicago: Encyclopædia Britannica, Inc.

Rubin, A.M., & Perse, E.M. (1987). Audience activity and soap opera involvement: A uses and effects investigation. *Human Communication Research, 14,* 246–268.

Ruesch, J., & Bateson, G. (1951). *Communication: The social matrix of psychology.* New York: W.W. Norton.

Ruitenbeek, H.M. (1963). *The dilemma of organizational society.* New York: E.P. Dutton.

Rushton, J.P. (1975). Generosity in children: Immediate and long-term effects of modeling, preaching, and moral judgment. *Journal of Personality and Social Psychology, 31,* 459–466.

———. (1976). Socialization and the altruistic behavior of children. *Psychological Bulletin, 83,* 898–913.

Ruud, G. (1995). The symbolic construction of organizational identities and community in a regional symphony. *Communication Studies, 46,* 201–221.

Sabido, M. (2004). The origins of entertainment-education. In A. Singhal, M. Cody, E.M. Rogers, & M. Sabido (Eds.), *Entertainment-education and social change: History, research, and practice* (pp. 61–74). Mahwah, NJ: Lawrence Erlbaum.

Sangari, K., & Vaid, S. (1989). *Recasting women: Essays in colonial history.* New Brunswick, NJ: Rutgers University Press.

Santee, Erin (2001, May 21). Weekly suppers offer free food, but also fellowship, diversity. *Athens News,* p. 2.

Sawicki, J. (1991). *Disciplining Foucault: Feminism, power, and the body.* New York: Routledge.

Scott, W.G., & Hart, D.K. (1979). *Organizational America.* Boston: Houghton Mifflin.

Sen, G., & Grown, C. (1987). Gender and class in development experience. In G. Sen & C. Grown (Eds.), *Development, crises, and alternative visions: Third World women's perspectives* (pp. 23–49). New York: Monthly Review Press.

Senge, P.M. (1990). *The fifth discipline: The art and practice of the learning organization.* New York: Doubleday.

Sharan, B.R., & Bhatt, D.K. (1992). *Status of women: A historical perspective.* New Delhi: South Asia Books.

Sharma, K. (1991). Grassroots organizations and women's empowerment: Some issues in the contemporary debate. *Samya Shakti: A Journal of Women's Studies, 6,* 28–44.

Shefner-Rogers, C.L., Rao, N., Rogers, E.M., & Wayangankar, A. (1998). The empowerment of women dairy farmers in India. *Journal of Applied Communication Research, 26,* 319–337.

Shehabuddin, R. (1992). *Empowering rural women: The impact of Grameen Bank in Bangladesh.* Dhaka, Bangladesh: Grameen Bank.

Shiva, V. (1989). *Staying alive: Women, ecology, and development in India.* London: Zed Books.

Shridharani, K. (1946). *The Mahatma and the world.* New York: Duell, Sloan, and Pearce.

Siddiqui, K. (1984). *An evaluation of Grameen Bank operation.* Dhaka, Bangladesh: Grameen Bank.

Singhal, A. (2001). *Facilitating community participation through communication.* New York, NY: UNICEF.

———. (2004). Entertainment education through participatory theater: Freirean strategies for empowering the oppressed. In A. Singhal, M. Cody, E.M. Rogers, & M. Sabido (Eds.), *Entertainment-education and social change: History, research, and practice* (pp. 377–398). Mahwah, NJ: Lawrence Erlbaum.

Singhal, A., & Chitnis, K. (2004). Community organizing for health: Toward a people centered vision of health. *MICA Communications Review, 2*(2).

Singhal, A., Cody, M.J., Rogers, E.M., & Sabido, M. (Eds.) (2004). *Entertainment-education and social change: History, research, and practice.* Mahwah, NJ: Lawrence Erlbaum Associates.

Singhal, A., Law, S., Kandath, K., & Ghanekar, D.V. (1999). Investigating (dis)empowering attitudes and behaviors of women dairy farmers and the effects of the three intervention programs in the Kolhapur and Jaipur district milk unions of India. In National Dairy Development Board, *Women's empowerment through dairy cooperatives in India* (pp. 102–132). Anand, Gujarat: National Dairy Development Board.

Singhal, A., & Obregon, R. (1999). Social uses of commercial soap operas: A conversation with Miguel Sabido. *Journal of Development Communication, 10*(1), 68–77.

Singhal, A., & Rogers, E.M. (1989). *India's information revolution.* New Delhi: Sage.

———. (1999). *Entertainment-education: A communication strategy for social change.* Mahwah, NJ: Lawrence Erlbaum Associates.

———. (2001). *India's communication revolution: From bullock carts to cyber marts.* New Delhi: Sage.

———. (2002). A theoretical agenda for entertainment-education. *Communication Theory, 14*(2), 117–135.

———. (2003). *Combating AIDS: Communication strategies in action.* New Delhi: Sage.

Singhal, A., Sharma, D., Papa, M.J., & Witte, K. (2004). Air cover and ground mobilization: Integrating entertainment-education broadcasts with community listening and service delivery in India. In A. Singhal, M. Cody, E.M. Rogers, & M. Sabido (Eds.), *Entertainment-education and social change: History, research, and practice* (pp. 351–374). Mahwah, NJ: Lawrence Erlbaum.

Singhal, A., Svenkerud, P.J., & Flydal, E. (2002). Multiple bottom lines: Telenor's mobile telephony operations in Bangladesh. *Telektronikk, 98*(1), 153–160.

Smitherman, G. (1977). *Talkin and testifyin: The language of Black America.* Detroit: Wayne State University Press.

Soeters, J.L. (1986). Excellent companies as social movements. *Journal of Management Studies, 23*, 299–312.

Sood, S., & Rogers, E.M. (2000). Dimensions of parasocial interaction by letter-writers to a popular entertainment-education soap opera in India. *Journal of Broadcasting and Electronic Media, 44*(3), 389–414.

Soul City (2000, September). *The evaluation of Soul City 4: Methodology and top-line results.* Paper presented at the Third International Entertainment-Education Conference for Social Change, Arnhem, The Netherlands.

Sparks, D. (2004). From hunger aid to school reform: An interview with Jerry Sternin. *Journal of Staff Development, 25*(1), 12–21.

Spreitzer, G.M. (1995). An empirical test of a comprehensive model of intrapersonal empowerment in the workplace. *American Journal of Community Psychology, 23*, 601–629.

Sternin, J. (2003). Practice positive deviance for extraordinary social and organizational change. In D. Ulrich, M. Goldsmith, L. Carter, J. Bolt, & N. Smallwood (Eds.), *The change champion's fieldguide* (pp. 20–37). New York: Best Practice Publications.

Sternin, J., & Choo, R. (2000). The power of positive deviancy. *Harvard Business Review,* January–February, 2–3.

Sternin, M., Sternin, J., & Marsh, D. (1999). Scaling up poverty alleviation and nutrition program in Vietnam. In T. Marchione (Ed.), *Scaling up, scaling down* (pp. 97–117). London, UK: Gordon and Breach.

Stewart, J., & Zediker, K. (2000). Dialogue as tensional, ethical practice. *Southern Communication Journal, 65*, 224–242.

Stohl, C. (1995). *Organizational communication: Interconnectedness in action.* Thousand Oaks, CA: Sage.

Stohl, C., & Cheney, G. (2001). Participatory practices/paradoxical practices: Communication and the dilemmas of organizational democracy. *Management Communication Quarterly, 14*, 90–128.

Strauss, G. (1982). Worker participation in management: An international perspective. *Research in Organizational Behavior, 4*, 173–265.

Sturgulewski, Carol (2001). No one goes hungry. In J.Canfield, M.O. Hansen, C. Buck, C. Sturgulewski, P. Stone, & C. Brian (Eds.), *Chicken Soup for the Gardener's Soul, 101 Stories to Sow Seeds of Love, Hope and Laughter.* Deerfield Beach, Florida: Health Communications.

Sypher, B.D., McKinley, M., Ventsam, S., & Elías. E. (2002). Fostering reproductive health through entertainment-education in the Peruvian Amazon: The social construction of *Bienvenida Salud! Communication Theory, 12*(2), 192–205.

Taylor, B.C., & Trujillo, N. (2001). Qualitative research methods. In F.M. Jablin & L.L. Putnam (Eds.), *The new handbook of organizational communication: Advances in theory, research, and methods* (pp. 161–194). Thousand Oaks, CA: Sage.

Taylor, C. (1989). *Sources of the self: The making of modern identity.* Cambridge, MA: Harvard University Press.

Taylor, H.G., Taylor, C.E., & Taylor-Ide, D. (2002). Getting started: Positive change is possible. In D. Taylor-Ide and C.E Taylor (Eds.), *Just and lasting change* (pp. 17–31). Baltimore, MD: Johns Hopkins University Press.

The Indian Express. (1996, September 2). Kurien gets two-year extension, NDDB board reconstituted. Ahmedabad Edition.

Thomas, H. (1999). *The slavetrade.* New York: Simon & Schuster.

Thomas, P. (1994). Participatory development communication: Philosophical premises. In S.A. White, K.S. Nair, & J. Ascroft (Eds.), *Participatory development communication: Working for change and development* (pp. 49–59). New Delhi: Sage.

Thompson, V.A. (1961). *Modern organization.* New York: Knopf.

Tompkins, P.K., & Cheney, G. (1983). Account analysis of organizations: Decision making and identification. In L.L. Putnam & M.E. Pacanowsky (Eds.), *Communication and organizations: An interpretive approach* (pp. 123–146). Beverly Hills, CA: Sage.

———. (1985). Communication and unobtrusive control in contemporary organizations. In R.D. McPhee & P.K. Tompkins (Eds.), *Organizational communication: Traditional themes and new directions* (pp. 179–210). Newbury Park, CA: Sage.

Tracy, S.J. (2004). Dialectic, contradiction, or double bind? Analyzing and theorizing employee reactions to organizational tensions. *Journal of Applied Communication Research, 32,* 119–146.

Trethewey, A. (1997). Resistance, identity, and empowerment: A postmodern feminist analysis of clients in a human service organization. *Communication Monographs, 64,* 281–301.

———. (1999). Isn't it ironic: Using irony to explore the contradictions of organizational life. *Western Journal of Communication, 63,* 140–167.

Trethewey, A., & Ashcraft, K.L. (2004). Practicing disorganization: The development of applied perspectives on living with tension. *Journal of Applied Communication Research, 32,* 81–88.

Tucker, C. (2003, October 20). Rich addict, poor addict: One disease, two very different treatment plans. *The Atlanta Journal Constitution*, A1.

UNAIDS (1999). *Comfort and hope: Six case studies on mobilizing family and community care for and by people with HIV/AIDS.* Geneva: UNAIDS.

United Nations Development Programme (2002). *Human development report 2002: Deepening democracy in a fragmented world.* New York: Oxford University Press.

Usdin, S., Singhal, A., Shongwe, T., Goldstein, S., & Shabalala, A. (2004). No short cuts in entertainment-education. Designing *Soul City* step-by-step. In A. Singhal, M. Cody, E.M. Rogers, & M. Sabido (Eds.), *Entertainment-education and social change: History, research, and practice* (pp. 153–176). Mahwah, NJ: Lawrence Erlbaum Associates.

Van Leer, C.A. (1998). Dialectical empiricism: Science and relationship. In B.M. Montgomery & L.A. Baxter (Eds.), *Dialectical approaches to studying personal relationships* (pp. 109–136). Mahwah, NJ: Lawrence Erlbaum Associates.

Vogt, J.R., & Murrell, K.L. (1990). *Empowerment in organizations: How to spark exceptional performance.* San Diego, CA: University Associates.

Von Mahs, J. (2005). The sociospatial exclusion of single homeless people in Berlin and Los Angeles. *American Behavioral Scientist, 48*, 928–960.

Wallack, L. (1990). Two approaches to health promotion in the mass media. *World Health Forum, 11*, 143–155.

Wallis, A. (1998a). Social capital and community building: Part one. *National Civic Review, 87*, 253–271.

———. (1998b). Social capital and community building: Part two. *National Civic Review, 87*, 317–336.

Warburton, D. (1998). A passionate dialogue: Community and sustainable development. In D. Warburton (Ed.), *Community and sustainable development: Participation in the future* (pp. 3–28). London: Earthscan.

Warren, M. (1998). Community building and political power. *American Behavioral Scientist, 42*, 78–92.

Warren, R.L. (1978). *The community in America* (3rd ed.). Chicago: Rand McNally.

Wasserman, K. (1999). Good works: A community of hope. Available online at http://good-works.net (Retrieved August 19, 2004).

Watkins, K., & Woods, N. (2004, October 2–3). Africa must be heard in the councils of the rich. *The International Herald Tribune*, p. 8.

Wayangankar, A. (1994). *The empowerment of Indian dairy farmers.* Unpublished MA Thesis. Albuquerque: University of New Mexico.

Wayangankar, A., Rogers, E.M., Rao, N., & Shefner-Rogers, C. (1995). Empowering Indian women dairy farmers. *Journal of Rural Reconstruction, 28*, 29–40.

Weick, K.E. (1979). *The social psychology of organizing.* Reading, MA: Addison-Wesley Publishing.

Weitzman, E., & Kawachi, I. (2000). Giving means receiving: The protective effect of social capital on binge drinking on college campuses. *American Journal of Public Health, 90*(12), 1936–1939.

Wellman, B., Carrington, P.J., & Hall, A. (1988). Networks as personal communities. In B. Wellman & S.D. Berkowitz (Eds.), *Social structures: A network approach* (Vol. 2, pp. 130–184). Cambridge, UK: Cambridge University Press.

Wendt, R.F. (1998). The sound of one hand clapping: Counterintuitive lessons extracted from paradoxes and double binds in participative organizations. *Management Communication Quarterly, 11*, 323–371.

White, S. (1994). Introduction—The concept of participation: Transforming rhetoric to reality. In S.A. White, K.S. Nair, & J. Ascroft (Eds.), *Participatory development communication: Working for change and development* (pp. 15–32). New Delhi: Sage.

White, M., & Epston, D. (1990). *Narrative means to therapeutic ends.* New York: W.W. Norton.

Whyte, W.H. (1956). *The organization man.* New York: Simon and Schuster.

William, C., & Windebank, J. (2000). Helping each other out: Community exchange in deprived neighborhoods. *Community Development Journal, 35*, 146–156.

Wilson, P.A. (1996). Empowerment: Community economic development from the inside out. *Urban Studies, 33*, 617–630.

Winant, T. (1987). The feminist standpoint: A matter of language. *Hypatia, 2*, 123–148.

Woolcock, M. (1998). Social capital and economic development: Towards a theoretical synthesis and policy framework. *Theory and Society, 27*, 151–208.

Wright, J.D. (2005). Introduction: Homelessness and the politics of social exclusion. *American Behavioral Scientist, 48*, 925–927.

Young, I.M. (1994). Punishment, treatment, empowerment: Three approaches to policy for pregnant addicts. *Feminist Studies, 20*, 33–57.

Yunus, M. (1983). *Group-based savings and credit for the rural poor.* Paper presented at the inter-country workshop sponsored by International Labor Organization at Bogra, Bangladesh.

———. (1984). *On reaching the poor.* Dhaka, Bangladesh: Grameen Bank.

———. (1997). The Grameen Bank story: Rural credit in Bangladesh. In A. Krishna, N. Uphoff, & M.J. Esman (Eds.), *Reasons for hope: Instructive experiences in rural development* (pp. 9 to 24). New Delhi: Vistaar Publications.

———. (2002). Fighting poverty from the bottom-up. http://www.grameen-info.org/mcredit/timeline.html (Retrieved November 18, 2004).

Yunus, M. with Jolis, A. (1999). *Banker to the poor: Micro-lending and the battle against world poverty.* New York: Public Affairs.

Zeitlin, M., Ghassemi, H., & Mansour, M. (1990). *Positive deviance in child nutrition*. New York: UN University Press.

Zimmerman, M.A. (1990). Taking aim on empowerment research: On the distinction between individual and psychological conceptions. *American Journal of Community Psychology, 18,* 169–177.

———. (1995). Psychological empowerment: Issues and illu-strations. *American Journal of Community Psychology, 23,* 581–598.

Zimmerman, B., Lindberg, C., & Plsek, P. (1998). *Edgeware: Insights from complexity science for health care leaders*. Austin, TX: VHA Inc.

Zoller, H.M. (2000). "A place you haven't visited before": Creating the conditions for community dialogue. *Southern Communication Journal, 65,* 191–207.

———. (2004). Dialogue as global issue management: Legitimizing corporate influence in the transatlantic business dialogue. *Management Communication Quarterly, 18,* 204–240.

Name Index

Subject Index

CPSIA information can be obtained
at www.ICGtesting.com
Printed in the USA
LVHW081513250821
696079LV00020B/458